THE
MAGNIFICENT
ROCKIES

These pages: The Sneffels Range of Colorado, in grand isolation. Beneath its gray exterior lies a heart of gold and silver.

Pages 4 and 5: Albert Bierstadt gave a nation in civil war this romantic portrayal of **The Rocky Mountains,** *1863.*

Pages 6 and 7: In the ten million years since their birth, the Tetons' craggy Cathedral Group have hardly lost their adolescence.

THE MAGNIFICENT ROCKIES

Crest of a Continent

By
The Editors of
American West

The Great West Series

AMERICAN WEST PUBLISHING COMPANY
PALO ALTO, CALIFORNIA

A relict of time and erosion — Canyonlands, Utah.

Members of the American West editorial staff
responsible for creation of this book:

Staff writers

Bette Roda Anderson   Donald G. Pike   Janet Ziebarth

Editors

Donald E. Bower   Patricia Kollings

*Lanphere B. Graff, geologist and naturalist,
served as special consultant.*

Library of Congress Card Number 72-82181

ISBN 0-910118-27-2

CONTENTS

PREFACE

IN THE AWESOME SILENCE of prehistoric times—perhaps a billion or more years ago—there began on the North American continent a gentle series of tremors. Over the next few million years, this portion of the earth became more violent, forming great troughs and uplifting the land into dramatic mountain chains. So radical was this upheaval that geologists called it the Laramide Revolution. "In the 40,000,000 years since rocks of the mountain region were first subjected to major and dramatic uplift," write the authors of THE MAGNIFICENT ROCKIES, "the Rockies have continued their evolution . . . continued to rise as a unit, adding another 5,000 feet of elevation to the crest."

Then followed more centuries upon centuries of erosion, eating away at the top layers of the mountain peaks, climaxed by extensive glaciation during the Great Ice Age. "But the ranges maintained their basic structures with integrity: the arched upfolds, the fault lines miles in length, and the remnants of molten rock extruded upon a sedimentary earth surface—these would remain to tell the history and sequence of the great revolution." By comparison to the earth's natural activities, the coming of man and his subsequent adventures appear as little more than the flickering of a match against a starry, mountain sky.

Only two centuries ago the white man first ventured into the Rockies, at the same time as politics and freedom were arriving on the American scene along the eastern seaboard. The colonies were seeking to unshackle themselves, cut the umbilical cord from Mother England, and find their own maturity. Thomas Paine's *Common Sense* had been published, George Washington had been named commander-in-chief of a revolutionary army, and Thomas Jefferson had authored the Declaration of Independence.

On July 4, 1776, while the Continental Congress was unknowingly creating a national holiday by adopting this remarkable document, a lesser event was happening in the wilderness far to the west, an event unrelated for the moment to the excitement at Philadelphia. At a busy little Spanish town called Santa Fe, Fathers Dominguez and Escalante were making preparations to find a trail from New Mexico to the Spanish missions in California. The expedition, ultimately unsuccessful in its objective, nevertheless made the first substantial penetration into the rugged heart of the Rocky Mountains. When Escalante camped with his party along the San Juans and named his bivouac Our Lady of the Snows, he was making history of sorts: this was the first named site in future Colorado. Before Escalante was turned back by the early mountain snows, he had seen some of the West's most spectacular attractions—the Black Canyon of the Gunnison, the San Juans, the Grand Mesa, and the Colorado River and some of its canyons. Escalante had, in fact, established what would become the initial portion of the Spanish Trail, predating American exploration by some twenty-seven years.

With the advent of the nineteenth century, valiant but frustrating efforts were made to penetrate this great mountain barrier. Lewis and Clark, Zebulon Pike, Stephen Long, and John Charles Frémont were the official explorers; their accomplishments, however great or slight, provided the eastern establishment sufficient information (and misinformation) to whet the appetites of a small adventuresome minority. It was, however, the unofficial explorer—the mountain man—who in his quest for the beaver pelt sought out the land and learned to know it. The authors of THE MAGNIFICENT ROCKIES have described him as "a paragon of anti-social behavior whose wilderness skills and instinct for survival have remained a part of the Rockies' heritage in the stories about Jedediah Smith, Hugh Glass, William Sublette, Jim Bridger, Thomas Fitzpatrick, and 'Black Jim' Beckwourth. These and others like them were the men who coursed the mountains and valleys, rivers and plains of the Rockies, learning the geography so important to subsequent settlement and challenging the British right of ownership to the Rockies and Northwest merely by their presence."

But the mountain men were not publicists. In fact, they abhorred civilization, fully aware that the first wave of eastern immigrants would erase their livelihood by driving the beaver into impossible hiding places. Nor did the early explorers provide any real incentive for a mass migration. The typical New Yorker or Penn-sylvanian or Bostonian of the early nineteenth century had only an indolent cur-iosity about the West—comparable perhaps to the average middle-class American's interest today in the exploration of the moon. At this point in time, there was no incentive for the quiet majority to leave their farms or villages for the unknown, hostile West.

In July of 1847, two years before John Marshall's discovery of gold in California, the quest for religious-freedom led a group of persecuted Latter-Day Saints from Nauvoo, Illinois, across southern Wyoming into northeastern Utah. When their leader Brigham Young beheld the Great Salt Lake and declared, "This is the right place," the era of permanent settlement of the Rocky Mountain West had begun. It was God, not gold, that lured the first settlers to this wild land—but it would be gold that would make it flourish.

En route to California, a group of Cherokees had discovered some traces of gold in Colorado (near present-day Denver), but the meager color could not deter them from the fabled glitter of the golden state. Not until 1858 did the headlines in Kansas City papers shout of gold discoveries in Kansas Territory—headlines that initiated the rush to the "Pike's Peak gold mines." No mountain was too high, no canyon too deep, no Indian too formidable to deter the lustful prospector from his appointed round. From that day until this, men have been combing the rugged peaks of the Rockies Front Range, of the Sawatch and the spectacular San Juans, seeking gold, silver, uranium, and a dozen lesser minerals that lie buried in this great cordillera.

This marked the beginning—the volatile imprint of the white man upon the formidable Rocky Mountain West. In the process of introducing civilization to this virgin land, he eradicated the buffalo, the Indian way of life, the gold that enticed him—eventually even the blue skies would be endangered. Americans came with militia, with steel rails to move their belching iron horses, with cattle and sheep, with housing developments and highways, with factories and mercan-tile goods.

Today, as the tourist moves along the freeway system of Denver and reflects on the endless man-made structures all the way from Boulder to Colorado Springs (a distance of more than a hundred miles); as he moves west into the mountains on four-lane divided highways and becomes entangled in the burgeoning resort community of the new Dillon, the sprawling ski center at Vail, the spreading city of Grand Junction; as he observes the dozens of bulldozers and subdivision skeletons at Steamboat Springs, the mushrooming growth of Teton Village in Wyoming or Alta in Utah, or the renovations at Taos, New Mexico, it would appear that man's mark has been all-encompassing and indelible. Progress has wrought change —for better, for worse, or a combination of both. The once inaccessible Bighorn River on the Wyoming-Montana border is now an integral part of the Yellowtail Reservoir, a fisherman's haven; a portion of the isolated Green River has become Flaming Gorge, a man-made lake surrounded by excellent facilities for the family and the sportsman; the virgin canyons of the Colorado have been opened up to the boatman, the water-skier, the fisherman, and the amateur explorer as part of dramatic Lake Powell.

Yet, paradoxical as it seems, the Rocky Mountain West remains a vast, untamed wilderness, virtually unchanged from the days of Escalante or Lewis and Clark— unchanged from the days when the earliest man migrated south from the Bering Strait. Most of the million-acre mountain West, in fact, has been but slightly altered since the end of the last great Ice Age a few million years ago. In relation to the whole, man's little pockets of civilization, his insignificant scars upon the mountain slopes, his narrow ribbons of asphalt, his ski-run gashes through the forests, are hardly more than flotsam and jetsam on the vast oceans of the world.

To escape from the Denver maelstrom, one swings westward for a dozen miles to the heights of the Front Range, to wander at will among the pine-covered slopes that are unchanged from ten centuries ago. From Jackson Hole, Wyoming, it takes but a few minutes to cross Jenny Lake and hike the rugged and magnificent Tetons. Yellowstone National Park, despite its millions of visitors, offers hundreds of acres of lonely trails and wilderness, far from the madding crowd. Man's ugly touch can be avoided for weeks and even months in the Uncompaghre Scenic Region in the heart of the San Juans in Colorado, or in the Pecos wilderness of New Mexico, the Canyonlands of Utah, the Bridger Wilderness of Wyoming, or the Beartooth country of Montana.

No single volume can comprehensively provide the entire story of this region arbitrarily referred to as the Rocky Mountain West. But THE MAGNIFICENT ROCKIES does relate the more significant facts of geology, climate, wildlife, and history, past and present. Technically, this book confines itself to the Central and Southern Rockies, but it also encompasses portions of the Colorado Plateau and the Great Basin, a recognition of the fact that parts of these regions are considered, by those who live in the Rocky Mountain West, a part of it.

Sam Foss wrote an oft-quoted verse:

> Bring me men to match my mountains,
> Bring me men to match my plains,
> Men with empires in their purpose
> And new eras in their brains.

This book, in some measure, tells of such mountains and such men.

—Donald E. Bower

PART ONE

SPINE
OF A
CONTINENT

Eons ago, from deep beneath an inland sea, the Rockies chain began its rise, slowly pushing to the surface, then on toward the sky. In our era it is the crest of the North American continent, the divide that intercepts the clouds and directs their waters to the two great oceans of the world. Constantly these mountains are being renewed, as young ranges like the Tetons (left) are thrust up; and just as constantly they are being worn down by erosion. Their granite fortress, so seemingly impregnable, is in slow surrender to the quiet seige of time and the elements.

The Tetons: Mount Moran and Jackson Lake.

CHAPTER 1

THE BEAUTIFUL BARRIER

*A view of the towering wilderness that long resisted man's efforts
to tame it—and now offers him refuge from too much civilization*

Rocky mountain history is above all a story of land, of the plants and animals that have adapted to that land, and of man, who is still learning to live as the land dictates.

This high, aloof region was born in the long prehistoric millennia when the earth's frame heaved and shifted and belched forth fire. Its continuing remoteness and its diversities of altitude, latitude, moisture, and exposure make it the home of a dazzling spectrum of natural life, running all the way from low-lying grasslands to alpine tundra.

The Rocky Mountains were a nurturing ground of North America's first civilizations, created by red men in response to what the land gave and withheld. For the mountain men, prospectors, entrepreneurs, cattlemen, and farmers of the nineteenth century, who saw the Rockies as a place to exploit and mold to the requirements of eastern or European culture, the mountains were a quirky and sullen host, dispensing gold and pelts and showers of wealth to some, bare dust and disappointments to many others. The region remained isolated and colonial, dependent on outside capital and markets, long after it had grown an indigenous American population.

Nowadays the Rockies are a land where the ultramodern and the primitive rub shoulders. One of the last islands of true American wilderness, they are a paradoxical place where cities, missile plants, giant mines, and oil rigs sprout amid grazing lands, forests, and salt flats; whose citizens cherish an ambivalence to the lucrative federal and corporate presence in their midst, fearing a growth that extracts irreplaceable natural wealth and a dependence that may someday turn "booms" to "busts."

The geologic heritage of the Rockies is clear on a relief map of the United States. A little to the west of the 105th meridian, the pale, unrelieved buff of the plains darkens and wrinkles, as if a giant hand had pushed the land from the west, leaving it puckered and contorted. From Montana to New Mexico, geography is complex and gnarled; names of cities and national parks lie on the land in twisted profusion, encircled by massive mountain ranges or nestled in foothills.

The land got this way through a billion years of alternating upheaval and quiescence, of erosion by wind, sand, water, and ice. Some of the energy for mountain-building came from magma and hot gases deep below the earth's surface, which expanding, forced the ground upward. Where the earth cracked, they exploded or oozed out, eventually forming mountain-sized deposits of volcanic rock. But mainly, the Rocky Mountains grew by folding and faulting, wherever the earth's crust wrinkled and pinched together, or where surface rock cracked and pressures from below pushed the rock on one side of the crack upward. The Absaroka Range in Wyoming is made of volcanic material, while the Teton Mountains and Utah's Wasatch Range are typical fault-block mountains, rising sheer and sudden above the plateaus on which they stand. Their steep scarps and crags are quite different from the mounded, rolling sides of Colorado's folded Front Range.

As they were squeezed upward, the mountains were

In Estes Park, the Stanley Hotel nestles below abrupt cliffs. Once a barrier that impeded travel and resisted settlement, the Rockies now provide a haven in the middle of a growing nation.

scoured and eroded from above by wind, dust, and slides of ice and snow. Rains carried much of their sedimentary covering down to form the foothills and valleys at the base of the Rockies, and as deposits piled up farther and farther east of the mountains, they formed the Great Plains, whose gentle westward rise attests to their origin.

Glaciers put the final touches on the Rocky Mountain profile during the Ice Age, which began around 3,000,000 years ago and lasted many thousands of years. Although the main block of ice which stretched from the Arctic into North America never reached as far south as the central Rockies, smaller regional ice sheets existed in the mountains as far south as New Mexico. Grinding with undetectable motion down the mountainsides, the great, crackling, blue-veined masses of ice smoothed off ragged peaks, scoured out huge, bowl-shaped indentations in the rock, widened narrow valleys, and shunted enormous boulders far from their original resting places, often leaving them strewn on mountain meadows in moraines.

To a great extent, the shape of the land determines the shape of life there—its limits and its possibilities. Each place has its rules of climate and resource and accessibility, sometimes successfully exploited or thwarted by man, yet never completely negated by his efforts. For the plants and animals of the area, these rules are the determiners of life, pure and simple.

Even to those who know the region well, the Rocky Mountains appear confusingly varied and even contradictory. One might say of the Rockies, as Wallace Stegner has said of the larger West, that "its life zones go all the way from arctic to sub-tropical, from reindeer moss to cactus, from mountain goat to horned toad. Its range of temperatures is as wide as its range of precipitation. . . . It is shortgrass plains, alkali flats, creosote-bush deserts, irrigated alluvial valleys, sub-arctic fir forests, bare, sun-smitten stone."

For all its variety, though, natural life in the Rocky Mountains reflects one basic reality—dryness. Geography dictates that the Rockies receive only the minutest portion of the moisture blowing in off the Pacific Ocean, for much of it is captured by the Sierra Nevada

lying between them and the coast. The air that continues across the Great Basin and the Rockies is hot and dry until, encountering the mountains' high ranges, it rises, cools, and precipitates its remaining moisture on their peaks and upper slopes. These high slopes just below timberline are the wettest parts of the mountains; here the snow piles deepest and stays longest, replenishing groundwater and nourishing the headwaters of rivers like the Colorado and the Green.

The breezes continue eastward over the Rockies, again wrung dry. All the eastern flanks of the ranges and the Wyoming Basin lie in the "rain shadow" of the mountains. Their only source of moisture is the runoff from rivers like the Yellowstone and Rio Grande and water accumulated on the slopes high above them.

Most of the flora typical of the Rocky Mountains— hardy grasses, ponderosa pine, juniper, piñon pine, and sagebrush—have survived there because they need little water and efficiently conserve what they have. Douglas fir and aspen, for which the mountains are also famed, are actually less widespread; they grow only at the higher elevations where there is plentiful water.

The animals most common to the area—coyote, mule deer, bighorn sheep, and wapiti—travel far and wide to find water and an equable climate in all seasons. Others, like the gopher, badger, and kangaroo rat, burrow underground, where the earth stays moist. Some of the most celebrated Rocky Mountain residents—the mountain goat and ptarmigan, for instance—survive there because they live in specialized spots, just below timberline or among the alpine meadows and peaks, where the climate is cold and wet.

The human spectrum in the Rockies is as broad as the natural. It goes all the way from the cosmopolitan urbanity of Denver to the loneliness of a sheepherder's covered wagon high in the San Juan Mountains; from the manicured amplitude of the Wyoming Hereford Ranch to the hogans, ancient crafts, and bare red earth of the Navajo Reservation; from the mechanized mines, smelters, and refineries of Butte, one of the world's most famous company towns, to the rural calm of southern Utah's farming villages.

But for human beings, too, the basic realities here are simple: the Rockies are generally an arid land,

In parts of the Pecos Wilderness Area of New Mexico, slopes are covered with a close-standing forest of conifers, stopped only by the harsh climate and resistant soil of timberline.

which demands much money and technology to support crops and cities—if it responds at all to such promptings; a land whose major wealth cannot be tapped by individual or regional capital alone, a land that has retained some of its isolation—with all its drawbacks and advantages—well into the twentieth century.

Only recently have the Rockies supported a white population, but from prehistoric times to the nineteenth century, Indian civilization survived and even flourished in the region. Unlike whites, Indians could live as minimally or as lavishly as the land dictated; while the white man attempted to bend the land and its resources to the standards of an imported culture, the Indian's culture was *of* the mountains, created by them. Thus, the Shoshonean peoples who roamed the arid plateaus and sagebrush flats of western Colorado and Utah lived nomadically in small bands, combing large areas for roots, insects, small animals—any food they could find. Their tools were few, their shelters minimal, their social and religious customs simple. In southwest Colorado, however, where the water supply and the terrain were more favorable, Anasazi and then Pueblo Indians built adobe edifices several stories high, farmed, irrigated, and created an elaborate religious and social structure. Between these two extremes lay a wide variety of Indian cultures, each formed in response to the specific conditions of the land from which it sprung.

White men first sought the Rocky Mountains in the eighteenth century, not to farm or settle there, but to seek out furs, mineral wealth, and grazing possibilities—pursuing ventures that were to become greatly dependent on outside capital and markets.

In the 1870s and 1880s, farmers came to the Rocky Mountains looking for permanent homes. Inspired by liberal but unrealistic homesteading laws, many farmers settled, without water rights or knowledge of irrigation and dry-farming, on land that was too dry to support crops. Many had to give up, and the history of those who stayed reaffirms the region's need for outside capital and controls. Farming here depends on the great dams and irrigation projects built by the federal government, and on interstate control of the water that all need so desperately.

Although twentieth-century development has changed much in the mountain economies, the Rockies remain relatively dependent on outside money. Since World War II, the area's main growth has been in aerospace and defense-related industries, in federal and state government agencies, in oil and mining, in manufacturing, in tourism, and in agriculture. Many people fear that the federal presence, which has so transformed the region, may prove to be ephemeral. The oil and mining ventures prompt a similar fear, because they extract finite resources and are run by giant corporations whose outlook is more national and global than regional. The Rockies' aridity has always made mountain farmers concentrate on one or two cash crops, and thus depend on outside markets for their livelihood.

Many mountain dwellers envision a future in which their economies will be more diversified, less dependent on outside interests, and more heedful of preserving the natural beauties and remoteness many sought in coming here. Further development of tourism and of manufacturing that depends on renewable natural resources like trees and grass may offer some answers to the region's problems.

In spite of new highways and industry, much of the Rocky Mountains remains a remote and beautiful wilderness, preserved by the federal government as parks, forests, wildlife preserves, and monuments. To a growing part of the American public, the Rockies, once a barrier to westward expansion, are now a barrier land of a different sort—one that offers a respite from the workaday world. Campers, hunters, hikers, and skiers flock to wilderness vacation spots, eager to put some distance, however small, temporary, or padded by modern comfort, between themselves and civilization. The ski industry, which has boomed since World War II, has shown the economic value of recreation and tourism. The mountains' isolation has itself become a resource, attracting a new income to the area. Already important in the mountain states' economies, tourism will play a crucial role in their futures.

From the austere grandeur of barren rock and snow above timberline to the gentle beauty of wild flowers and meadow grasses in aspen groves, the Rockies evince a rich variety of natural habitats.

CHAPTER 2

PROFILE OF THE ROCKIES

Peaks, plateaus, and mountain parks—a closer look at the varied physical features that make up the imposing Rocky Mountain chain

ROCK THROWN UPWARD, iced over by alpine glaciers, washed smooth by water in eons of geologic time only to be chiseled again into rugged silhouettes by a climate that compels rock to break—these are the Rocky Mountains. This imposing chain of peaks rises from the Great Plains and the Colorado Plateau more than a vertical mile into thin highland air, the domain of wind and sun, a long climb up and an arduous trip around.

The passes—river-cut valleys, intermontane "parks," and larger breaks of the chain—provided a select number of natural intermountain thoroughfares, which have themselves become almost as famous as the range. Raton Pass, east of the Sangre de Cristo Range; the "Gangplank" of Wyoming, a beveled sedimentary bridge over rocks of the mountain core (site of the right of way for the first transcontinental railroad); and South Pass on Wyoming's Continental Divide along the Oregon Trail—each one provided early routes through terrain men and wagons could cope with. Today the transmountain routes lead over the Continental Divide in spectacular high passes—Loveland, Berthoud, Rabbit Ears, Vail, Wolf Creek, Monarch, and others—winding through the mountains instead of around.

Variety is the key word of the Rockies in both southern and central branches of the great chain—variety in color, vegetative cover, altitude, structure, and geology. The long history of this region has resulted in broken patches of jumbled hard rock—massive groups of sediments, formed in great thicknesses, arched upward and folded, and then worn to reveal a beautiful core of red granite. Or, the rock is dark lava, extruded over an ancient land surface and then subjected to erosional forces of water and ice through periods of environmental cataclysm—the Great Ice Age, beginning almost 3,000,000 years ago, recent enough to leave its mark inscribed upon the land. There are no fresh lavas in the Rocky Mountains, just the volcanics of old fires that burned when the range itself was young and during its long growth. But uplift can originate in ways other than folding and volcanism; some of the earth's restlessness with confinement in millennia long past found expression in fault lines, which sheared the earth into giant sections of movable rock, making land ready for the uplifts that would gradually create the Rocky Mountain chain.

Weathering forces were to work vigorously against the preservation of these mountains in their original, post-upheaval condition. Water and ice would grind away hard rock, breaking it down to boulders, cobbles, pebbles, and fine grit, transporting the load outward for deposition upon the Great Plains. The high peaks were among the first to succumb, losing some of the original stature achieved in their upheaval, but in a peculiar way the climate and rock of these mountains have resisted the rounding forces that had already worn the Appalachian and other eastern chains into smooth forms; thus the high country peaks are serrated and dramatic—often more jagged than in their youth—still looming high above mountain valleys. Certainly in the span of a man's lifetime, the peaks seem only to be growing more jagged and craggy, more rugged in form.

The same great forces that uplifted the Colorado Front Range also canted ancient sands into "flatirons" in the Garden of the Gods, Colorado Springs.

Over the millennia, sporadic rainfall has eroded the clay walls of Fremont River Canyon in southern Utah.

But the forces that wear rock are legion. Weathering occurs constantly as rock is exposed to the atmosphere: to rain, which overruns rock surfaces, dislodging grains, dissolving soluble minerals, putting rock fragments in motion; to wind, which can batter airborne fragments against low ground obstacles; to desiccating sun. Or ice may be involved, developing its crystalline structure within cracks or between rock grains, later to wedge apart rock fragments that will be ready for transport. In massive quantities of highly crystalline rock, such as granite, frost-wedged fragments will tend to be large sized, breaking along jagged fracture lines and leaving the rocky face more angular in form.

That zenith of erosion, the Pleistocene Ice Age, repeated its cycle of advance and retreat four times. The continental ice that came from Canada chiefly affected the lowlands of North America, but the highlands had

their glacial counterpart in the alpine valley glaciers, which in many places swept down to 8,000-foot elevations. These valley ice fields were best developed on the eastern Rocky Mountain slopes, where their vigor and size were due to drifting summit snow and deep preglacial valleys; in their path they left a land transformed by the ice and anything ice could carry.

Ice erodes rock with many of the same techniques used by flowing water—exerting great force against an obstruction, breaking pieces from it, and then flowing past with the debris. Water has the advantages of higher speed and greater turbulence, but ice is more rigid, able to melt and refreeze while flowing around obstacles. Both carry fragments of rock, the tools a glacier will use to abrade the surface over which it must flow.

Because ice flows very slowly and will deform only

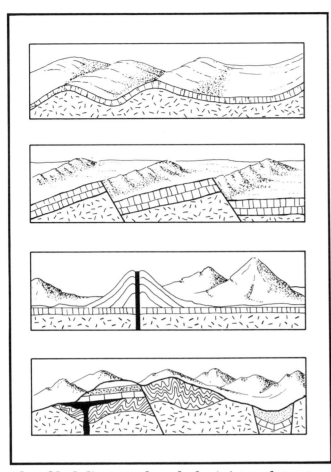

These block diagrams show the basic internal structure of mountains. Top to bottom: folded mountains, high scarps of fault-block mountains, lava flows with volcanic "plumbing," and an eroded composite range.

ments and carry away rock debris from the glacial headwalls. The multiply-jointed granite and thin sedimentary rocks of the southern and central Rockies are particularly susceptible. Amphitheater-shaped bowls, called "cirques," are seen almost everywhere among the high country peaks, the results of extended and vigorous glacial activity.

The typical alpine landscape of rough rock sidewalls and smooth valley channels continues downslope in what was likely once a crudely carved river valley. The postglacial walls are broadly curved and U-shaped, typical of a slope that once served as the trough for a moving channel of ice. But in this alpine setting of smooth valleys and high meadows there may be found peculiar landforms resulting from glaciation, as tributary rivers of ice joined the main flow. Being narrower and not as deep, the tributary glacier floor will usually lie far above the deep channel of the master glacial trough—forming the "hanging valley," an oddity almost as widespread as cirques in the Rockies, characteristic of this present geologic age but derived from times of massive ice accumulation, when ice ruled most of the land surface and carved the alpine features repeatedly preserved upon our present mountains. Those landscapes created by ice in the highlands are among the most profound and easily identifiable features; each range that has had ice upon its shoulders will bear the traces of this domination.

under massive pressures, rock fragments are trapped between the glacier and its channel, either dragged along at the glacial base, scratching grooves upon underlying rock and being itself ground flat in the meantime, or floating freely, incorporated within the ice. Only the larger rock fragments join the ice mass, carried alongside its outer walls; these are broken from mountain summits by a unique process of quarrying that happens only in ice fields of the temperate climate zones, high at the glacier head. Summit moisture—from blowing snow, avalanche, and direct snowfall—collects along any weak joints in the rocky highlands, initially to melt, then to refreeze and split the rock, permitting the permanent ice fields to incorporate loose rock frag-

P ROBABLY MOST FAMILIAR among all the various Rocky Mountain ranges is the Colorado Front Range, from whose central granite axis flanking sedimentary beds dip to the east and to the west, creating a fascinating secondary foothill topography. Distinctly north-south in trend, the Front Range rises steeply out of the Great Plains to timbered slopes, surmounted by alpine regions of sharp summits and great glacial amphitheaters. The Front Range is a broad upward fold, with many peaks rising to 13,000 and 14,000 feet.

Eastern foothills fringe this mountain base with sedimentary layers of hard rock, upturned to steep angles, often jagged, separated from the main range by long valleys. These foothills, also called "hogbacks," or "flatirons," dip sharply eastward—in part the result of upfolding in the main mountain block, during its long

While Colorado was casting up barriers of stone, the Wyoming Basin was filling with monumental sheets of detritus;

growth, climaxed by the onset of erosion. As rock layers were stripped away, only layers that were particularly hard to erode survived; among those was the Dakota sandstone, a rough layer of sediments forming the hogback ridgeline near Golden (northwest of Denver), and the spooky anvils of Fountain formation sandstone in Boulder's Flatirons and the Garden of the Gods near Colorado Springs. The rocky hogbacks present limited environments for vegetation. Nonetheless, some sheltered hillsides have stands of aspen, yellow pine, and sparse growths of juniper and piñon above 6,000 feet. In moist valleys, the hackberries and other hardwood trees develop moderate size, while cottonwoods align themselves along the lower stream channels.

Contrasts to the sparse tree cover of the foothills are found on the timbered slopes of the Front Range itself. This range's variety defies generalization; the images change constantly as summits rise from plateau to timberline, and the face of the range adapts quickly. Rising from the north end of the Front Range is a snowy range known as the Laramie; to the south are the lower Wet Mountains; and between, west and northwest of Denver, the Front Range crest rises skyward to become high and formidable. Even the passes are more difficult here, as they wind along deep, steepsided mountain gorges. The east face of Longs Peak rises in a sheer perpendicular cliff 3,000 feet from timberline to summit. All along the range's eastern face, there is little interruption to precipitous slopes as a continuous line of steep-walled Front Range amphitheaters face toward the plains.

Southward from the landmark of Arapahoe Peak, the glacial sculpturing and spire topography are less obvious; the crest of the Continental Divide rises dramatically above two levels of ancient erosion. But individual peaks—James, Evans, Grays, and Torreys—still

below its forsaken landscape lie trona, phosphate rock, uranium, and other valued minerals.

display turrets, buttresses, and other castellated forms. These are troublesome areas in which to fight fire, and in past blazes large acreages of the Front Range have burned. Lodgepole pine and aspen of this high country are second-growth vegetation.

The southern Front Range landmark is Pikes Peak, between Colorado Springs and Cripple Creek. Many other mountains are higher, but none rises on the very edge of the Great Plains, isolated from other peaks, with such commanding appearance. Zebulon Pike thought the peak was unclimbable, but ascents were made and eventually an automobile road was built to the summit. From the 14,110-foot top of this famous peak, neighbors—Cameron Cone, Sachett Mountain, Bald Mountain, Mount Rosa, and Cheyenne Mountain —seem puny in comparison. On a clear day, the viewer might see Blanca Peak by looking south to the Sangre de Cristo Range, and the strange Spanish Peaks, with

radial dikework branching outward from this ancient center of local Rockies volcanism.

A southern mountain group—represented by the Sangre de Cristo Range—continues the almost straight line formation begun by the Rockies' eastern front. The dark color of the Sangre de Cristo rock emphasizes the deep and razor-sharp crest line, with precipitous peaks boldly and majestically rising out of the bordering lowlands. Extending beyond Santa Fe, New Mexico, which is located low on a southwestern flank, is the Sangre de Cristo, which finally brings the Rockies to their southern terminus with a number of small ranges and dry mountain groups.

Parallel with the front ranges but immediately to the west are two ranges, the Sawatch and the Park, each with equivalent structures and topographic expression, each separated from the Colorado Front Range by a chain of intermontane basins—the "park" meadowlands, rolling interludes to the high mountain story.

Both Sawatch and Park ranges resulted from uplifts, but this common primary structure has been complicated by later events. The Park, which begins at the north as a rolling, timbered plateau with massive, sloped margins, grades into rugged summits bordered by glacially carved amphitheaters and steep cliffsides. Here erosion has been effective; deep canyons alternate with narrow ridges so incised by the glacial ice that some mountain spurs are merely skeletons of rock. Carved from hard granite, these slopes are steep; but at lower elevations, where the rock is sedimentary, descents tend to be flat faced and gentle. The Sawatch structure has also been complicated, but by volcanic flows, which wrap about the great granite-core rock and are a part of the widespread volcanism that occurred long ago to the south in the San Juan Mountains. The Sawatch is 100 miles long and bristling with major 14,000-foot peaks, including Mount Elbert (14,431), the highest in the long Rockies chain. But the range's national fame was to come from gold discoveries there in 1860, and silver-associated lead in 1877.

The intermontane valleys—North, Middle, and South parks, and the San Luis Valley—are basins of an exceptional nature; all lie in the midst of a rugged mountain region where dissection is profound, yet each one is a center of sediment accumulation. They are structural depressions in the earth's topography, relatively low in elevation but with high outlets, drained by the Platte (North Park), the Colorado (Middle Park), the South Platte (South Park), and the headwaters of the Rio Grande (San Luis Valley); thus all are headlands of major drainage systems. In essence, the parks are lofty, rolling meadows, enclosed by the pine- and snow-covered mountains, which offer protection from temperature fluctuation and screen out heavy snows. Each of the basins is also an island of lower rainfall, among peaks with higher precipitation.

Clues to the geological past are everywhere, as in this roadcut west of Denver, where the dynamic origin of a foothill is revealed by upturned layers of sedimentary rock.

*The wave of tension that built mountains from the Sierra to the Rockies totally bypassed
the Colorado Plateau, thus leaving rock layers horizontal at Canyonlands Park.*

Beyond the Sawatch and Park axes are western border ranges, a belt of interlocking mountains, more irregular in form than those of the east, with plateau and valley interruptions, offset with unusual mountain groups—many of them igneous in origin; they are the Elk, La Plata, San Juan, and Uncompahgre mountains. Access to these ranges is limited; there are few trails and hardly any permanent settlements within the rugged highlands. The San Juans represent many shared characteristics of these ranges, basically those that result when lava is poured upon a sedimentary landscape.

Surrounding country is arid, but the mountains themselves never fail to have abundant precipitation, supporting dense forests of white pine, scrub oak, piñon pine, and cedar on the lower slopes, with some spruce and aspen on the higher. Large areas of the interior above timberline are so deep in rock fragments that the slopes support no plant growth at all. Landslides also help to remove and discourage plant colonization of the high slopes. The regional rock is soft shale topped by well-layered lavas; they have been deeply incised from the canyon cutting of Ice Age glaciers. Once rain slicks the flat shale surfaces, landslide conditions prevail in every ravine head and on every steep ridge slope.

BETWEEN THE CENTRAL AND SOUTHERN ROCKIES, there is a large intermontane depression merging eastward into the Great Plains, embracing a great deal of topography unknown to the mountains; this is the Wyoming Basin. In late evening, shadows fall long upon the basin floor—cast by the low buttes, mesas, and ground-hugging vegetation. Semiaridity is a fact of life here, among parched reminders of water shortages: sagebrush, tumbleweed, badlands, alkali flats, and sand dune accumulations. But these dry flatlands have generated an excitement as profound as any that has ever

gripped the high country Rockies. Rock formations under the surface layers of the basins were found to be reservoirs for oil and natural gas, coal, and uranium, as well as oil shale within the central flatlands. At its borders, other natural resources were exposed—limestone, gypsum, phosphate rock, and building stones—fossil remnants from the incursion of a marine world in another geologic age. Upon this vast mineral wealth, the topography of the present day has been structured.

Going "up in the Basin country" has always meant traveling to the Bighorn Basin, located in Wyoming between a mountain range of the same name and the eastern Absaroka Mountains. The basin floor is typical badland country, carved by ancient and recent streams biting deeply into the red and purple clay stone. Other basins emulate this topography, but few are as widespread, or as well known for the fossil life preserved in these badland rock layers. East of the Bighorns, along the mile-wide-and-inch-deep Powder River, similar flat topography is repeated but portrayed in a different way; because surface rocks are stronger and more able to survive stream erosion, a unique butte and ridge landscape exists. Its origin is linked to what lies beneath—the coal beds, which often occur within basins of this area, and extensive natural underground burning. Coal fires beneath shales have baked clay rock to the hardness of brick, making so brittle a cap rock that its preservation became guaranteed in the form of the present tablelands.

The badland theme is repeated elsewhere throughout Wyoming—at Hell's Half Acre, where sedimentary rock is severely dissected, and to the southwest in the Green River, Washakie, and Great Divide basins, where intertonguing sedimentary rocks, both marine and continental, display their conglomerate, limestone, siltstone, and oil shale in vertical slices. Where badlands are not prevalent, the buttes and knobs of hard rock rise above light-colored, chalky sedimentary strata, devoid of vegetation so that every wrinkle, fault, and pinnacle is fully visible.

With its wealth of geologic history, intense water erosion, faulting, downwarps, flash floods, evaporation, and resources, the intermontane sag in the mountain world known as the Wyoming Basin hides many secrets beneath a shell of dry desolation. To the economic geologist, paleontologist, geomorphologist, and the casual tourist who is looking for a different kind of solitude and is not intimidated by vast distances, these basin lands can be beautiful.

Mountains of the Wyoming Basin are either local upwarps—Sweetwater Arch, Rawlins Uplift, and Rock Springs Uplift—or they belong to the Rockies. The Sierra Madre continues the Park Range, while the Medicine Bow and Laramie mountains cradle Laramie Basin but are part of the southern Rockies. On the north and west, the Wyoming Basin rubs shoulders with rock from the central section of the long Rockies chain —the Bighorn and Owl Creek mountains, and the Absaroka and Wind River ranges; while farther west the Wasatch and Uinta mountains, along with several small but dramatic ranges such as the Tetons and Gros Ventre, and the Yellowstone Plateau continue a heritage of high peaks begun in the south and contribute their own variations to Rocky Mountain landforms.

Ranges of the central rockies are broken and rugged, reaching to great heights, like their counterparts farther south. Most have occurred as great folds or wrinkles in the crustal surface, but some have arisen in other ways—in the displacement of mighty blocks, bounded by fractures, or (like the Yellowstone Plateau and the Absaroka Range) from volcanic activity. This central region is maverick and confusingly unpatterned, with respect both to the rock involved with its formation and to its irregularity of trend; many of the uplands are not even mountains.

A great concave arc sweeps from Montana-Wyoming borderlands, around Bighorn Basin, and westward to Yellowstone Park, with the highest and most rugged sector lying in the Bighorn Mountains. Asymmetrically folded, the range rises gently out of its western basin into a rolling upland, culminated by 8,000-foot plateaus—broad and flat, with only scrubby trees covering the rock-strewn summits. Large canyons trench the summit surfaces, and these moist, lower regions support growth of lodgepole pine (known locally as white pine) and yellow and jack pines. Wood of the white pine, the dominant species, is knotty, coarse-grained, easily warped, and not usually lumbered.

The central plateau ends in 13,166-foot Cloud Peak and then drops sharply down a steep east face, opening

The Spearhead defiantly dares the forces of wind, water, and ice to erase its massive granite pinnacle from the horizon of Rocky Mountain National Park.

into forested parks. On the eastern valley floor, hog-backs—standstone outcrops harder than the valley shales—rise to 200 feet.

Bold, thousand-foot precipices remain from the last glacial epochs, carved upon the compact and almost structureless granite of the central mountain crest. Small lakes dot the mountain highlands, and these too are remnants of the Great Ice Age.

A low range of mountains at the southern end of the Bighorns provides the setting for a magnificent canyon crossing by the Wind River, flowing north. East walls of the canyon are those of the Bridger Mountains; at the west, the Owl Creeks. The cross cut is so deep that a 3,000-foot section of mountain geology is exposed: the tilted fold line, with gentle northern slopes and steep southern exposures.

Headwaters of the Yellowstone, Shoshone, Greybull, and Wood rivers begin in a large range of broad rolling highlands known as the Absaroka; though the summits rise to 11,000 and 12,000 feet, peaks are few in number and the landscape of bogs, small lakes, and many small streams give no sense of altitude. The summit is basic-ally a plateau of volcanic debris accumulated from nearby lava vents, upon which have been incised the deep valleys that alone have developed this high moor-land into something resembling a mountain range.

On the Yellowstone Plateau, too, mountainous con-tours are due to the erosion of narrow valleys rather than the dramatic formation of peaks. The plateau is a conifer-covered, broad expanse amid a rolling general topography. A present reminder of its volcanic history is the continuing thermal activity in the form of geysers, hot springs, and steam vents, or fumaroles, which are by far the most abundant expression of this thermal energy, with steam appearing almost anywhere—in for-ested areas, by stream banks, and even beneath rivers. Under most of the Yellowstone Plateau, fire has been smoldering throughout geologic time; though thought to be waning, fire nonetheless persists, perhaps just 15,000 feet below the lava surface.

To the south, isolated and majestic, are the moun-tains of the Teton Range—serrated, razor-sharp crests, snow-covered yearly. The granite summits rise several thousand feet above timberline, lofting to their greatest height with the bold Grand Teton. Profound forces raised this block of rock out of the earth's shell, tilted back the granite wall, then slowed the upward move-ment, creating a range that now towers one and one-half miles above the Snake River plain. Tranquil in comparison, the chain of small lakes—Phelps, Taggart, Bradley, Jenny, Leigh, and Jackson—fringed by mead-ows and interspersed by forests, lie below this towering mountain front.

Other ranges lie to the south: the wild primitive area of the Wind River Range; the rugged Gros Ventre Mountains; a series of small mountain ranges along the Wyoming, Utah, and Idaho borders, more plateau than mountain; and then the strange configuration of an east-west-trending range, the Uintas, and its less radical neighbor, the Wasatch.

The Wasatch is different from the others; stretching past the Great Salt Lake, it has a complex formation. Along the western slope is a scarp equal in dramatic impact to the eastern Tetons or the eastern Sierra Ne-vada, formed along an old fault line and resulting from uplift along this line of weakness. Ten miles north of Provo, Utah, Mount Timpanogos rises 12,008 feet to survey the Uinta and Wasatch national forests, and from this height the southern high tableland of the Wasatch Plateau can also be seen, broken by many elaborate irrigation tunnels, developed by early Mor-mon settlers in this valley of the Great Salt Lake.

SINCE THE ROCKIES WERE FIRST UPLIFTED, and through-out most of geologic time, water and ice have been upon the mountains, altering the form of hard rock, decisively changing the evolution of landforms, setting fragments from high peaks awash toward the Great Plains. Water and ice have shaped the present range, carving its valleys and foothills into a rugged, bold to-pography. Not much is known about how the Rockies looked in the rough-hewn stages of their great uplift, but much is understood concerning how the range was formed. This story involves a geologic history and an "evolution" known definitely to have occurred because of the evidence preserved within the rock and land-forms of today's mountains.

With an elevation of 14,001 feet, Sunshine Peak near Telluride barely qualifies as one of Colorado's mighty "Fourteeners." Skyline Lake is at left.

*This wall of spooled pinnacles — fancifully named Goblin City — is part of the
Needles area, a remote southern section of Canyonlands National Park.*

*The pale granite of Pikes Peak rises above the red sandstone
of Gateway Rocks, Garden of the Gods.*

*Overleaf: The Great Sand Dunes National Monument lies in a mountain-rimmed cul-de-sac with
scant vegetation and strong winds — a perfect trap for blowing sand.*

Colorado's two tallest peaks are Mount Massive (center, 14,421 feet) and Mount Elbert (snow-capped at left, 14,433 feet).

39

CHAPTER 3

BIRTH OF THE RANGE

*The tumultuous geological story of the fires and seismic forces
that raised these mighty mountains from a tranquil inland sea*

ALMOST ONE BILLION YEARS AGO an area now known as western North America was beginning a series of formative events that would bring the entire Rocky Mountain chain into existence. Earth movements began quietly, required immense epochs of geologic time for their completion, and then passed to new eras of quiet and waiting, only to be followed by more movement and change. Eventually mountains arose out of the uneasiness, in an event so radical the upheaval is known as the Laramide "Revolution."

The revolution's prehistory began with the formation of a great, slowly sinking trough extending southward from what would later be the Gulf of Alaska to the Gulf of California. Sediments and other products of erosion were washed from inland sources outward to the continental margins and were caught within the sinking, sea-covered trough.

A sister trough—the Appalachian—was sinking in similar fashion along the eastern coast, subsiding slowly, at a rate of filling almost equal to the rate of its deepening; and between these two unsteady coasts was a vast interior, slowly being flooded by the sea.

For some unknown reason, the western trough suddenly split into inner and outer sections, each essentially keeping its own previous north-south trend in what was to be a period of unstable conditions within the western lowlands. To the east, the Appalachian Mountains were beginning their rise, developing the folds and structures of mountain uplift long before western ranges were ready.

A great many seas would sweep over the western trough before the land was high enough to keep out invading water, and during these repeated floods new layers of sediment would be laid upon the continent. Some were limestone and shale, deposited in marine environments; others formed while the continental landmass was most exposed, and these would be sandstones and coarse conglomerates with large, angular rock fragments. Interwoven among the fluctuations of the seas was the development on land of the first plant species—simple in structure, lacking true leaves, and reproducing by spores grown at the ends of their branching stems. More advanced varieties appeared later—species with stronger stems and branching root systems, growing in the lowlands and along shorelines. They would provide the peat and fossil vegatative matter that would become the coal beds of Colorado and Wyoming.

An inner section of the great trough began to buckle and fold, forming a small mountainous unit—the Ancestral Rockies—in what is now the Utah–Colorado–New Mexico area. Erosion on these highlands produced large aprons of debris on mountain slopes and in the basins between ranges. (Red sandy shale and sandstone, upturned by even more massive earth movements, were one day to be the Colorado Front Range foothills and the archetypal hogback ridges of the Garden of the Gods.) The climate was warm, even at higher elevations; deposits of salts found within the mountains of eastern Utah and western Colorado tell of a full climatic change—from a consistently humid climate to drought and temperature diversity, as coal swamps

*Square Top Mountain and a forested, glacier-carved valley stand at the headwaters
of the Green River, high in Wyoming's Wind River Mountains.*

GEOLOGICAL TIME CHART

YEARS AGO (Approximate)	ERA	PERIOD	EPOCH	IMPORTANT EVENTS (Italic type indicates events in Rocky Mountains)
10,000—	Cenozoic	Quaternary	Recent	*Time of continuous Rocky Mountain growth, warmer climate, and glacier recession.*
3,000,000—			Pleistocene	*Glaciers cover the Rockies in at least three major ice advances.* First evidence of man.
11,000,000— 25,000,000—		Tertiary	Pliocene	*Mountain streams are rejuvenated and begin canyon cutting; the Tetons rise along a fault line.*
			Miocene	*Period of extensive erosion in the Rockies.*
40,000,000—			Oligocene	*The Rockies are entirely above sea level, ending the Laramide Revolution.*
			Eocene	*The last major pulse of mountain building in the Rockies, arching the Uinta Mountains and forming many Wyoming ranges.*
60,000,000— 70,000,000—			Paleocene	*The Front Range is uplifted and the parks are established between ranges; the Garden of the Gods is formed.*
135,000,000—	Mesozoic	Cretaceous		*A second mountain building pulse in the Rockies.* *The Sierra Nevada are again uplifted.* *Beginning of the Laramide Revolution.* *Extinction of the dinosaurs.* Flowering plants appear.
180,000,000—		Jurassic		*The Morrison Formation is deposited as a continental ocean retreats.* Mountain building begins in the Sierra Nevada. Birds and mammals evolve.
225,000,000—		Triassic		Dinosaurs first appear. *Ancestral Rockies are eroded and buried under their own debris.*
270,000,000—	Paleozoic	Permian		*A major period of mountain building begins as the Ancestral Rockies develop.* *A shallow sea covers Wyoming.*
305,000,000—		Pennsylvanian		Conifer forests appear. Coal swamps form. Reptiles evolve. *Sediments begin to fill the Rocky Mountain trough.*
350,000,000—		Mississippian		Insects first appear. *There is restlessness and early mountain uplift in the Rocky Mountain trough.*
400,000,000— 440,000,000—		Devonian		Vertebrates appear on the land. Fish evolve.
		Silurian		First land plants.
500,000,000—		Ordovician		The marine world grows with the addition of corals and sea urchins.
600,000,000—		Cambrian		Mollusks, trilobites dominate. *Marine sediments are deposited within the Rocky Mountain trough.*
		Precambrian		*The Rocky Mountain trough is initiated.*

were replaced by upland and desert vegetation, as reptiles gained land supremacy, and as spore-bearing plants were replaced by hardier, seed-bearing trees.

Another mountain-building event was started in north-central Nevada. The land was becoming restless. Regions west of the Rockies were the first disturbed by uplifts as a swell of activity spread eastward from the coast. Upwelling in the Sierra Nevada area signaled the presence of forces that would later buckle crustal layers of sedimentary rock. Slow eastward-moving streams carried rubble from the new mountains down to the last inland sea, where 500 feet of multicolored clays and coarse sediments—the Morrison deposition—were to record the epic dynasty of reptiles in the Rocky Mountains. Within this layer of rock exposed at Dinosaur National Monument, in western Colorado, paleontologists would find a rich trove of well-preserved dinosaur bones along with fossil remains of the first primitive mammals, many plants, and freshwater invertebrates, which would date the time of deposition at around 150,000,000 years ago.

The force that signaled a geologic revolution swept upon layers of rock as great as 50,000 feet thick; rock was crumpled by the jaws of a global vise, torn along lines of weakness, thrust upward over other rock layers, sometimes recrystallizing under tremendous pressures and heat, sometimes being severed by jets of hot, pressured lava. Folding was most severe within the western ranges; as deforming pulses moved east, they began losing strength. Folding became less complex, and alteration by heat and pressure was minimal.

In the 40,000,000 years since rocks of the mountain region were first subjected to major and dramatic uplift, the Rockies have continued their evolution; regional deformation resulted in tilting of the massive Great Plains region, arching sedimentary rock into the "flatiron" foothill topography. The Rockies continued to rise as a unit, adding another 5,000 feet of elevation to the crest, presenting a rain barrier that would stand before moist Pacific winds, shielding the plains from western rainfall and so altering plains ecology that all the browsing herbivorous mammals were replaced by animals adapted to feeding on the harsher grasses of the semiarid plains. Many cycles of erosion followed in which the mountains lost much of their top layers of rock to the persistent erosive power of water and the extensive glaciation introduced by the Great Ice Age. But the ranges maintained their basic structures with integrity: the arched upfolds, the fault lines miles in length, and the remnants of molten rock extruded upon a sedimentary earth surface—these would remain to tell the history and sequence of the great revolution. A record of the events that shaped individual ranges would remain frozen in time within the rock layers of this impressive mountain chain.

RESULTS OF MOUNTAIN UPLIFT in the Rockies are displayed within the peaks of the Front Range and on the plains near Denver. By traveling west from that city, one crosses a succession of rocks that turn back the pages of geologic time—from the high plains and South Platte River Valley, to older rocks of the upturned foothills, to rock of the ancient mountain core.

The Front Range came into existence as a large, upward-folded arch, lifted gradually, between periods of lowland elevations and encroachment of inland seas. With each successive vertical movement, the forces of erosion vigorously renewed their attack upon the highlands. Sediments, laid like carpet upon older rocks, were worn away on the mountain crest but not along the base. Because much of its history is recorded in their sedimentary layers, the foothills west of Denver provide a key to understanding the geology of the Front Range upheaval.

Seventy million years ago, the sedimentary foothill

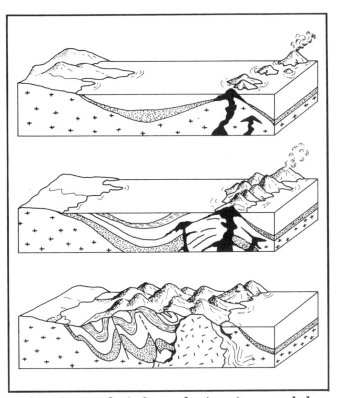

Activity in a geological trough, since it occurs below the earth's surface, is best seen in block diagrams. Stage 1: Land sinks slightly and the trough develops, collecting debris from higher ground. Here it lies beneath a sea dotted with volcanic islands. Stage 2: More and more sediments flow into the sinking trough, building distinctive layers, which harden to rock. Stage 3: The rock is folded and faulted into mountains, and the sea is expelled. In time, molten granite seeps up into the mountain mass (center right).

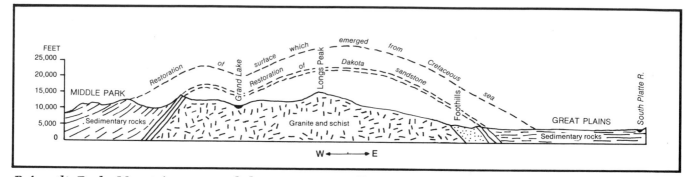

Before the Rocky Mountains were eroded, an east-west profile north of Denver would have shown a sedimentary cap covering the granite core (dashed lines), arched in a nearly perfect mountain fold.

layers bent sharply upward, and molten lava oozed out through great fractures along the mountain flanks; molten granite also intruded along fracture lines to build an ancient core. These granites cooled to form the light-gray Silver Plume granite found near the towns of Silver Plume and Georgetown (west of Denver), the gray Boulder Greek granite of Mount Evans and west of Boulder, the red Pikes Peak granite west of Colorado Springs, and the red Sherman granite of the Colorado-Wyoming border. Then a second granitic mass of rock appeared at the center of the range, permeated with hot gaseous solutions spreading through open fissures deep within the rock, introducing the gold, silver, and lead ores whose discovery would cause a fever in Central City and Idaho Springs in 1859.

Immediately surrounding granite-core rocks are types that are even older; igneous and metamorphic rocks, so changed by pressure and heat that their original characteristics have become obscured. By measuring the decay of some radioactive minerals, the age of these ancient rocks is fixed at one and one-half billion years, certainly the first rock to be involved in mountain-building within the Rockies.

The rock layers become younger and sedimentary as their distance increases from the mountain core and its associated volcanics and metamorphics; in traveling east one essentially moves from ancient geologic history into the history of more recent times. Unfortunately there are gaps within the record. One of the first recognizable flanking sedimentary layers lies in an unusual way right

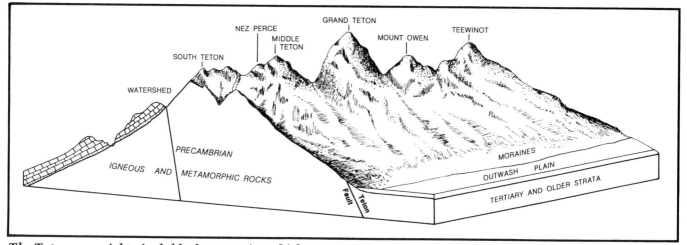

The Tetons are mighty fault-block mountains which were raised up along the Teton faultline.

upon the ancient core, and is exposed at the spectacular Red Rocks Amphitheater. These colorful red monuments of sandstone lie unconformably upon core rocks, a reminder of the sinking trough that spelled the beginning of the mountains. But the mountain core and its adjacent sedimentary rock layer were formed in different geologic ages, 300,000,000 years apart in time, with no depositional rock record or other information remaining to tell what happened during the gap in earth history.

Farther to the east lie the upturned hogbacks, the pronounced blades of Dakota sandstone still younger than the Red Rocks. They were sandy beach deposits of an ancient sea at one time and are still ripple-marked upon the surface. These sandstone layers were formed in the shallow water of another age, when dinosaurs walked the beaches and left footprints to tell of their presence here.

Eastward of the hogbacks, the land is linked more to recent geologic events than to the past because rivers and streams have done far more than mountain uplift to shape the land into contemporary form. An array of ridges, mesas, and hills stands between the mountains and the Denver Basin; one of these—Green Mountain—has been capped by naturally cemented gravels, now rock hard and known as conglomerate. The cap was deposited by an old channel of the South Platte River, which in those times followed a course through volcanic mudflows. Since then the river channel has dropped, but remnants of its heritage still remain. Several other gravel-capped, sloping surfaces, known as pediments, stand 400 feet above present stream levels, rising westward toward the mountain front. These pediments were formed thousands of years ago by streams emerging from the highlands, planing off bedrock and depositing gravels upon the eroded surfaces.

Denver lies twelve miles east of the mountains in the broad valley that the South Platte River has eroded into the rock of the eastward-sloping high plains. As the river slowly lowered its bed, old channels were abandoned; one such old streambed—Broadway terrace—is now downtown Denver. In excavations made as the city was built, fossil bones of mammoths and camels, as well as artifacts of primitive man, were found among the loose sand and gravels. Other tools of man—scrapers, arrowheads, and stone implements—were found lying about upon the terrace surface.

In many respects, there is a more detailed story to tell about sedimentary rock layers because fossil bones, teeth, shells, and footprints can be found within this rock, to be dated and to tell the evolutionary events of the region. Primordial rock layers do not contain the same type of evidence. The granite mountain core is a crystalline rock, composed of many different types of minerals, but without fossil remnants. Individual minerals tell relatively little about the rock they are found within, thus the detailed, irrefutable story of how emplacement of the Front Range core came about remains unavailable. Most of what is known about the primordial core rock has been learned by circuitous routes, an evolving technology, and the ability of the geologist to use every scrap of data available.

GRANITE CORES remain basic to other parts of the Rockies. They lie at the heart of Longs Peak, the Mount of the Holy Cross, the Black Canyon of the Gunnison, Royal Gorge, and the San Juan Range of southwestern Colorado (the Needle Mountains); other areas are the core of the Beartooth Range, Cloud Peak of the Bighorn Range, the Teton Mountains, and the Wind River summits. All have been formed of one of the oldest rock masses known to man.

The Tetons are a different mountain type within the Rockies. Early geologists thought that this group was nearly all granite and was really the core of a mountain range stripped of its eastern sedimentary half, but recent observers conclude there is a totally different explanation. The Tetons are the product of uplift along a fault at the eastern foot of the range, believed to lie at the juncture between the mountains and the flatlands of the Snake River Valley but unobservable because deposits of the last Ice Age and debris shed by the range conceal the line of movement. The presence of the fault must be inferred from the absence of foothills, the straight east face of the Tetons, and small steep slopes along the eastern mountain front.

A fault zone is subject to great tension, tending to pull apart the crustal skin of rock and causing adjustments of the earth beneath. The Teton mountain block is anchored on the west, along the Idaho-Wyoming border, and able to move only along the line of the

Folded rock layers of Dinosaur National Monument recall the upheaval that raised the Rockies.

fault. With displacement limited to the eastern scarp, its peaks have become among the most spectacular of any range in the Rockies.

The youngest of those mountains created by the Rocky Mountain uplift, the Tetons are known to be still rising. Current movement is indicated by small faults cross-cutting recent deposits on the range's eastern side, but judgments concerning rate of movement are best derived from displacement along the original fault, which has averaged one foot per 500 years. Movement has occurred in a series of violent jolts, rather than continuously. Small earthquakes have been frequent in the Teton region in recorded history, and observers say that larger ones can probably be expected.

Granite in the Tetons is exposed continuously along the backbone of the range, from Buck Mountain north toward upper Leigh Canyon, forming Grand Teton and most of its surrounding peaks. Unlike many granites of the Colorado Front Range, Teton granite is composed of gray quartz crystals and white feldspars, with flakes of black and white mica resembling pepper grains scattered through it. But the range is not entirely granite. Somber gray-colored masses surrounding paler granite disclose even more ancient, layered metamorphics seen along trails near Static Peak, Indian Paintbrush, and Death canyons (the northern or southern parts of the range) or as isolated inclusions among the high peak granites.

Light-colored veins of granite (igneous dikes) trace a webbed network through the darker metamorphics. These inclusions range from just a few inches in diameter to slabs hundreds of feet thick and thousands of feet long. One of the most conspicuous dikes, a black one on Mount Moran, formed as molten rock welled upward through an almost vertical fissure. The intruding hot rock crystallized rapidly between cold granite on either side of the fissure, while hot solutions also rose to permeate Moran's metamorphic peak, staining the main wall rosy red in color.

While the dikes were being intruded on Moran, Middle Teton, and Grand Teton, many thousands of feet of sandstone were being deposited in western Montana, 200 miles northwest of Grand Teton National Park. Reworked, recrystallized, and recemented fragments of this rock became quartzite. In time, thousands of hard, rounded gravels from this source were carried eastward by glacial meltwater, to be deposited finally in a huge Jackson Hole gravel sheet, 80,000,000 years ago. They had been jolted, tumbled, and pushed by streams of ice and tremendous glacial runoff, yet these almost indestructible gravels retained the structure and characteristics of their original sediments.

Once the Tetons were formed, the slow process of erosion began to carve down the topography; the concept of "everlasting hills" is a myth within the realm of geologic time. Small faults at the bases of Mount Teewinot, Rockchuck Peak, and other peaks; a block of land forming Jackson Hole that continues to drop and tilt downward along its western edge; gravel-covered land that once tipped southward but is now dipping westward toward the mountains; Fish Creek (a minor tributary of the Snake River) following its streambed fifteen feet lower than the Snake—these effects of continued disturbance indicate that mountain uplift is not yet stilled in the Tetons and that the erosive forces don't yet have dominance in the mountains.

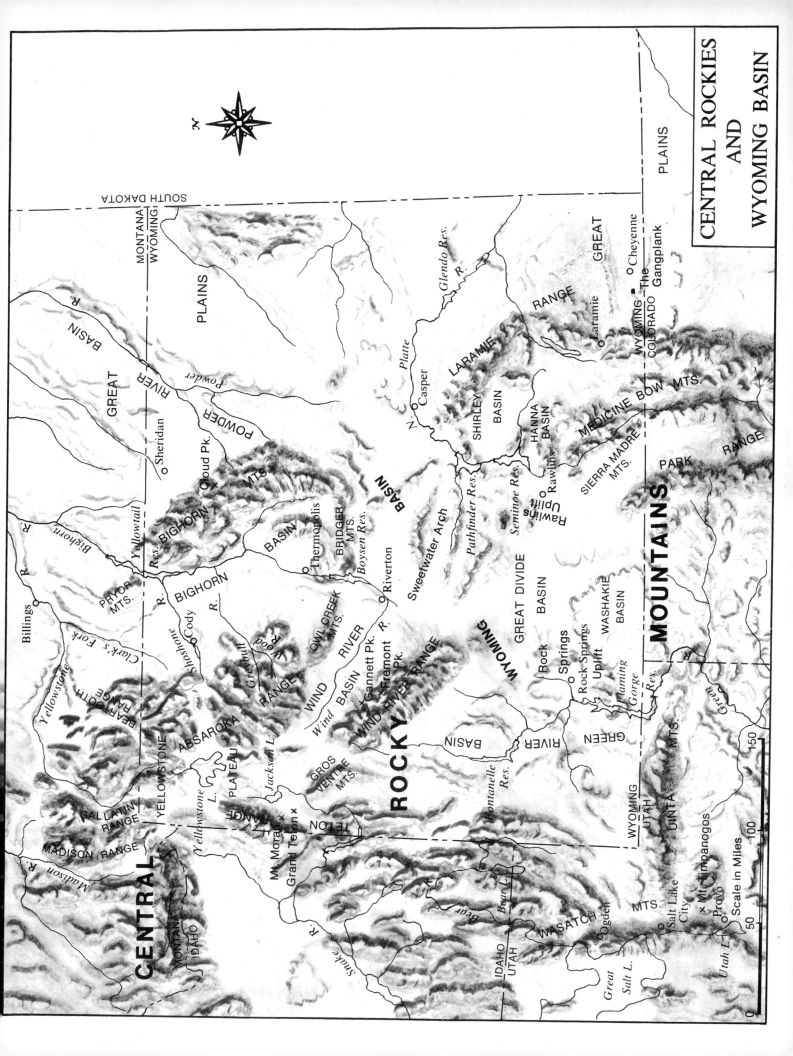

CENTRAL ROCKIES
AND
WYOMING BASIN

Yellowstone Indians knew of the "valley of many smokes" long before John Colter "discovered" these geysers.

CAPPING THE NORTHERN TETON RANGE are enormous ancient lava flows of the Yellowstone Plateau, an unusual tableland among peaks. The Rockies have no contemporary volcanoes within their confines, but examples of active volcanism still abound.

Surrounded by mountains, the forested volcanic plateau of Yellowstone National Park is anomalous for its broad, flat topography, its stream-cut and occasionally rolling hills. Cycles of volcanism produced first a basement layer of lava flows, best exposed in the Absaroka Mountains and at the margins of Yellowstone. In Barronette Peak, near the Absarokas, are layers of these old lavas in which each flow can be distinguished by the color of its weathered horizontal surface.

Flows from a later cycle of volcanism have covered the southern plateau, producing a rocky front as high as 1,000 feet and a surface with many lava pressure ridges twenty-five to fifty feet high. When seen from the air, the now timbered land resembles an ice field with crevasses on its surface. These original flow structures and those on the western Madison and southern Pitchstone plateaus have been largely unmodified in their structure, remaining as they were at the time of their deposition, even though the effects of glaciation were to radically alter much of the central Yellowstone area.

Glaciation proceeded three times into Yellowstone Park—the work of two glaciers fed by ice streams from the nearby Snowy Range and Absaroka Mountains. Glacial deposits in Lower Geyser Basin were left as ice encroached across the Continental Divide and extended to the headwaters of the Madison River, while ice from another glacier crossed into Jackson Hole, dropping its debris and forming the natural dam for Jackson Lake.

Far south of the Yellowstone lava source lies another site of local volcanism—the only Rocky Mountain remnant of an active volcano. Rising 13,623 feet at the southeastern margin of the Colorado Rockies, the Spanish Peaks are a massive monument to volcanic eruption.

Deep within any volcano lies magma—a mixture of molten rock, dissolved gases, and liquids. Birth of the ancient Spanish Peaks began in the rumblings, earthquakes and subterranean shifting brought on by building pressures and the rise of molten rock, carrying heat ever nearer to the earth's surface. Cracks developed, releasing volatile gases from the molten mass; water was vaporized, and then the first lava appeared in great eruptions. A small crater was formed to vent the rising column of molten material, and periods of eruption brought lava surging over the crater's rim. But there were also times when the volcano cooled, solidified, and lay dormant. Subsequently, renewed discharges of heat would blow off the crest, enlarge the vent, heave vast amounts of rocky fragments into the air, and add to the mountain's height. When the volcano's size became overwhelming, fissures developed on its flanks, and lavas rose around the craters.

The Spanish Peaks are not a weathered version of this ancient volcano but remnants of subsurface volcanic pipes and feeder lines, which supplied molten rock to the surface—the volcanic pipeline now laid bare

48

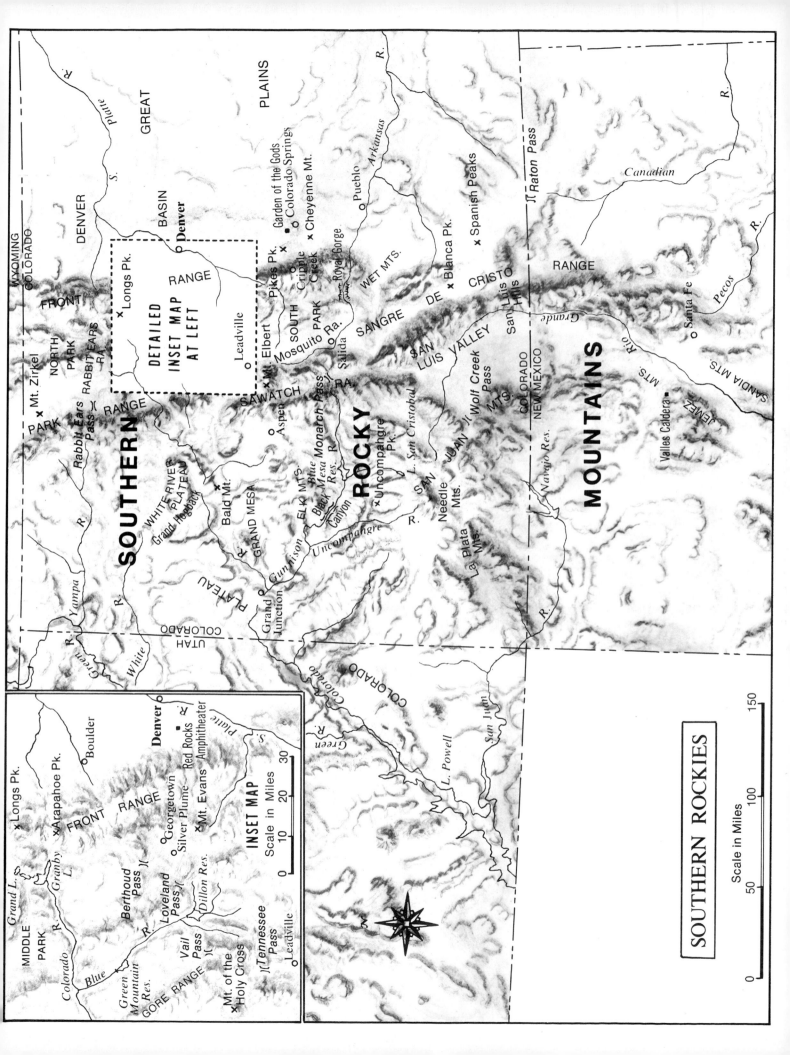

SOUTHERN ROCKIES

Scale in Miles

0   50   100   150

Main map labels

WYOMING
COLORADO

GREAT

PLAINS

DENVER
BASIN

Denver

S. Platte R.

FRONT

NORTH PARK

Mt. Zirkel x

RABBIT EARS RA.

Rabbit Ears Pass

PARK

RANGE

SOUTHERN

WHITE RIVER PLATEAU

Grand Hogback

Bald Mt. x

GRAND MESA

PLATEAU

Grand Junction

UTAH
COLORADO

Yampa R.

Green R.

White R.

Colorado R.

Gunnison R.

ELK MTS.

Blue Mesa Res.

Black Canyon

Uncompahgre R.

ROCKY

Uncompahgre Pk. x

L. San Cristobal

SAN

Needle Mts.

La Plata Mts.

JUAN

Wolf Creek Pass

MTS.

Navajo Res.

COLORADO
NEW MEXICO

MOUNTAINS

Detailed inset / central area

DETAILED INSET MAP AT LEFT

x Longs Pk.

RANGE

Leadville o

Mt. Elbert x

SAWATCH

Mosquito RA.

Aspen o

Monarch Pass

Salida o

SANGRE

DE

CRISTO

SAN LUIS VALLEY

San Luis Hills

RANGE

Front Range / plains cities

Garden of the Gods
Colorado Springs
Cheyenne Mt. x

Pikes Pk. x

SOUTH PARK

Cripple Creek

WET MTS.

Royal Gorge

Pueblo o

Arkansas R.

Spanish Peaks x

Blanca Pk. x

Raton Pass

Canadian R.

Santa Fe o

Pecos R.

Rio Grande

JEMEZ MTS.

Valles Caldera

SANDIA MTS.

Colorado River / southwest

COLORADO

Green R.

L. Powell

San Juan R.

Colorado R.

Compass rose

N

Scale bar (lower)

Scale in Miles

0   10   20   30

INSET MAP

Boulder o

Denver

Red Rocks Amphitheater

R.

S. Platte R.

Longs Pk. x

Arapahoe Pk. x

FRONT RANGE

Georgetown o

Silver Plume o

Mt. Evans x

Grand L.

Granby L.

MIDDLE PARK

Colorado R.

Berthoud Pass

Loveland Pass

Dillon Res.

Green Mountain Res.

Blue R.

GORE RANGE

Vail Pass

Mt. of the Holy Cross x

Tennessee Pass

Leadville o

INSET MAP

Scale in Miles

0   10   20   30

by ages of erosion. Radiating through a 360-degree arc are conduits for the magma, twenty-five miles long, stretching out into the Great Plains. Their superior resistance to erosion has enabled these conduits to endure as huge rock walls, fifty feet higher than the plains.

More recent volcanic activity has centered to the west of the Spanish Peaks, near the Jemez Mountains in northern New Mexico. Located in the Jemez is Valles Caldera, one of the most unusual topographic features of the Rockies. Originally thought to be a meteor crater, this fifteen-mile-diameter hole in the ground is now known to have had a volcanic origin. Early in the age of glaciers, almost 3,000,000 years ago, there was a group of catastrophic eruptions. First, the crater floor was arched to form a central dome with volcanic cones around its border, and then fifty cubic miles of volcanic material was blown out of this depression, creating a void and an associated subsidence, and forming the present caldera. Circular faults ring the crater and thermal activity exists below its surface; as at Yellowstone, the ground fires still burn deep.

Volcanism of the Yellowstone type also occurred in the San Juan Mountains, where lava came from many crustal fissures, coalescing into local flows and producing plateau topography. Lavas flowing directly upon sedimentary rock layers produced a rock sequence so unstable that landslides have always been dramatic and frequent. One of the largest landslides, the huge Slumgullion mudflow, moved downslope from a glacial cirque 11,000 feet high to dam the Lake Fork of the Gunnison River and form Lake San Cristobal.

Lavas make other appearances in the Rockies at Grand Mesa east of Grand Junction where huge lava flows have formed a cap rock highly resistant to erosion; Flattop Mountains, also a lava cap rock; and the Ten Mile District, north of Leadville, where limestones, sandstones, shales, and lavas interleaf. But volcanism has created no recent cones from a single vent. Where the recent lavas have flowed, they have been fluid and have easily poured upon the land, covering large areas and creating plateau highlands.

THE WYOMING BASIN is a major break in the continuity of the Rockies, yet it was a product of the same upheaval that raised the mountains. It is divided into a series of smaller basins—separated by uplifts and bordered by mountains—whose bowl-shaped surface reveals none of its underlying structure. Beneath the individual basins are downfolds, formed in as complex a folding experience as any that gave rise to the Rocky Mountains.

While mountains were being uplifted, the Wyoming Basin was acting as a collection area for debris. As a result, many thousands of feet of sediments, representing all epochs of geologic time during the Laramide Revolution, are found here—coals, limestones, shales, and mud deposits from temporary lakes, as well as the associated fossil life from those eras.

The basic structure of the Wyoming Basin is exposed in varying degrees; in some small basins the separating uplifts have been prominently displayed by erosion, while in others mountain structures seem to be lacking. Because most individual basins have no apparent symmetry, some geologists began to believe that they performed a passive role while the Rockies were building. But the semblance of no structure may be a delusion. A later theory contends that the basins did participate—by actively downfolding as adjacent mountains were involved in upward movements.

As folding, faulting, and buckling continued in the Rockies, some of the nearby separate mountain blocks were pushed in toward their adjoining basins. They broke apart from the main mountain mass, and then were thrust into the basin floor. Thus, the deepest parts of each separate basin are located, not in the center, but near the perimeter, adjacent to the mountain uplifts.

Economically the basins are extremely useful. Artesian water conditions (where major sandstone layers are water saturated and able to relinquish a steady water supply to a tapped well) prevail in all the Wyoming basins. Oil shale, oil, gas, and coal accumulations are to be found in many.

The reason for this wealth of natural resources lies with the basin configuration and the sedimentary type of rock layers it contains. The basins have been a collection storehouse for local organic material, for water-soluble minerals, for minerals that have been washed in from elsewhere and for those that form in place.

The presence of many water-soluble minerals, among them trona (used in making soda ash), alters the usefulness of the artesian basins. Though water is chemically adequate for drinking when tapped near basin margins, a well deep in the basin center will issue water with as much as 60,000 parts per million of dissolved salts—unpalatable to summer pasturage animals.

Petroleum and natural gas also occur in the basins where water is contained within the rocks. Derived from the organic material of some fine-grained rock, like shale, the petroleum and gas migrate into such porous rock as sandstone, limestone, or dolomite. Since oil is less dense than water, the oil globule will rise through the water-saturated rock. Movement continues until a barrier, such as impermeable shale above a slight arching of the rock layers, traps upward progress of the oil. Most Wyoming oil fields are of this type.

Other treasures lie among the sedimentary rock layers of the basins. Uranium ores (the second largest national reserves are here) have been disseminated among the sandstones and conglomerates of the Wind River, Powder River, and Shirley basins; washed in from other sources, they are present only in light concentration (less than 0.5 percent) and must be recovered using strip-mining techniques. The rare element titanium, present in "black sands" now being washed along the beaches of the Carolinas, has also been discovered among "fossil beaches" found in Wyoming.

Least exotic of the basin minerals is the coal found in all of Wyoming's lowlands. Formed in the same geologic epoch as the titaniferous sands, coal represents the remains of swamp vegetation that grew during temperate or subtropical periods in ages long past. Recovered by strip operations, most Wyoming coal is directly converted to electrical power on the mining site, but large amounts are also transported east by rail to markets in the Missouri Valley.

One mineral found within the basins and also available in the surrounding mountains—gold—was the source of periodic booms in the Rockies. Here in the lowlands, however, it is far from its source. Free gold, weathered from mountain veins, was long ago transported out in the river currents, and concentrated in favorable places along channel beds. Placers kept prospectors happy for a century, but no big strikes were ever made in the basins.

THE STORY OF GEOLOGY in the southern Rockies, central Rockies, and the Wyoming Basin would not be complete without mention of the Ice Age, though it was to influence landforms in the Rockies more than it affected earth movements. Geologic conditions took a major turn toward cold climates after the Laramide Revolution, as glacier ice covered most of the Rockies' highlands and even moved down upon the plateaus. Ice joined the ongoing erosive attempt of water to destroy a highland region, built upon a restless landscape millions of years before. When climate began moderating, the glaciers retreated to permanent ice fields, cradled in shaded recesses among high peaks. Moving ice fields left behind gouged, U-shaped valleys, serrated peaks and ridges, and great piles of broken rock.

Some experts believe the Ice Age is gone; if so, it was the last great episode of geologic change seen among the high country peaks. Young glacier-fed streams still continue the work of downcutting in the mountains and foothills, picking up and moving sand and gravel onto the plains; but these rivers are part of the present evolution by which landscapes are slowly changing—not part of the past. Their channels are narrower, their yearly discharges a mere fraction of the glacial volume; the earth appears to be a quieter world.

Though natural events no longer happen as dynamically as in the days of the revolution, the earth still is restless and transitory—nothing remains stable to the winds of change. The climatic revolution, though less intense, does continue in the Rockies—breaking rock, undermining hillsides into landslides, flooding the riverbanks. An often-gentle revolution of time and low energy persists over the highlands.

CHAPTER 4

WHIMS OF MOUNTAIN WEATHER

Global winds and local land profiles that produce hail and blizzards,
chinooks and intense sunshine in an ever-changing climate

UNLIKE ROCK AND THE LAND ITSELF, climate is annually, daily, even hourly variable, shifting subtly many times within a decade—more radically within a millennium. Warming or cooling trends are established, causing permanent glaciers either to recede or, as in the present era, gradually to advance.

For the mountains it is difficult to make predictive weather generalizations, even with a net of widespread, well-situated weather stations and computers working full-time. Storms weave and dodge the instruments, and snowfalls always seem to take their biggest accumulations elsewhere, avoiding observation. Forecasting the weather becomes speculative even for the experts, but understanding the wiles of weather is easier. Winds and pressure systems control weather patterns, and so are the starting point in explaining mountain climate.

A colorless, odorless, tasteless, expandable, compressible, mobile blanket of gases—the atmosphere—envelops the earth in a substance called air. Driven to move by variations of heat within this mass, winds circulate the lowest layers of air around the earth in known patterns; the Rocky Mountain region lies squarely within the westerly wind belt. Most storms are controlled by an aspect of the basic easterly-moving wind pattern— two independent pressure systems, each stationed over the Rockies during specific seasons. The high pressure cell, an area where air gathers, remains throughout winter months. Winds of the cell rotate in a clockwise direction, occasionally bringing cold Canadian air south to the mountain states, instigating winter storm

conditions with impressive snow accumulations. The low pressure cell mediates summer weather over the Rockies with winds that move in a counterclockwise direction, drawing warm, buoyant air from the Gulf of California and giving the mountains their characteristic warm, dry summer.

Light, local afternoon or evening showers in the valleys and almost daily thunderstorms in the mountains may interrupt the clear mountain sunshine, but in the foothills these warm months are almost always dusty and dry. It's a good climate—when extremes of hot or cold temperatures descend on the mountain states, their effects are always tempered by the dryness of the air and the clear sunshine. Because of the stable pressure systems located over the mountains, the higher elevations rarely are visited by the sudden, irregular, severe intrusions of outside storm systems. To a large degree, many storms that are forecast for Denver never reach the mile-high city.

On a yearly average, precipitation for the Rockies is very low—eight inches in the lowlands to twenty on the peaks—confirming the area's status as semiarid. Except for high mountain ridges, north-facing slopes, craggy peaks, and some high areas of sheltered intermontane valleys (North, Middle, and South parks), rain- and snowfall are so deficient that irrigation is essential for Rocky Mountain agriculture to survive. Most storms bring moisture in the spring and early summer, and again during winter months. This is the water that reservoirs now collect to give the dry lowland plains a way to survive the fluctuations of climate.

Cold air pockets, drifting into warmer valleys at night, run into a forest "dam," where the cloudy
vapors hover until morning winds dissipate them around the peaks—here, Longs Peak.

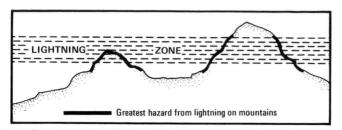

Lightning can strike either slope or mountain peak.

THREE BASIC VARIABLES provide a key to understanding many facets of weather in the mountains: exposure to sunlight, topographic relief, and (most of all) altitude.

Perpetually altering the pattern of warmth and cold, light and shadow upon mountain slopes, the angle and path of the sun are ever changing—from dawn to dusk, week to week, and season to season. Mountain summits receive first warmth only moments after sunrise, as heat is swiftly transmitted through the thin, clear air, but on the slopes the sun's heat comes slowly or not at all. Eastern and southeastern faces (at the Rocky Mountain latitude) will be warmest throughout the day, but they never receive the full measure of heat as do the summits; many western slopes and sheltered intermontane valleys remain in shadow even as the sun is setting. Thus, snowdrifts remain the longest in cul-de-sac valley heads, on north and northwestern slopes. When the wind blows hot in the summertime, these slopes are cool refuges for deer and other browsing animals.

An intense sun together with the advantage of longer daylight hours implies that on the summits there is more time for the ground surface to receive heat, more time for rock surfaces to become fryingpan hot. Since the earth conducts heat poorly, the heat it absorbs remains upon outer rock and ground surfaces on the sunny slopes. This heat can become so intense that surface temperatures leap above air temperatures. The balance reverses after sunset, when the ground heat radiates back into space. The repeated response of rock to this daily fluctuation in ground temperatures—expansion and contraction—spells disaster to unprotected rock at the ground level; cracking, splitting, and peeling become major forms of "dry" weathering at these high elevations.

Six thousand feet is a point of change in the atmosphere of this mountain land: below is nearly half the air's moisture and well over half its dust particles; above is cleaner, more rarefied air. Only the slightest sun screen mutes the ultraviolet rays, which pass almost unhindered to high slopes and cause the severe sunburns experienced by mountain climbers and skiers.

Remarkably clear highland air presents an entirely different visual world to the observer; overhead the sky can be a deep violet-blue, and land features stand out in sharp detail—in their own earth colors. Blue shades are gone from distant landscapes, and the sunset sky is often not red, but yellow from low water vapor and lack of haze. In the transparent atmosphere of high country, the sun's disc gleams with a sharply defined perimeter, gone is the nebulous corona of diffuse light that fades into the blue shades, as is usual with skies seen at sea level.

As sunshine falls on the local bumps, jags, and pinnacles, the unique shape of individual parts of a range will set up small microclimates—variations based more on mountain form than on anything else.

The most dramatic effects of local topography are the morning and evening breezes over mountain and valley, generated not by sweeping wind systems but by ground surface heating and regional contours of the land. With evening, drafts of cool air drain downward, bringing lower temperatures into valley lowlands. Cooled by the gradual loss of heat from the soil, this chilled layer of air slides downslope under its own weight, moving toward the warmer, less dense air below. The air moves valleyward in pulses and avalanches, with five to thirty minutes separating each surge. If its descent is blocked by anything large and formidable— a grove of trees, an artificial dam, or a narrowing of the valley—the air stagnates, forming a cold air lake, and the area experiences nighttime frost.

Day begins, and sunshine again warms the mountain slope; its air will heat, rise aloft, and be replaced by valley air, creating a daytime breeze out of the mountain valley and toward the peaks. The valley air is moist, and as these breezes cool at higher elevations, clouds form near the mountain peaks, frequently bringing afternoon showers.

When local showers have passed and clear skies returned, some unusual, small, cigar-shaped clouds may form—hovering east of pinnacles and isolated high peaks, riding the crests and waves of a turbulence set up by the mountain peak obstacles. On the lee side of the mountains, the airflow begins a roller coaster ride downward, following the mountain slopes. At the bottom, rushing air currents bump into flat foothill terrain and are deflected skyward again, to produce vertical currents traveling fifteen miles an hour or more—enough to elevate sailplanes or gliders, making the east face of the Rockies an excellent playground for the growing sport of soaring.

Whenever winds are strong and gusting, they affect the weather in nonlocal ways, spreading their influence over the entire Rocky Mountain region, and it is here that altitude reaches full relevance.

The dry, warm wind of a chinook may occur from any unobstructed major wind system west of the Rockies. In making its ascent of the mountain barrier, an air mass cools, losing fourteen to twenty degrees for every mile of upward movement. Water vapor condenses into snow or rain on the windward slope. The process of condensation adds warmth to the air, just as the evaporation of moisture removes it. As the air descends the eastern slopes its temperature increases, and by the time the air reaches the plains it is both warmer and drier than when it assaulted the western side of the mountain barrier.

Along the Montana, Wyoming, and Colorado mountain fronts, a chinook can begin at any hour of the day or night, continuing for hours or even days; or it can start up in short spurts of warm, dry air, interrupted by colder and calmer conditions before the full chinook wind is felt. The temperature may rise twenty to forty degrees in fifteen minutes; the mountain sky remains dark and cloudy, with rain or snow falling at mountain summits. On the plains, the sky is fair with good visibility and lens-shaped clouds following the dry wind, a pleasing change where winter weather lends monotony to the landscape. But stockmen are not impressed by the winter's respite; in the Wyoming basins, when sudden thaws melt the top few inches of snow, cattle mire; when the snow crust refreezes, an icy top layer injures the feet of animals who must move about to find fodder.

The mountains are a haven of moisture in an otherwise semiarid land. Clouds concentrate here and bring rain that is always adequate for existing conifer growth

but never enough to foster verdant forests. If winds are high, the air clear and dry, sunlight burning, plants scarce, and the ground bare, conditions may be such that even in the mountains the soil will parch. The winds never blow as dusty as those in Grand Junction, or on the high plains, but the mountains aren't always a refreshing haven from heat.

Generally, big snowstorms come south from Canada after the autumnal equinox, around October 1, and reach an annual climax in late March. Snows will linger for weeks on shady mountainsides, some melting only after the sun's peak elevation at the summer solstice. But big storms are not the only ones that leave huge accumulations as they pass, as was shown when a single, small offshoot of a big storm in April 1921 passed across the face of the Front Range in eastern Colorado, was blocked at North Arapaho Peak (elevation 13,502 feet), and left eighty-seven inches of new snow at the valley weather station of Silver Lake—all in just twenty-eight hours.

Coming quickly and lying deep, the snow, once accumulated, can move down steep, unforested mountainsides in the thunder of an avalanche. Hundreds occur every year in the Rockies, usually intermittently and in a variety of places, ripping downslope just after heavy snowfalls, unusually active drifting, a sudden cold snap, or a quick thaw. Other forms of destruction are well represented too—flash floods producing road washouts, dry lightning setting fires upon high peaks

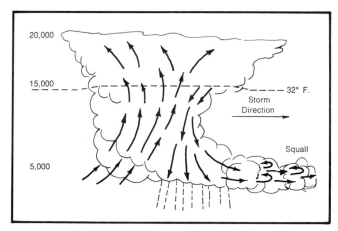

Powerful air currents are capable of generating massive hailstones within the anvil of a cumulonimbus cloud.

Overleaf: Clouds result directly from the presence of mountains. As Pacific winds slip into higher elevations, invisible water vapor condenses into opaque clouds of water droplets.

Clouds veil the summit of Grand Teton; as they are driven eastward by the winds, more will form.

and severe hail damaging the lowland truck gardens. When it comes to Rocky Mountain weather there are no half measures.

Hail, considered to be the most destructive form of moisture, is cast out of only the most dramatic of thunderstorms, usually on spring and summer afternoons when the air is unstable and drafty. Hailstones vary in size from fractions of an inch to two or three inches in diameter. The biggest ones have onion-skin-like shells, with a small ice-seed core. They have come from great turbulence within a cumulonimbus storm cloud, in which liquid water (cooled below the point of freezing), snow, and ice are simultaneously present. Tremendous vertical currents of air catch raindrops in the updrafts, carrying them through repeated cycles of melting and freezing, adding layers of cloudy snow and clear ice, as they move up and down through the cloud. Growth of the hailstone stops when a temporary lull in the updrafts sends the hail falling out of the cloud and plummeting down to earth. Alternatively, the hail may overflow from the top of a cloud, above the freezing level, and spill down the margins, where upward-moving air currents are weak and cannot prevent its fall. Hail is one of the most interesting phenomena of mountain weather, but it can also be the most destructive to agriculture—a point well known among the truck gardeners of the Denver Basin.

IN THE ROCKIES, one can change the weather simply by changing position. What is a hundred-mile-an-hour wind in Boulder may be only a breeze rustling the trees in Denver; the winter snowstorms that roar across Wyoming may never stretch south along the Colorado Front Range. The variables producing climate vary themselves so widely that nowhere in the Rockies are

thistle all summer, return to the job of restraining snowdrifts on the major highway links between Wyoming's towns and cities.

Most highways remain open across the basin country through the winter months, except for roads into the high mountains, which remain snowed in for several days after a storm, or roads lying directly in the storm path. Standard procedures for travel across Wyoming include a survival kit of blankets, water, and food, should ground blizzards require stopping along the highway and a long auto-bound wait for the blinding snows to pass.

Spring can hardly be found in Wyoming. Snow persists until June in the basin lands, longer in the high country, until summer's hot winds settle upon the open land. The snows that have watered antelope through the winter provide a start to rangeland grasses, which green quickly while the water is plentiful. Small artificial catch basins hold water for the cattle, sheep, and antelope.

With peaks rising north and south from the basin, the mountain structure implies an even more uncompromising weather pattern. Legendary snowfalls of 350 inches annually—400 inches on the high peaks—have been recorded here, but the snow is heavy, large flaked, and not driven by dangerous, blinding winds. High in water content, the snows fall on slopes down to the 4,000-foot level, supplying the meltwater that permits mountain streams to be constant water carriers to the arid lowlands.

The problem of avalanche control is a real one in the mountains, so trouble-shooting forest service teams have been set up to try to "defuse" avalanche situations before they become hazardous. In the Front Range and the Sawatch, in the "parks" and mountain towns west of Denver, and around the highly populated ski resorts, highway department patrols shoot explosive charges into snowbanks before they have a chance to avalanche spontaneously. That this kind of care is now being taken is partly the result of larger winter populations and an increased use of the mountains west of Denver. All the major Colorado intermountain highways are open during winter, except Trail Ridge Road, from Estes Park to Grand Lake.

Weather has been among the factors bringing tremendous growth to the Denver-Boulder cosmopolitan

conditions the same; the weather is bipolar, with Wyoming Basin conditions at one extreme and Colorado at the other.

Winter comes early in the flat basins of Wyoming and beside the Front Range, bringing the first snow in September, interrupting summer with the realities of an approaching storm season. The first storm often travels alone and is followed by another month or more of warm days and cool nights; the Wyoming and Denver Basins will wait through a pleasant Indian summer before stronger storms develop their tracks across Wyoming and a cold high-pressure system builds over the mountain state to the south.

In Wyoming, storms follow a path from the northwest, with winds and ground blizzards moving across the lowlands, drifting fine, hard snow and laying bare the low bunchgrass frozen in a stony soil. Sturdy snow fences, which have only collected tumbleweed and

areas. Mile-high Denver's early winter climate includes forty-degree daytime temperatures, cold nights, and bright sunlight, which rapidly melts the traces of snow left by storms that have slipped in from Canada.

As the Denver new year continues into spring, the weather turns less pleasing. Wet, heavy snows kill the ambitions of early foliage, and days are overcast and cold. But these late spring storms represent the last influences of the midwinter high pressure system, and summer quickly takes over the weather pattern once its low pressure system moves into the mountain states.

Middle months of the year bring ninety-degree days to Denver, but nights are cool and the air is always dry, giving much relief from the intense sunlight.

THE WINDS OF CHANGE are bringing new, unnatural weather conditions into the Rockies. Smog in Denver is on the increase as the city grows. Subdivisions as far away as Evergreen, twenty miles from Denver—and some fifty miles from the downtown area—create a transportation need, with only the automobile to meet the demand. Local public service operations and the huge power generator plant of the Four Corners region have been accused of creating atmospheric pollution problems for Denver, but the individual automobile seems to be causing most of the worry Denver people have about the quality of their skies.

Weather and climate cannot cause air pollution, but conditions in the atmosphere greatly affect the diffusion and elimination of contaminating agents. The Denver Basin is not favorably structured for the natural dissipation of smoke, dust, gases, and vapors—the contaminants of clean air. Herein lies much of Denver's problem: it is flat-lying and allows stable air to concentrate pollutants near their source. When air stagnates in the basin, it prevents natural nighttime radiation of heat and promotes what should be a most unusual occurrence for Denver, the mile-high city—slow morning warmup. Air pollutants are insulating Denver from the sunlight for which it is famous, thereby lowering its average temperature. And as the city has grown, so has this disparity between city and open-country temperatures, sometimes by almost two degrees.

Pollution normally alters the visibility and sunshine over an affected city because the contaminants act as centers for condensation, creating haze or fog. The water droplets formed from the polluted haze are more stable than their normal counterparts, failing to evaporate as readily when heated. Oily substances in particular will surround a droplet with a protective coating, thereby retarding evaporation. Chemical reactions among the many contaminants create new compounds, some more dangerous than the original waste products; these increase the number of different gases in the atmosphere, reducing the quality of the air and the quantity of sunshine able to penetrate the haze.

The atmosphere has been an unstable element upon this earth since the earliest epochs of its formation, when methane gas, not nitrogen and oxygen, was a primary constituent. Paleontologists can watch the beginnings of an oxygenated planet and follow the trace of climate throughout geologic time, paying particular attention to the fluctuations from warm to cooler climate in the mid-latitudes. Back in the 1950s, scientists first noticed the present cooling trend in climate; in the 1970s they wonder what degradation of the air around us will do to the climate of the future.

THE ROCKY MOUNTAIN CLIMATE is wily and fast moving, sudden and unpredictable, yet always under the control of a simple set of circumstances—two contrasting pressure systems and their associated summer and winter weather patterns. Because Rockies weather is not influenced by the constantly changing pressures that normally control worldwide temperatures and precipitation, this land standing in the westerlies is in fact isolated from the rest of the country. Weather controls are inborn, stemming from deflections caused by the mountain barrier, the altitude with which prevailing winds must cope, and the many ins and outs of a chain of mountains having little continuity. The region has its own weather, its own climate, and the many anomalies expected where weather is controlled by topography.

Atop a six-hundred-foot-high mesa near Boulder, scientists from the National Center for Atmospheric Research tackle problems of weather prediction, climate modification, and air pollution.

CHAPTER 5

WATER ON THE GREAT DIVIDE

Rivers and reservoirs—some born of nature, some of technology—
that conserve the most precious resource in the Rockies

A BREEZE CHANGES DIRECTION, the temperature cools, and rain falls earthward to the hard, jagged mountain peaks below. Born in the atmosphere, carrying gravitational energy to spare, the drops plummet toward the earth's mass and impart some of their energy to rock and to rock fragments, setting the smaller ones into temporary motion. The water itself may disappear into the ground or pool up, conforming to the shape of the ground below and the layer of air above, reflecting any light that strikes its outer surface and gleaming just slightly. As the pool enlarges, it breaks through whatever has been its retainer and starts rivulets moving downgrade, their speed determined by the pitch of the landscape, the roughness of the surface, and the obstacles in their path. Eventually the rivulet becomes a brook, then a stream, and finally a broad river flowing seaward.

The Rocky Mountain rivers as we know them existed before the mountains and were simply rejuvenated in the uplift. Earlier, when the land surface was flat, the rivers, gorged with mud and silt, pushed lazily along in sediment-filled valleys. The scene held every aspect of permanence. But the earth did not remain quiet—mountains folded upward, canting the river gradients and throwing streams out of their old, idle habits. Still following the same courses, the rivers began actively removing material from their channel bottoms. Alluvium was easily carried away, leaving exposed the hard rock of the mountain core. Rock proved almost as weak. In their truculence, the mountain streams went straight down into the granite, holding their courses, and cross-ing the mountains in their effort to get out. The canyons cut by these streams—Royal Gorge, Black Canyon, and countless others—are reminders of river persistence to keep drainage patterns at all costs. Though no longer cutting as violently, the Rocky Mountain rivers still remain fundamentally out of harmony with the barrier mountains.

Water that has fallen out of the sky and onto this land has, since the last Great Ice Age, followed particular courses toward the seas; since the Rocky Mountains have stood, they have been master of the circumstances, determining the direction of surface water flow. The Continental Divide serves as administrator. It is the crest line along the cordillera, arbitrating to which ocean water will flow. Smaller divides are the crests that delineate individual valley basins, deciding which river will receive their runoff. Generally, the major rivers begin in the snowpack, either directly on the Continental Divide, like the Snake, Colorado, and Arkansas, or in single ranges, where the San Juan, Rio Grande, Pecos, Green, Bighorn, and Yellowstone arise. The water moves quickly out of these highlands, seeping only slightly into the ground, leaving very nearly just a channel to mark its path.

As a river flows seaward, it passes through (potentially) four erosional phases, determined by how extensively the river has matured from source to outlet. The peaks claim its birth and infancy; the slopes are where its youth is spent; the flatlands bring about maturity. Interruptions in the river's slope (gradient) form the *rites de passage* from one river age to another.

In spring this unnamed creek in Maroon Canyon in Colorado is swollen with meltwater from the winter's snow. By summer its flow will be considerably reduced.

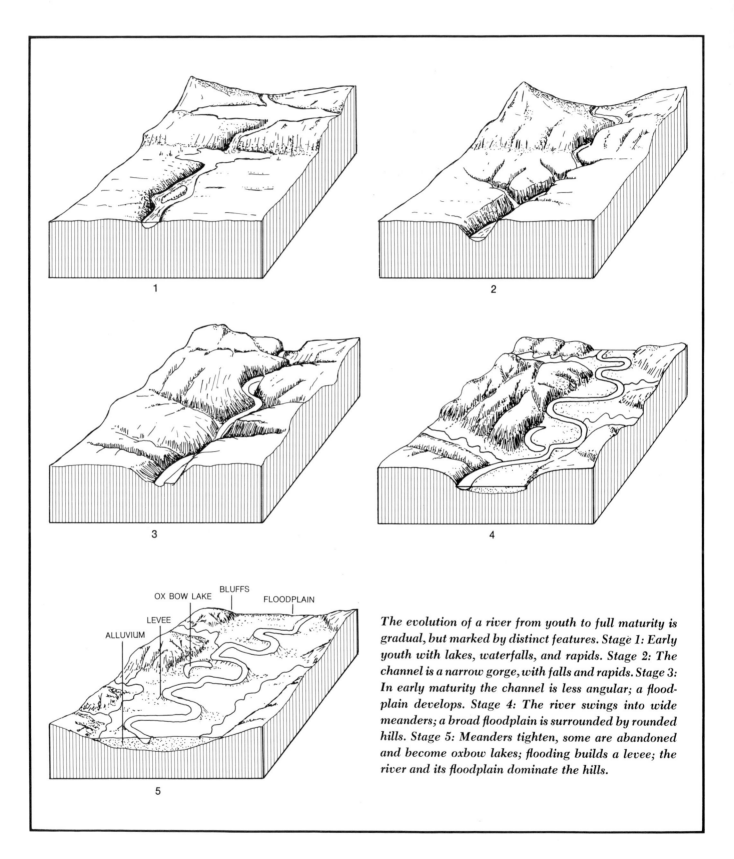

The evolution of a river from youth to full maturity is gradual, but marked by distinct features. Stage 1: Early youth with lakes, waterfalls, and rapids. Stage 2: The channel is a narrow gorge, with falls and rapids. Stage 3: In early maturity the channel is less angular; a floodplain develops. Stage 4: The river swings into wide meanders; a broad floodplain is surrounded by rounded hills. Stage 5: Meanders tighten, some are abandoned and become oxbow lakes; flooding builds a levee; the river and its floodplain dominate the hills.

An infant stream is short; it flows intermittently and is full only after a rain or the spring snowmelt—but in power it is mighty. The gradient of the brook can be so great that after a single heavy rainfall its gully is deeper, its head noticeably cut back into the upland, but still it is ephemeral.

Once downward erosion has sliced into rock or ground that is wet year round (the water table), the brook will have permanent flow. Throughout youth, the channel continues to deepen, remaining narrow, but encountering layers of harder rocks, producing waterfalls and rapids along its course. Its valley is V-shaped and steep.

When the falls and rapids have disappeared and the stream is flowing steadily, it has reached maturity. It is now widening its bed by swinging side to side in the channel, undercutting the outward bend and leaving sand on the inner bank; the valley shape is approaching a broad U, and the valley walls have been reduced to slopes, rising gently to distant ridges and hills.

Late maturity merges almost imperceptibly into old age. The meanders become longer and more tedious to navigate; the floodplain is broader. At times of high water, the river will break over its bank and inundate the bottomlands; natural levees are built sloping away from the river; the valley rises gently to low hills.

Among Rocky Mountain rivers, the Arkansas is a good example of the erosion pattern; within its 1,450-mile length, it passes through four phases. For the first 100 miles, from its rise at 11,500 feet in Tennessee Pass of the Colorado Sawatch, it is a typical mountain stream, losing altitude through pine-covered slopes, past Leadville and Salida, and carving its way through the Royal Gorge. Once out of the mountains and onto the dry plains, the river flows past the iron and steel city of Pueblo and into an arid land of flat-topped mesas and horizontal sedimentary rocks. On into eastern Oklahoma, the river channel becomes restricted by natural levees and sandbars. Here the valley is spacious from river meanderings; the winding river moves lazily on to join another old-timer, the Mississippi.

JUXTAPOSED TO THE WATER that flows on the surface is the water that moves underground. The composition and structure of the earth's outer layer make retention of groundwater possible. If the earth were a china plate, there would be no water that soaked into the ground—no springs, wells, or geysers, and precious little clear, convenient water for man or other living things to use. Copper, gold, aluminum, and some iron ores would never benefit from the concentration that results on redeposition of these valuable minerals, and selective removal of others in the presence of groundwater. Originating in the downward trickle of rainwater or melting snow, water moves into the soil by filling openings between clay particles, mineral grains, and rock fragments. Lower and lower the water moves, until a layer of already wet rock is met—where spaces are water filled—in a zone known as the water table. (See figure.) Ground above may be bone dry for several feet, but at the water table the rock is thoroughly saturated. The water table runs unevenly, following paths that conform to a region's particular land surface—high beneath hills and low beneath valleys, spreading out laterally, always seeking lower levels. As rivers cut their gullies, ravines, and valleys, they encounter groundwater—thus tapping the earth's water storage vat. Rivers are not the only profiteers of subsurface water; for some lakes, groundwater is the main source of water intake.

Water is able to move about underground because of three major forces—capillary movement, gas expansion, and gravity. Capillary action draws water in any direction—upward, downward, or sideways—in defiance of gravity. But its powers are limited to only small water trickles through only the tiniest of fissures, those that are initiated by evaporation in clay soils or by plant root prying in both soil and rock. Gas expansion is the primary force behind geyser eruption, and has much to do with generating hot spring bubbles. It tends to push water from spaces where the gas is generated under the ground to less confining spaces, eventually surfaceward. Gravity is by far the most effective force, and is also the most easily observed. It simply encourages fluid to move downslope.

Moving under gravity, water is able to flow through rocks that are "permeable"—that is, those having many pore spaces and the ability to accept water through them. The Rocky Mountain Dakota sandstone is such a rock layer. Not only are its thick beds especially capable of bearing water, also its watershed covers

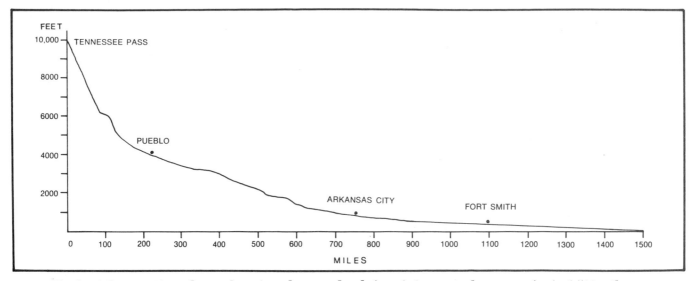

In profile the Arkansas River shows elevation changes that brings it from youth to maturity in 1,500 miles.

wide areas of the mountains, gathering groundwater from highland seepage, and channeling it to the foot-hills of the Front Range, where this sandstone out-crops before it dips eastward and flattens its gradient beneath the plains. Overlying the permeable sandstone is a layer of impermeable shale, positioned in such a way as to act as a "dam." Water enters the sandstone at the 8,000-foot level in the Rockies and flows east with the gradient. Forced upward against shale by the decreasing elevation, the water develops a "head" of pressure. If a well is drilled through the shale and into the water-carrying sandstone layer at these low eleva-tions, water will be brought up far above the water table. In theory, it may gush upward to the level it had at the mountain intake, but in fact it falls short of this mark because there is an associated loss of water pressure to friction, produced as water has moved through the sandstone.

All of the Denver Basin, north and south of the city, is part of a large artesian system; drilled water has been easy to find, allowing municipal, industrial, and do-mestic uses. However, farmers of the region irrigate their land with only small amounts of artesian water; the majority of their needs comes from water resources found at shallow depths in the terrace and flood-plain acquifer deposits of the South Platte River.

When Denver's artesian basin was discovered in

1883, about four hundred wells promptly sprang up with the first surges of interest. They maintained good pressure and flow at first, but seven years later all but six of the city wells required pumps to draw out the water, and in many the water no longer flowed. Was nature failing man, or man failing nature? Investiga-tion revealed that the very low porosity of the sand-stone, which had given the Denver basin its artesian properties, had also brought on the eventual failure. The first water withdrawn from the wells had been part of a supply that had been slowly collecting in the rocks over time, but once heavy drafts on the cache were made, the reserve couldn't be replenished fast enough.

With the centrifugal pump and modern equipment, deeper and deeper wells have been drilled; today six thousand wells tap the area's artesian resources. But as the groundwater becomes depleted it sinks to even lower strata. Technological advances in the mining of water so far have been able to keep stride with retreat-ing supplies, but the supplies are finite, and the mining operations are becoming technically more difficult. There is every likelihood that existing underground water resources alone won't produce water stability in the Rockies.

Today's geologic age follows a peak of deformation, volcanism, and erosive activity—extraordinary and large-scale geologic events that have left a legacy of, among other things, the lakes of our contemporary age.

The lake basin is a container—which must first be formed in order for a lake to exist. Usually the bottom is rock or alluvium, but almost never is it watertight; some seepage moves out, while some groundwater percolates in through basin sides and bottom.

Lakes are transitory features of any landscape because, once formed, many have the tendency to create their own destruction. At least part of the year, the feeder stream carries sediment which will be deposited at the entrance to the lake basin. Rock fragments fall where fast moving water meets quiet lake water, and its speed begins dropping to zero. The alluvium is dumped according to its size and weight—the heaviest near the inlet, the lightest or flattest farther from shore. If allowed to follow its natural course, the lake may literally "silt up" and lose its basin. Lakes without outlet spillways, relying on outward seepage and evaporation to compensate for the almost constant inflow, have a short life, for basin-filling will go ahead at a rate commensurate with the river's access to fresh sediment sources and its ability to carry the load. Even if an outlet is present, the lake may still be in trouble— if it serves as a route through loose rock, the outgoing water will take on the aspects of an actively eroding stream, swiftly picking up and holding bed material, and carrying it elsewhere. What was once a lake will be no lake at all.

A landslide-formed lake provides a good illustration of lake instability. One that was created in 1925 across the Gros Ventre River, near Kelly, Wyoming, is a classic. First the dam formed: a wall of mountain sandstone estimated at 50,000,000 cubic yards came down into the valley on a June afternoon. Rock on the mountain must have fractured rapidly, snapping free from other surrounding rock along a line of weakness and slipping downward, with some rock finally coming to rest 350 feet up the opposite side of the valley. Within a minute or two, the slide had created a main wall of rubble 250 feet high, and behind it was forming a lake that would rise 60 feet in the next eighteen hours; by the end of three weeks that figure was 200 feet, at which point apparent growth of the lake stopped, due to seepage and dry weather, so that in the next two years no water topped the dam. Then in May of 1927

a heavy snowmelt brought lake water to the brink of overflow and finally over the top. More than fourteen billion gallons were dissipated in the next six hours, through an overflow channel cut 300 feet wide and 100 feet deep. The first foot was the hardest to erode, after that an increased water flow deepened the channel, and the deeper channel increased water flow; it seemed regenerative. A huge wall of water sprang down the lower valley, churning up all that it met. But even while the interaction between flow and channel persisted, conditions were beginning to balance. The outlet was lengthening more than it deepened, the Gros Ventre Lake was shrinking, and seepage was allaying the rest of what pressure remained. Once equilibrium was reached between inflow and outflow, the disaster was over. The lake remains today, though small in size, but in geologic reckoning it will have been a temporary feature of the landscape.

The catastrophe on the Gros Ventre might have been avoided by construction of an artificial outlet for controlling the overflow, as was done after the 1959 Madison Canyon landslide in west Yellowstone. The Army Corps of Engineers constructed a spillway channel that was flat bottomed, nearly level for the first 300 feet before the dam, and 250 feet wide. The plan was to give the stream a durable bed and spread out the water so that as much water surface as possible would "feel" a drag from the bed roughness. The spillway succeeded.

Lakes have been formed by glacial activity as well

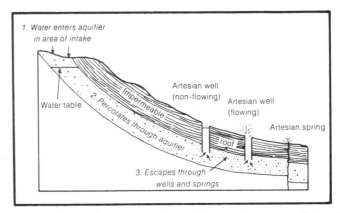

Groundwater in an artesian system seeks any outlet— a drilled well or faultline (far right). Pressure increases with distance from intake, hence only lower wells flow.

as by landslide. Glacially initiated scouring—the slow scrape of bedrock by an overriding ice sheet—and removal of rock blocks by the ice mass work to produce shallow basins in hard rock, usually well above timberline. Thousands of these small rockbound basins were left when the glaciers of the last Ice Age completed their retreat from the mountains, and they started fill-

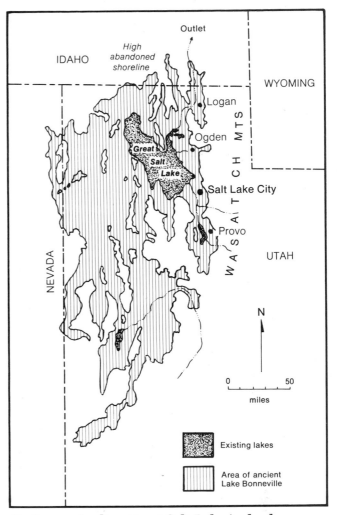

Shallow and saline, Great Salt Lake is slowly shrinking by evaporation, as its predecessor Lake Bonneville did.

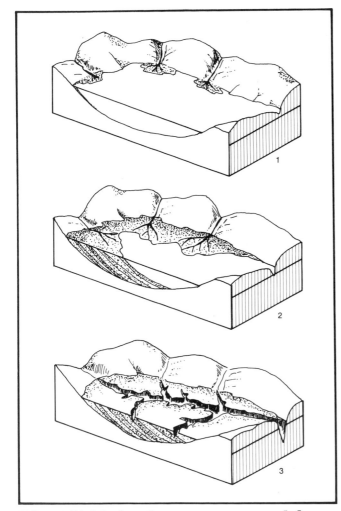

Sides of this lake have been cut away to reveal changes in its history. Stage 1: Sloping lake basin and high outlet channel (at right) favor water storage; a layer of sediment veneers the lake bottom. Stage 2: More layers of sand, silt, and mud line the basin; erosion deepens the outlet. Stage 3: The lake is totally drained and replaced with debris brought in by streams. The streams have stopped depositing and now wash away sediments.

ing with water at the first heavy downpours. The Beartooth Range, the Bighorn Mountains, and the Uintas all hold small ice-carved lake basins at valley heads, sometimes beneath a carved cirque wall.

Natural faulting of mountain blocks can also shape lake basins, but the necessary factors of proper climate, rock type, and crustal movement are rarely so in accord as to produce a durable container for lake water. If the climate is too wet or the rock too weak, the basin may be inundated by its own fill before any depth of still water can be established. But it is not impossible; an ancient Rio Grande was ponded in the San Luis

Before the last great mountain upheaval, the Arkansas River flowed atop a plateau. But as the Rockies rose, the river's bed sank ever lower; today it is almost lost in the shadowy depths of 1,000-foot Royal Gorge.

Estes Lake Dam, part of the Big Thompson Project, is no scenic attraction, but it provides needed water.

Valley, by a faulting of land and volcanic eruption that was to form the San Luis Hills.

Lakes that survive the struggle and maintain themselves do so only with the help of fortune. A flow of lava formed Yellowstone Lake and instigated western discharge to the Snake River and the Pacific, but this drainage was to have a short life. In the meantime, a meager tributary to the Yellowstone River was lengthening headward, on a beeline with the lake's basin wall. Rotten lavas withered under the tributary's erosive attack, until the stream accomplished its goal, seizing drainage and forming a new, lower spillway east to the Yellowstone, the Missouri, and eventually the Gulf of Mexico. Somehow the lake didn't entirely

dred feet high, right across the Lake Fork canyon of the Gunnison River, backing up the river waters. Three miles upstream the water found an outlet at the edge of the mudflow, far enough away from the point of highest pressure so that the lake did not self-destruct.

One great lake—now barely a ghost of its former self —had its heyday in the Pleistocene, when melting glaciers produced more than enough water to go around. Huge Lake Bonneville, unmatched in the West, was the ancestor to Utah's more diminutive and shrinking Great Salt Lake. Its wave-cut shorelines notching the Wasatch Range lower slopes, this great lake covered an estimated 20,000 square miles of northwest Utah and measured 1,000 feet deep at its maximum. Its overflow was north to the Snake. As the Pleistocene ended, with climate becoming drier and warmer, water supplies were diminished, the outlet was abandoned, and evaporation became dominant. Inflowing streams carried low percentages of dissolved mineral matter, derived from the chemical weathering of rock in the area surrounding the lake. Without the continuing high precipitation, cool climate, and northern over-flow conditions that had fostered the growth of Lake Bonneville, these dissolved salts became trapped in a lake basin with no exterior drainage and subsequently concentrated by evaporation until the lake was highly saline. Surviving today in its place is a twelve-foot deep, 3,000-square-mile Great Salt Lake—also Sevier Lake and Lake Utah. Testifying to the past are the Bonneville Salt Flats, the thousand-foot former shore-lines, and a slow rebound of the earth's crust—upwarping centered on the vanished lake—as the land recovers from the weight of the water.

As a result of good timing in man's evolution on earth, he has had access to a pleasurable season of *natural* lakes. With his ingenuity, man has also found ways of sculpting the earth himself—and building lakes —both to hold water where a large supply is needed and to drain undesirable water. Swamps appear to be doomed by the scheme, except where they may be important to wildlife, and lakes are on the increase. Man is saving some natural lakes from degeneration, and artificial ones are multiplying through water use projects. These projects have critical importance in the Rocky Mountain states, where water needs are great.

dissipate itself in the subsequent flood.

Colorado's famed Lake San Cristobal arose dramatically and has managed to sustain itself. A thick mass of volcanic dust accumulating on the San Juan Mountains became saturated by heavy rains, and the ooze started moving downslope under gravity's pull. It spread out fanlike in a broad barrier two to three hun-

MAN HAS BEEN BUILDING DAMS across streams in order to store water since before history was recorded, and the material that has always been most accessible—earth—is still the most commonly used. Though the spectacular large dams are usually concrete, the earthen variety is solid and stable.

Usually the water behind a storage dam will radically change life in the region—providing water for cities, industries, power production, and recreation—as it changes the earth's appearance by regulating the river, providing flood control, and producing water for irrigation. Such a metamorphosis has been under way in the Rockies, where rivers have become some of the most highly managed in the nation. Dams with the names of Flaming Gorge, Seminoe, Alcova, Blue Mesa, and Yellowtail—all have provided water for man's use in the Rockies.

The mountains stand as reservoirs of water in a desert where water is precious. Without artificial reservoirs, less than one-quarter of the total mountain runoff could be considered a steady and dependable water supply. Use of surface water takes much of the burden off groundwater resources, which have been fragile and easily overdrawn.

The need mountain states have for water has dictated that dams be built, but not without some local hardship. The town of Dillon, Colorado, had to be moved to make way for the Dillon Reservoir; ranchlands have been lost, as has other valuable acreage. However, advantages have outweighed the difficulties —advantages in accessible water and in greater recreational possibilities. Further, most dams are of moderate size and located low in the mountains; for these reasons those who are watchful of wilderness recreational interests in the Rockies have never seriously challenged

the plans for water development.

Water has been important to the Rockies in many ways—both to the land and to man. Water must be credited for the sculpture of today's landscape of canyons, valleys, and waterways. It was already at work while the mountains were pushing their way from the interior of the earth into the clouds. Every grain of rock removed was a challenge, every inch of deepened bed a triumph. In the beginning, streams flowed to land of ever lower altitude, just as today, with basic drainage networks changing little since they were established long ago in the geologic past. But there has been some individual change, as rivers are never associated with permanence. The mountain streams have been developing their channels, smoothing out the course at one point, building valley floor at another, being held back temporarily in a mountain lake, dropping underground and out of sight.

For man, holding onto water has been one of the challenges of the Rocky Mountain states. The Rockies snowfall is greater than at any other high region of the continental West, yet the lifeline is fragile between land use and the land's capacity to meet the water demand. Water is a precious commodity to own in the Rockies, and one not freely given with purchase of the land. Its use is taxed, in payment for the storage reservoirs behind man-made dams—the only arrangement practical enough to distribute great volumes to water users. Water development of the Rockies is unique in this way: cities built with water borrowed from the past (ground resources) now place future reliance upon the water project reservoirs. A secure future for mountain cities now depends upon their almost complete control of water resources. To the Rockies, water is the crucial commodity.

The San Miguel, like all mountain rivers, means more than musical rapids and beautiful scenery to the mule deer, wapiti, beaver, and other creatures that live along its banks.

Moist morning air over Lake Como and low storm clouds on the Bitterroot Range reflect the first rays of the sun in a golden haze.

Some whims of a mountain stream are sudden changes of direction, bubbling rapids, and abrupt cascades, such as these near Skalkaho Pass, Montana.

Overleaf: In a land where 400 inches of annual snowfall is normal, the gentle shoulders of Mount Elbert beckon the cross-country skier to the top of the summit.

Natural reservoir: Maroon Lake, with its cold glacial waters held in an ice-carved basin, is a typical, jewel-like tarn.

Man-made reservoir: Flathead Lake, in the Northern Rockies, was designed for water storage and recreational use.

Cirque lakes and the remnant of a glacier lie just below Cloud Peak in the Bighorns.

PART TWO

COMMUNITIES OF NATURE

The great variety of landscapes within the Rockies —soaring peaks and plunging canyons, forested slopes and barren, sun-soaked plateaus—offers a wide choice of environments for living things. In each community plants and animals, imposing and humble, have adapted to their surroundings and to one another, flourishing until the whole mountain West seems to burst with sprouting, flitting, wandering wildlife.

Aspen grove after an early spring rain.

Spiderwort.

Alpine lily.

Goldbloom saxifrage.

Purple thistle.

Showy daisy.

Alpine daisy.

Forget-me-nots.

Globeflower.

Columbine in bloom along Sneffels Creek, Uncompahgre National Forest, Colorado.

Black-billed magpie.

Western tanager.

Great horned owl.

Bullock's oriole.

Horned lark.

Mallard ducks.

Steller's jay.

White-tailed ptarmigan in winter.

Red-tailed hawks.

Mother raven with young.

Sage grouse.

Mule deer.

Black bears.

Porcupine.

Bull moose.

Wapiti, or "elk."

Mountain lion.

Yellow-bellied marmot.

Mountain goat.

A rabbit's white winter coat provides nearly perfect camouflage.

CHAPTER 6

LIFE ON THE SHELTERING SLOPES

Residents of the many mountain neighborhoods—dense green forest and foothill grassland, bubbling stream and vertical canyon wall

DRIVING WEST FROM THE MISSISSIPPI, through the grasslands and foothills that roll to the snow and granite climax of Pikes Peak, one travels three or four different lands, with no more passport than a gas tank and curiosity. The empire is Nature's; the border guards are the dominant plants that silently signal one's entry into each new country. The inhabitants of these lands write a history that lives for millennia in the war of wind, rain, and lichen upon the rocks, or decades in the mute struggle of fireweed, aspen, and ponderosa pine over a foothill, or only moments in the death-shriek of a jackrabbit felled by its ancient predator the coyote. Change is constant here, but not anarchy; each life zone follows strict and intricate laws. One need only learn the language to read their stories.

Altitude and *latitude* are the basic words in the mountain lexicon; adding to them a few terms like *moisture, exposure to the sun,* and *steepness of slope,* one understands how and why Rocky Mountain plants and animals live where they do.

Climbing a high mountain in North America, one can go from desert heat to arctic cold, for with every thousand feet of altitude, the temperature drops three degrees. But life grows by latitude, as well. Timberline, for instance, is relatively low on northern mountains, and rises as one travels south: the forests that cover the shoulders of New Mexico's Rockies would lie more like a lap robe around the knees of Wyoming's Absaroka Range. The farther north one goes, the greater the domain of alpine meadow, snow, and ice.

If the Rockies were a single ridge, running like an arrow north to south, the life zones would rise above each other in straight, orderly rows. But each range has its canyons, its ridges cutting east to west across the grain of the mountain chain. And on either side of each ridge lies a north- and a south-facing slope. Face north, and the forest canopy is dark and dense, the ground damp and littered with rotting branches; here the winter snow persists into spring, soaking into loam and rock. Face south, and the forest is more like a park, with sun glistening through pine needles and bathing a meadow here and there; winter runoff and the occasional rain trickle quickly through this warm soil, leaving it well drained and dry. Depending upon the quirk of canyon and ridge, life zone jostles life zone on the slopes, and much of the existence here depends upon traveling and interchange between communities.

In the foothills of the Colorado Rockies, where the altitude rises to around 5,000 feet, one can apply this new knowledge. To the east falls a sea of grama and buffalo grass, and to the west springs the Front Range of the Colorado Rockies. Just west of Colorado Springs, on the way to Cripple Creek and Leadville, the highway squeezes through a granite notch known as Ute Pass; here, at 6,000 to 8,000 feet, one begins to read the story of life on the slopes. Later chapters will explore the wind-battered peaks where no tree can stand and the high, semiarid plateaus veined with canyons; the shortgrass country and the aspen, pine, and spruce forests that clothe the mountain slopes are this chapter's concern. By Rockies standards, the life of the

*Startled outside their native peaks, bighorn sheep prepare to escape into the twilight forest.
Predatory mountain lions and wolves follow the bighorns' migrations from peak to timberline.*

Nature's neighborhoods, like man's, are never static. One day this sunny aspen grove may be engulfed by the forest of conifers on its fringes, and all its residents must adapt or find new homes.

slopes is luxuriant and abundant, constantly moving and changing.

From the bottom of Ute Pass, one gets intimations of the variety the mountains offer. At the base of the notch, scrub oak, piñon, juniper, and even some yucca cling to the steep, dry, gravel foothills. Where a stream runs, taller cottonwood trees—lowland cousins of the mountain aspen—suck up the precious moisture. A little higher, small ponderosa pines grow on sunny, south-facing slopes. This is where the plains and the foothills reach out to one another from east and west like giant interlacing fingers.

The road rises, and on the shadier, north-facing slopes, one begins to see the big trees, first singly, then in groves: white fir, ponderosa, Douglas fir, and Colorado blue spruce. Then, as one rounds the last curve of the pass, a whole horizonful of densely forested mountain—the beginning of the montane zone at 8,000 feet. Driving farther, one sees the forest frontier on still higher mountains: the subalpine zone, and fin-

ally timberline, where Engelmann spruce, Alpine fir, and limber pine bend under the force of gale and snow, where life is best for the humbler grasses and flowers of the meadow.

But these are only intimations. The plants that signal a change in life zone are like flags; they tell the traveler where he is—but to really understand the place, one has to know its more retiring citizens as well, for each natural community is the product of its members' interactions.

The grasslands meet the foothills in the rain shadow of the Rockies. Here, the dominant plants are short and compact: grama grass, needle grass, buffalo grass, plants whose narrow leaves hoard water, whose roots need only one season to dig deep into the soil. Grass seeds depend on only the wind for dispersal, and they are so minute that marauding birds pass them by. A few short trees grow along streambeds—rock pine and ponderosa, mingling with spiky juniper. The ponderosa penetrates low on the mountainsides because it

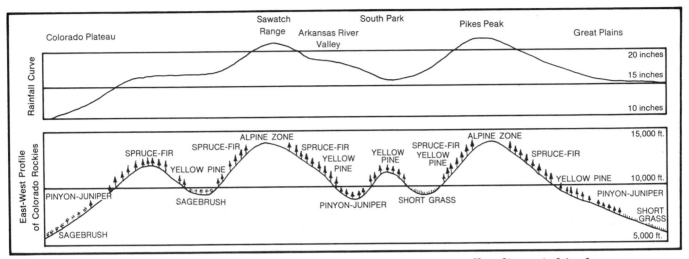

*In this cross-sectional slice through the Rocky Mountains, rainfall is seen to follow lines of altitude
(top chart). Zones of plant life also vary with the altitude (bottom chart).*

thrives on a warmer climate than other pines can tolerate, and because, like the hardy grass, it sends down deep roots to capture groundwater.

In this borderland, cleft with cool canyons and checkered with groves and grassy parks, mountain and plains life meet. Here the destinies of the plains badger, the kit fox, and the prairie falcon intertwine with those of the Colorado chipmunk, the mountain lion, and the golden eagle. When spring freshets swell the mountain water table, earthworms—a key food in this transition zone—come to the soil's surface, where ants, ground beetles, and magpies snap them up. When the worm-laden magpie flies out over the plains, a prairie falcon dives upon the plump morsel. Or perhaps a mountain chipmunk enjoys a beetle that has just eaten a worm, only to end its life in the jaws of a kit fox that has stolen into the canyon from the grasslands.

Some animals come to the foothills for a longer stay. The pronghorn, distant cousin of the deer family, finds shelter against winter gales in the low-lying canyons, foraging there for mountain shrubs. In the summer, though, it prefers the high plains, to which it is most adapted. It is the swiftest mammal on the continent, and its keen eyes spot a predator as soon as it appears on the stark horizon.

Between the foothills and the subalpine zone, anywhere from 6,000 to 9,000 feet, lies the montane zone of the central and southern Rockies. On the sunny,

south-facing slopes, the ponderosas stand at equal distance from each other, their long boughs not quite touching, their tops arrayed evenly against the sky, as if a gardener had surveyed their planting. On north-facing slopes, Colorado blue spruces mingle with an occasional Engelmann spruce, native of higher, colder climes. Douglas firs grow on both warm and cool slopes, their seedlings needing more light than the spruce but less than the ponderosa. Here and there among the darker conifers, aspens shimmer in the breeze. Alders, willows, and birches grow near streams, and piñon and juniper bristle on dry, exposed sites. The juniper, which wastes no time or energy in sprouting deciduous leaves or strengthening upright branches, grows from the foothills all the way up into the subalpine zone. The floor of a ponderosa grove supports a modest plant life —grasses, juniper, mountain mahogany, all of which are well equipped to stand the big trees' shade and the poor soil. Under the darker spruce forests, even fewer plants thrive.

Evergreens dominate the montane zone, because they can live in the cold, dry weather. They and other Rocky Mountain plants have needle-like leaves covered by a thick layer of wax and a tough, fibrous cuticle. When one holds up a pine needle against an aspen leaf, the difference in their shapes reveals why the pines conserve their water so well. A single vein carrying water and nutrients runs up the center of the needle,

while on the aspen, a whole network of veins sends water to the edge of the leaf. The needle, with fewer pores, allows less moisture to escape into the air.

Standing on one of these wooded slopes with only the wind and an occasional birdcall in his ears, a person would swear that this is a place of serenity, secure from change. Yet, like any other natural community, this one has its disasters, its wars of succession, its aggressive intruders. Change here may be imperceptible, but it is constant. Each forest strives to reach an equilibrium with the land on which it lives, but it often has to grow through many ragged stages to reach the manicured elegance of a mature ponderosa park.

Even the rocks that stud the open spaces of the mountainside are in flux. The lichens, clinging to their sides like green and orange medallions, are the earliest pioneers of the land that will become forest centuries later. The lichens live, die, and are followed for many years by their descendants until a thick layer of crumbling rock and dead lichens collects to hold a little moisture and dust. Soil begins to form in the rock crevices, and leafy lichens appear, preparing the way for moss and grasses. Soon plants like fireweed and kinnikinnic invade the pockets of earth. Fireweed is one of the most aggressive settlers of the Rockies; tufted with silky hairs that act as parachutes in the wind, its seeds roam far and wide. The kinnikinnic, like the trees that will later claim this spot, is an evergreen, with narrow, leathery leaves and has, like the juniper, a determination to colonize the poorest soil in the West. As alumroot, juniper, and pine seedlings join these plants in the rock crevices, their leaves drop down, decay, and cover the rocks with earth. Underneath their new soil coat, the rocks themselves are slowly crumbling, cracked by expanding plant roots and seasonal frosts. More seedlings invade from the surrounding areas and germinate in the shade and moisture provided by the pioneer nursery. Finally, after hundreds of years, the rocks have disappeared, and giant yellow pines, Douglas firs, and ponderosas wave above a grassy slope.

The plants are not the only pioneers. As soon as there are soil and roots, ground squirrels and gophers tunnel into the area, scattering seeds and droppings, which further enrich the soil. In its constant search for the next juicy root, the pocket gopher makes an efficient gardener. It turns the soil, aerates it, buries dried top

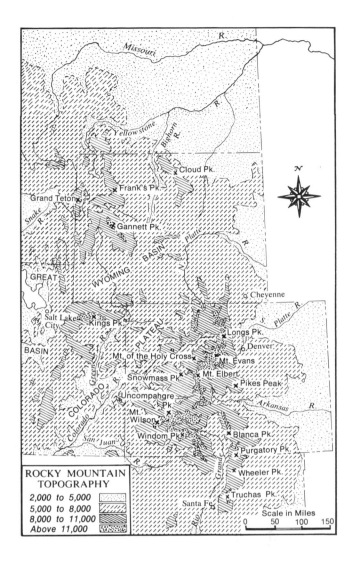

ROCKY MOUNTAIN TOPOGRAPHY
2,000 to 5,000
5,000 to 8,000
8,000 to 11,000
Above 11,000

grasses, and brings subsoil to the surface—all of which deepen the mountain sward.

Predator birds and coyotes follow the rodents. Deer and wapiti (commonly but erroneously known as elk) flock to the young forest to feed on seedlings, and then, as the conifers grow large, they leave for more promising forage. Soon a complex of food chains will link trees to bark beetles to woodpeckers to birds of prey, or pine nuts to squirrels to coyote and mountain lion.

When lightning-kindled fire razes a mountainside in the montane zone, some soil is left, and seedling descendants of the big trees spring up through the ashes. Here again kinnikinnic and fireweed are among the first to claim the land. Aspen seeds, carried by rodents and the wind, take root in the moistest open spots

High on a rock point near Leadville, silhouetted against the Sawatch Range, a lonely pine struggles to survive. Its very presence — its probing roots and fallen needles — helps new soil to form.

93

A small evergreen, the kinnikinnic, sprouts in land stripped by fire or logging operations, and thrives by its own system of conserving energy — bearing flowers instead of cones.

among the seedlings. The aspen needs much more sun than the larger conifers, and a recently burned-out area is the perfect place for it to grow. After several years, fallen leaves and rodent burrowing have thrown a rich carpet of loam over the hillside, and the ground is ready to nurture the lodgepole pine, which, like the aspen, thrives on sun. It is an aggressive, gregarious tree; thirty to fifty young lodgepoles crowd together on one square yard of ground, thrusting their contorted branches out in all directions. Smaller plants that cannot survive the growing shade die out. But in time the lodgepole and aspen, too, will be overtopped by the spruces and large firs that have grown up in their shade. Only then will this forest have reached equilibrium with the land; it will remain like this for the natural life of the trees, barring a plague of insects, loggers, or further destruction by lightning.

Animals of the montane zone follow a seasonal clock similar to these slower changes in plant life. The mule deer are migrants between the foothills and the lower montane. In the summer, they congregate on the edges of aspen groves and seedling stands; the grassy inlets between the large trees offer the mule deer the best forage, and when enemies come, it can bound off into the forest shadows. During the heat of the day, it takes cover in the shade, where flies are fewer, coming out at twilight to feed on meadow clover. Its pruning activities and preference for clover rather than grass keep the meadows open and grassy.

In the late summer, the scent of mushrooms draws the mule deer into the dense forest, where it feeds until late September. Then, following well-worn trails, it migrates down the hillsides to the piñon and juniper foothills, and stays there as long as snow covers the slopes above. In April and May, it is on the move again, browsing up through the montane. The deer's life depends upon its ability to migrate and to assimilate many different kinds of plants, since it neither hibernates nor stores food.

Mountain lions and coyotes are travelers, too, partly because they follow the deer herds, hoping to pick off the young and the sick. The coyote is not often so lucky as to fell a mule deer, though, and its main diet is rodents. In a slim winter, when even the prolific rabbit is scarce, the coyote will not scorn juniper berries and wild rosehips. Because of its ravenous and unselective appetite, the coyote is an important part of mountain life; without it the rodents would overpopulate and kill grasses and shrubs, and squirrels would devour all the pine seeds, preventing the spread of large trees. For the mountain lion and the coyote, the dense cover of the north-slope spruce forests offers the best hunting ground.

It is easy to miss seeing the deer, coyote, or mountain lion; they are all shy, and since they are large animals, there are relatively few in any given area. But one can hardly spend a minute on the slopes without glimpsing a ground squirrel or hearing the high-pitched bleating of the pika, a short-eared relative of the rabbit. And here and there in the dry parts of the meadows, one is sure to notice the mounded tunnels of the pocket gopher. Like the larger animals, rodents shape their life styles according to the seasons.

The golden-mantled ground squirrel eats pine nuts and other plant food voraciously throughout the spring and summer; in winter, it burrows under the ground and hibernates.

The important birds of the montane zone are common everywhere on the continent. Bluebirds and robins eat an enormous number of the grasshoppers and Mormon crickets, which would otherwise devastate the grass and trees. In summer, large flocks of common ravens descend on the mountain meadows to feed on these insects.

The Black Hills beetle—known as the "engraver" because of its tree-bark handiwork—wreaks havoc among the ponderosas. This insect hollows out galleries under the bark of the tree, where it feeds and lays its eggs.

Only the woodpecker and particularly cold weather keep the "engraver" from destroying whole groves.

CLIMBING above the 9,000-foot mark in the Colorado Front Range, one reaches the subalpine zone, where spruce is king. Gone are the tufted, olive-colored ponderosa, the dry meadows. This zone receives more snow than any other in the mountains; the slow runoff nourishes a deep silt and clay loam, makes marshes and ponds of the meadows, and keeps the moisture-loving spruce alive.

In these twilight forests, undergrowth has even less of a chance than in the montane zone. Kinnikinnic and juniper try, but they are less successful than shade-tolerant mosses and lichens.

The advantage here goes to the larger animals and predators, who often enter the forest from the exposed alpine meadows above to find shelter or to hunt. Wapiti browse the meadows in the daytime and bed down at night under the trees. Mountain sheep migrate to the forest in the winter. For the mountain lion, the wolf, and the coyote, the spruce forest is an extension of their montane zone hunting grounds, an ideal spot to stalk and ambush prey.

In this somber forest, one reaches the end of the slopes. Below, the animals travel from life zone to life zone, wresting from each what they need. Some of the most intense hunting and foraging goes on at the borders between zones. Plants crowd against foreign plants in the struggle to colonize slopes of different shade and exposure. And some cosmopolitan species, like the juniper and the kinnikinnic, send emissaries into all the life zones of the slopes.

Above are two or three thousand feet of timberline, alpine meadow, and snow-locked peaks, where life runs to a different rhythm. On the peaks, life is sheathed in ice for much of the year, and the rules are more unbending. Many of the plants and animals who have adapted to life up there could not live on the slopes below. So their story is really a separate one—a sequel to the story of life on the slopes.

CHAPTER 7

LIFE ON THE HIGH PEAKS

*Tundra plants and hardy animals that make their homes in the barren
beauty of the windswept crags and meadows above timberline*

THE HIGHEST PEAKS of the Rocky Mountains—in the Wind River Range of Wyoming, in the Uintas of Utah, in Colorado's Front Range and San Juan Mountains, in even the southernmost Sangre de Cristo Mountains of New Mexico—are snow locked and arctic much of the year. On Wyoming's ranges the domain of bare rock, snow, and alpine meadow reaches as low as 9,500 feet, while to the south, in Utah and Colorado, it begins at 11,000 to 12,000 feet.

From timberline to mountaintop, extremes are the rule. The peaks are colder, windier, and drier than the slopes; because the air at high altitudes is thin, rock and meadow receive an intense solar bath, and the temperature often rises sixty degrees during the day, only to plummet again during the night.

In such an environment life is more restricted than it is below. Where the breeze grows to a gale, where summer shrinks to a six-week pause in the icy year, the meek and enduring inherit. This is a land of grasses, sedges, and tiny flowers. The clumps of ancient, stunted trees that toil against the wind at timberline are sometimes known as "elfinwood."

Commuting between life zones is less constant than it is on the slopes, because the heights demand more specific adaptations from their inhabitants. From June to September, tourists from the slopes—deer, wapiti, rabbits, and their predators—bring a brief burst of activity to the alpine meadows. The natives of this high country, however, are not travelers; marmots, ptarmigans, and pikas are old settlers who know how to make do when the snow flies.

Because their life is more specialized, less accommodating of outside influence, the food chains linking these animals are shorter, simpler, and more fragile than those of the slopes. Decimate one of the native populations on a mountain peak, and it may never grow back, as it probably would lower down.

At timberline Engelmann spruce and limber pine take their last stand—for the animals of the slopes, the last place of shelter before the open meadows. Prevailing winds, snow, and frost shape this rugged garden. Wind is the most constant of these forces; it is wind, with its teeth of ice and sand, that strips the tree trunks of bark and prostrates them against the mountainside. Like their counterparts below, the timberline trees try to send out branches on all sides, but the gale batters their buds and dries up their store of water; only those on the lee side of the trunk can grow. Here and there sheltered by rocks or larger trees, ordinary seedlings spring up; but when they grow above their protection, they too become gnarled and denuded, bending away from the wind like tattered flags. On the forest frontier, the deformed are the normal.

Snow and frost also sculpt these trees; each seedling can grow only as high as the winter blanket of snow, which insulates it against the frost. Like any other forest, elfin timber sprouts new green shoots in the summer. Each summer the young tree grows a bit taller, and each winter the snow protects it; temperatures below the snow crust may be fifty degrees or more above those on the surface. But finally the tree's tender growing tip pierces the snow blanket; wind and frost quickly

*Marmots are an engaging sight, lumping along over the high meadows, as here above
Trail Ridge Road. Protected by heavy fur, they sleep away the harsh alpine winter.*

The snow coney, or pika, survives winter on the peaks in a snow-insulated, rocky burrow with a cache of sun-cured grasses gathered during the summer.

absorb its moisture, and it dies. Undaunted, the tree may go on producing such new shoots year after year, though none can live past the winter. A cluster of dead brown twigs tops each mature tree at timberline, telling of the harshness of winter.

But if they cannot grow up, branches grow out, away from the wind. The energy that would normally impel the tree upward toward the clouds here sends it outward, parallel to the ground, in a dense fretwork sometimes as high as a man's head, sometimes only a foot from the earth. When winter comes, the snow's weight reinforces the horizontal growth.

Timberline trees are thus smaller than those of the lower elevations, but they are much older for their girth. Their seasonal growth is much more modest, and one needs a magnifying glass to read the history that

lies encoded in their rings.

Timberline, like forests of the slopes, is a place where animals of different life zones mingle. In the summer, elk and mule deer on their way to the alpine meadows find shelter here against the fierce sun of high altitudes and against their major predators, the mountain lion and the ever-present coyote. Surprised in its browsing of forest meadows, the snowshoe rabbit hops into the matted timberline forest. Summer visitors to the peaks reenter timberline at the time of their autumn migration down the slopes. Deer, bears, coyotes, rodents, and birds all come here for a mountain delicacy—the blueberries, which ripen in the fall. As in normal stands of spruce, the soil under elfin timber gets little sun and supports little underbrush; dank and smothered in needles, this ground is extremely acid. Blueberry is

Mule deer may be found within alpine meadows and at timberline during warm months of the year, but they migrate into lower forests when the snow falls.

one of the few plants that can grow in such conditions.

During July, August, and September, blueberries are the bears' staple food. The bears, in turn, help spread the plant, since blueberry seeds often pass through their digestive tracts intact, to be dropped miles away.

Traffic moves into the elfin forest from both above and below: some alpine residents who do not hibernate or are otherwise unequipped for the alpine winter come in under the forest canopy when snow falls. Pine grosbeaks and golden-crowned kinglets, some of the most typical birds of the peaks, move to timberline for shelter and stay through spring to breed and raise their young. Bighorn sheep, which forage for grass and sedges among the rockiest parts of the peaks, retreat to timberline or lower as the weather grows cold.

INEVITABLY, although reluctantly, timberline gives way to grass, shrub, bare rock, and glacier as the altitude rises. Much of the plant and animal life on mountaintops from Montana to New Mexico is similar to that on the high mountains of Europe, Asia, and Alaska. Relics of the last Ice Age, when arctic tundra covered many portions of North America, these flora and fauna maintain a highly specialized life-style suited to extreme conditions.

The plants are the most specialized of all. Grass is one of the few familiar to travelers from the slopes. It grows here because its modest size, narrow leaves, and deep roots conserve what little moisture the peaks provide. Even the smallest, most limber trees lack the flexibility of a grass stem, which bends but does not break in the highest wind. And because it is so short,

The Wind River peaks are rigorous winter strongholds of pikas, marmots, and mountain goats.

grass can be assured of a warm winter snow cover; unlike spruce and pine, it loses no energy in putting forth shoots that must die in winter.

The green mat covering the peaks contains sedge as well as grass. Alpine sedges are shorter cousins of plants that grow on the prairies and in the foothills—all hardy, grasslike colonizers of arid soil.

But two-thirds of alpine plants can live only in arctic conditions. Because the growing season on the peaks is so short, they would have to rush through their entire life cycle in a few weeks if they lived like the plants of the slopes. Most alpine plants spend years between germination and first blooming. Plants like the alpine avens are relatively speedy growers, but bear grass must work for five to seven years before it can put out its showy yellow flowers.

Predictably, the succession of plants over an alpine meadow is painfully slow. Below, a hillside can run the gamut from bare rock to forest in eighty or a hundred years; here the lichens alone may need several centuries to create enough humus to nourish grass and shrubs.

Typically, alpine plants clump together in low, dense mats, which absorb the sun's heat much as an animal's fur does; the intense color of their flowers and the deep green of their stems and leaves mean also that they absorb heat rather than reflect it. These plant clusters thus create their own microclimate in a harsh land. Often the ground temperature around them is only a few degrees above zero, while within the plant colony temperatures rise to forty or fifty degrees.

Unlike the plants of the slopes, the peak-dwellers depend very little upon bees for fertilization. Insects better adapted to the heights perform the bees' function. Here sphinx moths, butterflies, and dragonflies travel from bloom to bloom with their freight of pollen. The insects, too, are specialized species—darker than their lowland cousins, and so more able to take in the sun's warmth.

Because of a short growing season, alpine flowers require years between germination and first bloom.

Though there are no trees here, some plants look like tiny evergreens. The mountain heath bears small, dark-green needles whose margins roll downward and inward when the frost bites, protecting their precious moisture by exposing less surface to the air. Narrow, sheathed in wax, and stiffened by a thick cuticle, these leaves are well formed for life on the peaks. The heath, however, bears flowers, not cones; in this frigid world, the energy output required to produce a cone would be prohibitive.

SUMMER COMES SUDDENLY to the alpine world. Snow drifts linger into May and June, but underneath the snow's crust plants are putting forth tentative shoots in response to the longer days and more intense sunlight. Often buds pierce the snow blanket, to burst into bloom when the snow melts. One day all is white and severe, seemingly bare of life; the next, flowers of every hue cover the ground. The blue of sky pilot mingles with the gold of avens, the pink of mountain heather, and the purple of saxifrage. July and August are full of fierce activity, since these plants must make the most of the short season.

The sky pilot, or polemonium, like other alpine plants, has adapted its leaves to the harsh weather. Each of these plants is actually a plant cluster, whose leaves are composed of thirty to forty small, whorled, roundish leaflets covered with a sticky coating that keeps water in. Polemonium grows in the shelter of rocks and, when crushed, emits a disagreeable, skunky odor that wards off hungry foragers.

Alpine sunflowers and bluebells are reminiscent of their relatives on the slopes, but their stems—short, stiff, and covered with insulating hairs—are adapted to the more severe climate of the peaks.

Amidst all this unlikely extravagance, the purple saxifrage, pioneer of rock slides and boulder piles, is

Once plentiful, in herds that extended to the horizon, the bison today survives only in sanctuaries.

the unlikeliest of all. "Saxifrage" means literally "rock-breaker," an appropriate name for a plant whose roots grow best in rock crevices. Using whatever humus and moss they find in these fissures, saxifrage roots actually split the rocks as they grow; centuries later, the granite they have pulverized will have become soil and finally meadow.

The avens, too, are constructed to thrive in alpine conditions. This evergreen's low, woody stem scorns wind and frost; its rolled leaves store up moisture. Its flowers mature quickly, producing a multitude of seeds to ensure survival of a few in the harsh environment. The plant also stores nutrients in its root nodules, as a legume does. Once established, the avens slowly extends itself year after year like a carpet over the surrounding rocks.

Animals that live on the heights year round must bear winter cold and lack of food. The northern pocket gopher is one of these hardy residents; in summer and winter it finds a constant food supply in the roots of perennial plants like the sky pilot and the avens, and in the tuberous, nutrition-packed roots of sedges. During warm weather it burrows just as it does on the slopes, but in the winter it packs soil into snow burrows, which look like casts when the snow melts. Other rodents, like the long-tailed vole, follow in the gopher's path, using its abandoned burrows as a home.

Rock slides and fragments provide the pika with an ideal home; though some pikas exist in isolated rocky patches lower on the slopes, the peaks are their real habitat. This short-eared relative of the rabbit, about the size of a guinea pig, must work hard to survive, for it lives above ground and does not hibernate. In late summer it frantically harvests grasses, cures them in the sun, and then stores them in the rocky crevice it calls home; in one short season it may gather a bushel or more of food. Then, when the blizzard howls, it stays warm in the rocks next to its fodder.

The marmot, which looks something like a giant pika, also remains all year among the rocks and glaciers of the peaks; during the winter it burrows in the soil and hibernates.

Grasshoppers survive all year on the peaks, often spending the winter dormant in a natural deep freeze of snow or under cover of rocks or piles of droppings left by large animals; when the spring melt arrives, they jump to life again.

The ptarmigan is at home in the alpine meadows through the winter. During the summer, this small grouse lives much as other birds do, feeding on insects and plants. But in winter it molts its gray and brown feathers for a new coat of pure white and becomes almost invisible against the snow. Fringes of long feathers on its toes serve as snowshoes, and when other birds are long gone, the ptarmigan roams the snowfields in search of buds exposed by the wind. Because this bird is so secure in its camouflage coat, it expends little body heat in flying; when predators threaten, it huddles close to the ground, hoping to be passed by.

Of the large animals, the mountain goat—found mainly in Montana and Idaho—comes closest to making a year-round home of the peaks. This shaggy-haired member of the antelope family subsists mainly on the lichen-like moss covering the rocks of the peaks. Since its food supply is perennial and available wherever the wind or its own pawing have uncovered rocks, it need not migrate like the deer. The mountain goat may seek shelter against the bitterest cold in elfin timber, but it prefers to remain high and remote among the rocks, because its main protection against predators is its ability to live where others fear to tread. Its thick pelt repels ice and snow, and its hooves are suited to the most precarious spots on the mountains. The goat's hoof has a hard, sharp rim for cutting into ice and a thick ball of flesh that gives traction on the slipperiest surfaces; a space between the two forms a suction cup, ensuring the animal's grip on the ground.

SUMMER BRINGS MANY VISITORS to the peaks. In July and August, Swainson's hawks skim higher and higher above the forests, until they are searching for rodents among the peaks. Mountain bluebirds and ravens come to feed on the newly revived insects. Summer is the only time most large animals appear on the heights, but they come then in great numbers and variety. During these lush months, mule deer and wapiti arrive, followed by coyote, mountain lion, and wolf. In August, bears on their way to a winter den come here for rodents, berries, and other vegetation. The coyote and western red fox find good mouse- and gopher-hunting here, as well as insects, birds, and an occasional snowshoe rabbit that has ventured into the open to browse. Mountain sheep come from the valleys to eat grass and moss at the edge of snowfields, retiring in the fall to the pine glades below.

These summer visitors live by different rules from the alpine residents; when snow flies, they have retreated to more protected spots. The bear is in its den, the deer are on their way to the foothills, and predators are finding better hunting on the slopes. Marmot, ptarmigan, and pika dig in for the long winter. Silence falls over the alpine meadows; snow piles up; life settles into its seven-month arctic sleep.

CHAPTER 8

LIFE ON THE ARID FRINGE

*Denizens of the near-desert reaches that lie at the foot of the Rockies
—the Wyoming Basin, the Great Basin, and the Colorado Plateau*

THINKING OF MOUNTAINS, we think in verticals. Foothill, slope, peak—each is a signpost on a climb. But for the Rockies, this is only half the story. Anyone who has crossed the Continental Divide in Wyoming, or the border between Utah and Colorado, where the highland unrolls in basin and plateau, can tell the other half. A relief map writes the same message large: the Rocky Mountains are as much plateau as peak. They contain three vast, arid highlands—the Wyoming Basin, the Colorado Plateau, and the Great Basin.

The Wyoming Basin sweeps southwest between the Bighorn and Laramie mountains, fanning out flat and grassy across half of Wyoming to the Uinta and Medicine Bow mountains on the south. This great indentation is part of the Rockies, framed on three sides by their distant, pale-blue profile, and yet its terrain and natural life are of the high plains and the cold desert, dominated in the northeast by shortgrass ecology and in the southwest by sagebrush.

South of the Wyoming Basin, along the line where Utah and Colorado meet, canyons and forested peaks begin to appear. The earth flames out in reds and yellows, heaves up forested mounds and mesas, and splits apart into terraced gorges where the rivers run. The Colorado Plateau is actually a thousand plateaus, separated from each other by the chasms and trenches that the Colorado River and its tributaries have cut: Split Mountain and Flaming Gorge on the Green River, the Black Canyon of the Gunnison, the Great Goosenecks of the San Juan, and Zion Canyon on the

Virgin. This is a land of contrasts, where ponderosa pine and spruce forests rise abruptly out of low-lying desert, where the lizard on the canyon floor and the pika on the cool heights live as close as the tenants of a high-rise apartment building. Here life takes every form the mountains can offer—from desert to foothills to slopes, and even, where volcanic remnants rise above timberline, to peaks.

West and north, across Utah and into Idaho, stretches the Great Basin Desert. In a land of little water, this region is the driest of the dry. Ancient glaciers scooped out its basins and left behind a long-vanished, landlocked sea, Lake Bonneville. Modern remnants of this glacial water, including Great Salt Lake, are almost as much mirage as lake; issuing in no rivers, receiving so little rainfall that they rarely overflow their banks, they are so full of salts and minerals that they often kill, rather than give life. Some of the smallest and shallowest appear only for the rainy season, evaporating when the weather is dry. This horizontal land of sagebrush and salt flat is frequented by some of the most adaptable animals from other life zones—the coyote, the mule deer, and the jackrabbit. Other animals, like the kangaroo rat, seem designed expressly for the formidable environment.

The Wyoming Basin, the Colorado Plateau, and the Great Basin share some characteristics: all are high, dry, and intensely radiated. In such inhospitable lands life cannot range freely; it must find or create islands of congeniality for itself. Man does this by building airconditioned houses and cutting himself off from the

Few places are more hostile to life than the high, dry alkaline wastes of the Colorado Plateau,
yet armed with an instinct for survival, many organisms compete against the odds and win.

105

outside atmosphere. When he steps into his home, he enters a very different habitat from that around it. Plants and animals do the same thing; each living thing "chooses" a miniature world—a certain kind of soil, a burrow, or a shrub root—that best suits its needs. Different organisms living only a few feet or inches apart may be in very different environments: a jackrabbit reclining in its lightly shaded "form," or nest, under a shrub has a very different kind of resting place from the moist, cool burrow of the kangaroo rat below the ground. Although sagebrush and other shrubs seem to grow indiscriminately over arid spots, they, too, live in different communities. Sagebrush dominates the northern parts of the basins and plateaus, while shad scale, which can withstand heat and aridity even better, grows in the south. Saltbush appears on the salty or alkaline margins of salt lakes or on playas, where the other shrubs cannot grow.

Take these plants and animals away from their microhabitats for even a short time and they will probably die, just as a person stranded in the desert without cooled air and running water will soon perish. A naturalist has told of taking a rattlesnake only a few feet away from its daytime home: "Desiring a picture, I hooked him out from the dense growth into the bright sunshine for photographing. It was a very hot July day, about midafternoon; in a short time he turned belly-up and died before I could pose him and focus the camera."

Microhabitats are particularly important to the animals of the basins and plateaus because usually their bodies are not, like plants', especially adapted to the environment. They are no more capable of standing heat and dryness than animals anywhere else, but they are practiced in the art of avoiding them. Burrowing underground, staying there during the day, and appearing only at night, is one of the commonest ploys used. A burrow provides cooler temperatures and retains the moisture the animal loses through breathing; the humidity inside a burrow is usually much higher than in the air above. Caves offer the same kind of relief to canyonland dwellers. In the Great Basin the large pools of water that collect during the rainy season become important microclimates for animals that need large amounts of water.

For most animals survival in these regions means

Plateau plants huddle in arroyos, leaving barren rock stark against the sky (Arches National Monument).

being active or dormant at the right times, as well as finding the right place to live. During the day, hawks, vultures, insects, and the heat-loving lizard are often the only moving things on a sagebrush flat. As evening falls, however, the pace of life quickens. Jackrabbits, kangaroo rats, and other rodents that have spent the day in burrows and shady nests come out to feed on shrubs and seeds. A whole new set of predators appears from daytime shelters; owls, coyotes, kit foxes, and badgers are on the prowl for rodents. New interrelationships and "food chains" appear. In the day the lizards who prey on insects are eaten by daytime birds. After dark, rat eats seeds, and owl eats rat; or rabbit eats sagebrush leaves, and fox eats rabbit.

Much of the night's frenzied activity takes place around the water hole, lake, or stream, because night is the time when most animals can afford to venture into the air to replenish the water they have lost in the day's heat. Because many predators come here not just to drink but to eat, the watering spot is a dangerous place, and those who can drink fastest or need the least water hold trump cards. Night also brings dew—an important

Dominating the jackrabbit and sagebrush country of southern Utah is Rainbow Bridge, a monument to all that is powerful in the high desert — flash floods, wind, and rain.

By its sharp eyes, antenna-like ears, and a galloping stride, the ubiquitous jackrabbit seems made with but one design — to elude its predators.

source of water for the animals that can lick it off the surfaces of rocks, soil, and plants, or eat the plants that have just been moistened by it.

Since they cannot move about, plants must adapt more rigorously in growth and structure to their environment than most animals. Their major problem in the basins and plateaus is aridity. Water is life to all plants; through water they receive the soil's minerals, and by combining it with the sun's energy, they produce their own food. When a plant's cells are full of water, they are swollen and stiff; drought causes wilting. And like animals, plants in warm climates lower their temperatures by "perspiring" or sending off water vapor into the air through tiny pores in their stems and leaves.

Many plants in these arid regions are either "drought evaders" or "drought resisters." The first produce seeds coated with a chemical that rejects all but the best conditions for flowering. When just enough water washes the chemicals off the seeds, they burgeon, quickly putting forth roots, flowers, and leaves in a brief burst of vitality—and rush through their whole life in one season. "Drought evaders" thus live only when the basins and plateaus are wettest.

"Drought resisters" are perennials, which establish lasting roots and branches, growing new leaves and flowers only when they have enough water. Since they grow in this sun-baked soil all year round, perennials must have superior powers of getting water, saving it, and making do with small amounts of it. Once grow-

Herds of pronghorn antelope can be found on the high plains, sharing the grassy rangeland with sheep and cattle. They have not always been welcomed by ranchers.

ing, annuals in these regions are no different from plants of moist areas, but perennials here look and act very different. Some are able to go through a plant's version of hibernation: the penstemon and the mariposa and sego lilies of the Great Basin grow stem, leaves, and showy flowers for only one short season a year. The rest of the time, they exist only as roots and bulbs, under the ground where it is cooler and moister. Some perennials, like sagebrush and greasewood, grow above ground all year long. They are able to do so because their roots are extremely efficient and their leaves are constructed to lose very little water. Annuals can renew themselves only by leaving behind seeds full of dormant energy, but weather permitting, perennials manage to store enough food in their underground or-

gans to sustain new leaves and flowers each year. Because they can do this, perennials produce fewer seeds than annuals and require less specific conditions for germination. The life of an annual is brief, flamboyant, and prodigal; that of a perennial, long, slow, and economical.

Aridity is not the only obstacle to plants of the Great Basin. On the salt flats surrounding shallow inland seas, only saltbush can grow. It can do so because it is particularly fitted to withstand high concentrations of salts within its cells, and can excrete excess amounts through special glands.

Except for the shortgrass region of the Wyoming Basin and the forested spots of the canyonlands, a thin cover of shrubs dominates the basins and plateaus. The

Inquisitive but wary, the white-tailed prairie dog resides in a gregarious community. Prairie dog towns often cover tens of acres.

pale, diminutive plants stand far apart from one another with only bare ground or sparse grass between them. In the competition for the meager water supply, each shrub must spread its roots deep and wide, searching out the last drop of moisture. These high flatlands impose a strict husbandry on plant life; when a bush dies here, many seeds of the same kind will try to spring up in the same place, but ultimately only one new shrub will grow. Succession here is simpler than in moister areas. Cut down a stand of trees on the slopes of the Front Range, for instance, and a dozen different foliages will follow each other in the struggle to claim the land. In the basins and plateaus, however, the uprooted shrub is likely to be replaced by its own kind.

Although the basic conditions of life are similar in the three plateau regions, each has its own distinctive qualities. The Wyoming Basin is mainly shortgrass country, an extension of the high plains; geology and climate have made it suitable for only the hardiest plants—grama, buffalo grass, needle grass, and in the south where overgrazing has occurred, sagebrush and greasewood.

Grasses exhibit a remarkable talent for life. As one naturalist has said, "These humble growths live in the polar regions and on mountain tops; they endure the dry conditions of deserts, and the constant immersion of marshes and tidal flats. They are efficient and uncomplicated mechanisms for survival and dispersal. A grass stem is constructed of solid joints, from each of which arises a single leaf consisting of a sheath that

Both windswept peaks and high plateaus are colonized by bristlecone pines, trees even more ancient than the giant sequoia. Some survive over four thousand years.

fits around the stem like a split tube. The flowers are minute, attracting little attention from humans or from insects. Since they are wind-pollinated, they need neither fragrance nor inviting colors." While trees take decades to grow to maturity and send out seeds, grass can do so in only a year; if destroyed by fire or drought, it will grow back much more quickly than trees.

Like grass, sagebrush and greasewood are compact and low, exposing little leaf and branch surface to the sun's rays. Their leaves are narrow and wedge shaped, covered with silky hairs that insulate against heat and deflect radiation.

Some of this region's most typical animals are grazers and wanderers—keen of eye, swift of foot, able to subsist on the toughest grasses and shrubs. The American antelope, or pronghorn, for instance, can spot an enemy on the distant horizon and outrun the fastest mammals on the continent—crucial abilities in a land where there are no forests to hide in. As wary as its distant cousin the deer, the pronghorn has extra means of warning other members of its herd when danger appears. A natural historian notes that the animal uses a white patch on its rump to signal to other members of the herd; when the pronghorn becomes frightened, its muscles contract so that the white hairs rise and the patch flashes in the sun. At the same time, the pronghorn emits a musky warning odor. Thus, though the herd may be widely scattered over the plains, they can communicate common danger to each other very effectively.

This great horned owlet will grow to become one of the most active nighttime predators in the basins and plateaus; it is one link in nature's food chain.

Pronghorns migrate with the seasons; their life depends on being in the right place at the right time—wherever the weather is most clement, and food and water most abundant. In winter they congregate in the mountain foothills, where they find shelter against snow and gales that sweep across the plains; in spring they return to the plains as the grass and shrubs sprout once more.

Another Wyoming Basin animal that relies on speed and alertness is the jackrabbit. This large hare has a keen sense of smell, huge sensitive ears, and vision sharp enough to spot enemies miles away. Add to this a pair of especially long, wiry hind legs, and one understands why jackrabbits so often elude their predators. Some, known as antelope jackrabbits, will leap as high as

fifteen feet in the air, probably to get a better view of the area around and behind them. If they are hard pressed, their leaps become ground-hugging bounds, which soon leave all pursuers far behind. Many humans look long and hard, and never see this wily animal at all.

Like other animals here, the jackrabbit is not choosy about its food. It eats grass, sagebrush, and other shrubs, and though spines pose a problem, it will even eat cactus.

Even if one should miss seeing a pronghorn or a jackrabbit on the plains, one is sure to spot the bare, sun-hardened mounds of soil kicked up by the white-tailed prairie dog. On top of each mound may be several small, plump, cinnamon-colored rodents, barking out a warning to the rest of the "town's" inhabitants. Before the plains were settled, prairie dog towns in many places stretched as far as the eye could see. Nowadays, they still often cover tens of acres. Prairie dogs live on grasses, roots, and seeds, and their habitat, alertness, and warning system protect them from the hawks, coyotes, and foxes that are their main predators.

On the high alkali and sagebrush stretches of the Wyoming Basin, sometimes at altitudes of more than 7,000 feet, sage grouse travel in flocks, searching for food. Their eating habits, indicated by their name, and their strong wings, which carry them beyond the reach of enemies, make them well adapted to this area.

THE HIGH FORESTS dotting the Colorado Plateau region have been likened to islands in a sea of desert. As one naturalist has said of the Paunsaugunt Plateau, above Bryce Canyon, "It shares the same rich forest community as neighboring plateaus, a community that includes ponderosa, limber, and bristlecone pines, Douglas fir, white fir, blue spruce, quaking aspen, and manzanita."

The plants and animals of these tabletop communities are generally those we have already seen on the slopes and the peaks. On the highest, which reach 11,000 feet in Utah, grow wildflowers of the peaks and high slopes—lupine, mountain buttercup, and mountain bluebell—and some of the oldest trees on the continent, the slow-growing bristlecone pines, which twist along the ground at timberline. Here are visiting mule deer, marmots, ground squirrels, porcupines, and pikas.

Traveling into these canyons, one encounters the varied life of the slopes. Ponderosa pine, oak, juniper, and sumac grow in the sunny, dry spots, and where a stream runs, willow and cottonwood wave. Here, depending on numerous variables such as exposure, altitude, and moisture, one finds occasional beaver and

mountain lion, the ubiquitous mule deer and jackrabbit, and the brilliant black-and-white magpie. The life of the canyons is astoundingly intricate and varied, a study in contrasts. Within the close confines of a single canyon, one finds as many variations as on a whole mountain slope. North-facing canyon walls, like north-facing slopes, are colder, wetter, and more heavily overgrown than those facing south. Altitude, too, affects the life of a canyon, just as it does on the slopes.

MOST OF THE ANIMALS that frequent the Great Basin are not especially adapted for life in this hottest and dryest of the flatlands; many, like the kit fox and mule deer, must stay near water holes or make forays into the region from moister areas. One animal, however, seems made to live in this forbidding environment—the kangaroo rat. Like other burrowing animals, it emerges only at night; during the day it stays in its burrow, which it closes with a plug of dirt to keep heat out and moisture in. But there is more to the story: amazingly enough, the kangaroo rat drinks no water at all and subsists on a diet of dry seeds. It can do so because the very process of digesting the seeds produces water within its body, and because its system uses and conserves water in a highly efficient manner.

Varied as it is, the story of Rocky Mountain plants and animals has a common thread. On the peaks, in the basins and plateaus, even on the greater part of the slopes, life must contend with high altitudes, much sun, and very little water. In a land where the necessities of life are often an issue rather than a given, the struggle for survival takes on an intensity suggested in the alpine meadow's brilliant six-week flowering, and sometimes a touch of the bizarre, as in the case of the kangaroo rat. Pondering the conditions for life in the Rocky Mountains, one concludes that the most amazing fact of all is the profusion and variety that exist.

PART THREE

THE COMING OF MAN

Man carved a tenuous foothold for himself in the mountains—seeking a place to work and play, live and die—in experiences that told of a remote and often hostile land: Indians who learned to live with the high country, but as nomads, subject to Nature's benevolence; Spaniards intimidated by the interior of the chain and Americans interested more in what lay on the other side of the mountains; mountain men who plunged into the wilderness and emerged the undisputed authorities on geography and survival; and scientists who mapped and classified until the mountains lost their mystery.

"The Summer Rendezvous" by Thomas Hogan.

CHAPTER 9

BEFORE THE WHITE MAN

The Indian—from the first Siberian emigrant to the horseman
of the buffalo plains—living in harmony with the land

BEFORE RANCHERS, before prospectors, before government surveyors, before the U.S. Army, and before the mountain men—Indians had created the Rocky Mountains' first civilizations, following very different patterns from those that later colonizers would use. The diverse cultures of these native Americans had all grown out of accommodation to the land; their technology was largely of the Stone Age, and their religion revered the many forces of nature.

The red men's ancestors had come to the continent thousands of years before from Siberia. During the last glacial advance of the Ice Age, ice absorbed much of the earth's waters, ocean levels fell, and submerged land appeared. A land bridge at least three hundred miles wide linked Siberia and Alaska. Warmed by temperate Pacific breezes and covered with willows, alders, and grasses, this rolling plain must have offered lush pasturage for Ice Age mammals like the big-horned bison and the hairy mammoth. As the huge beasts browsed across the Bering Land Bridge and down into North America, primitive hunters of Mongolian stock followed their prey southward along the flanks of the continent's western mountain ranges. During a three-thousand-year migration, some fanned out over the high plains to the east of the Rocky Mountains; others settled the Great Basin and Colorado plateaus between the mountains and the Sierra Nevada. The westerly group subsisted on the small game and plants they found in this relatively dry area; the plains dwellers continued to hunt big game. Today, the high plains are arid shortgrass land, but in the moist late Ice Age,

they were a hunter's paradise.

Scanning the plains from Rocky Mountain foothills, Ice Age nomads easily spotted herds of mammoth and large bison; trailing them on foot through the tall grass, they drove the animals over bluffs or surrounded them, slaying them with stone-tipped spears. Probably their kill provided them with most of life's necessities: food, shelter, clothing, and tools of bone and sinew. So many large mammals flocked on the plains that the Indians probably gathered few plants; at least, they left behind no implements for grinding berries and chopping roots. They lived like this until, about 10,000 years ago, the glaciers began to recede, water became scarce, and their big prey died out.

Out of necessity, the big-game hunters began to live in the Desert Culture way; like the peoples of the Great Basin and the Colorado Plateau, they learned a highly flexible way of life, geared to exploiting the whole spectrum of food resources their rigorous climate offered. Since the rain fell in different places from season to season and year to year, the concentrations of plants and animals varied greatly, and Indians moved often. They combed the land for antelope, rabbits, reptiles, plants—even insects; a locust plague was a feast.

Although the Desert Culture people had to be extremely mobile, their technology was more varied and sophisticated than that of the big-game hunters. They made seed grinders, scrapers, and choppers from stone; digging sticks, fire drills, and spear throwers, from wood. From grasses they wove some of the earliest known basketry of the world.

The Sun Dance, a rite de passage of plains and mountain tribes, is depicted by Frederic Remington.
Tethered to a pole, the warrior danced until the hooks tore free from his flesh.

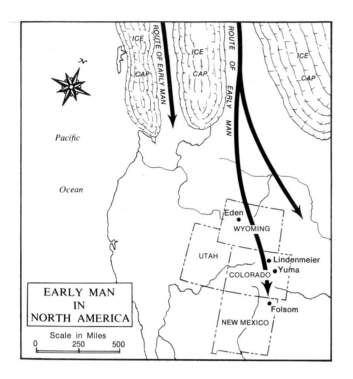

EARLY MAN
IN
NORTH AMERICA

Scale in Miles
0   250   500

They roamed their territory in small families. Occasionally, when berries, rabbits, or fish abounded in a certain place, word passed from family to family, and groups gathered to harvest or hunt together. Families of the region's colder areas formed bands for the fall nut harvest, and during the winter, lived together off the food, which they stored in baskets.

ABOUT 9,600 years passed between the glaciers' retreat and the white man's arrival on the continent; during this time, three distinctive cultures arose in the Rocky Mountain region: Great Basin and Colorado Plateau Indians lived much as they had since coming to the area. Plains Indians, borrowing from their neighbors to the south and east, added farming to their hunting-and-gathering economy and lived a semi-sedentary life; the men hunted on foot for buffalo and small animals, and the women planted crops and made crude pottery. Pueblos of the Southwest learned from tribes farther south to farm maize and to irrigate; they built permanent adobe houses, and became skilled potters and basketmakers.

Plains and Desert Culture life changed little from

this stage until the horse and the gun arrived in the West; but before the first Spaniard glimpsed their villages, the Pueblo civilization had developed, flourished, and declined. Their high, arid canyonland home seems to promise little, but by using the available rivers and pockets of rich valley land, these Indians became comfortable farmers. Known as Basket Makers because of their greatest skill, they first lived in the Desert Culture way, but by around A.D. 500 some Pueblo settlements had domesticated maize, beans, squash, and turkeys. Now known as the Anasazi, or "Ancient Ones," they built large clusters of pit houses, lined with stone slabs and roofed with wood—clearly not the kind of dwelling one made expecting to move often. During the next hundred years, they moved above ground, stringing together rooms of adobe and stone. The people now stored their surplus grains, experimented with new strains of corn, wove textiles, and adorned themselves with shell, wood, and turquoise.

From 1100 to 1300, the Anasazi expanded, settling throughout the Southwest in many-tiered villages wedged into protected cliff recesses or crowning the mesas. They had learned to irrigate and use the bow and arrow. Above all, they had created the most cohesive society of the North American West around a complex religion that involved the whole community in innumerable and elaborate public ceremonies. They now set aside one large building—the Great Kiva—for exclusively ceremonial and religious purposes.

Sometime in the fourteenth century, the Anasazi gave up their cliff dwellings and their sophisticated way of life; they dispersed into the canyons and the desert, some taking up the old Desert Culture again. No one knows for certain why this happened, but probably a combination of drought, raids by hostile Navajos and Apaches, and feuds within the villages caused the people to move. The Rio Grande Valley towns the Spaniards found were really the displaced remnants of the great Pueblo society.

AS THE DIVERGING PATHS of the three main Indian cultures suggest, the land dictated social structure as well as the material way of life. Predictably, the simplest society was that of the Desert Culture peoples, known in historic times as the Shoshoneans—a collective name for the Ute, Wind River Shoshoni, Gosiute, and other tribes who lived in Utah, Wyoming and Colorado. To the whites who encountered these Indians, they were wretched, half-human beings, contemptuously nicknamed "Diggers" because they dug edible roots from the arid soil.

But the Shoshoneans were supremely well adapted to their environment, which required mobility and sparse population. Because food was so scarce, they lived most of the year in single, extended-family units, both men and women sometimes having several spouses. Men and women split labor between them, the wife gathering plants, making baskets, and cooking food while the husband hunted. Both cared for the children. No one in the family had final authority over the others, but the wisest members, known as "talkers," offered advice.

Because they were nomads, the Shoshoneans felt that natural resources belonged to no one in particular; any family could go anywhere in search of food. Once a family camped in an area, though, they were its temporary "owners," unless the place was fertile enough to support more people. The Indians established their exclusive right to a thing or place simply by working on it or using it for a time; whatever a person made—a fishnet or basket, for instance—was his property. It was only later, in historic times, when some Shoshoneans acquired horses, that a wealthy class of horsemen grew up among them.

The Shoshoneans had no priests, but people who had especially powerful dreams became shamans, called "medicine men" by whites because their main duty was to cure people. Shamans were also considered especially wise and gave advice. Generally, though, each person practiced his religion alone by acquiring his own spiritual protector.

Primitive though their life seemed to whites, the Shoshoneans managed to avoid at least two crucial problems that still bedevil modern man. Contrary to popular opinion, they did not constantly grub for food; in fact, they had more spare time than the average industrial worker today. Because they had no way of preserving meat and no farming, they spent no time drying and preserving flesh, tilling the soil, watering crops, constructing irrigation systems and food-storage containers, or distributing food from family to family. The Shoshoneans had no leisured class of priests, aristocrats,

Ute petroglyphs in Arches National Park depict riders (top and right) in a successful sheep hunt.

or artists to support; each produced the minimum he needed to survive.

Unlike many more sophisticated cultures, the Shoshonean had little or no warfare. Since these Indians recognized few territorial rights and rarely organized for concerted action, war was impractical. In contrast to the Plains Indians, they had no system of military honors; when attacked, they often simply ran away.

THE BLACKFOOT and Crow tribal groups inhabited the high plains of Montana; to the south of them, in present-day Wyoming and Colorado, lived the Cheyenne and Arapaho. During historic times, Apaches migrated south from the Northwest through the plains, adopting many traits of the tribes they met there.

Until they acquired the horse and gun, these Plains Indians were little like the dashing equestrians of the movies. Nor were they, as the Spanish explorers imagined, a wealthy, indolent people who drank from golden goblets. They had, however, learned to live comfortably on their land. Most were farmers, gath-

Because Indians depended so heavily on the buffalo for food, shelter, and clothing, the shaggy beasts often assumed ceremonial importance. Here George Catlin depicts a buffalo dance.

erers, and small-game hunters first, and big-game hunters only secondarily, since hunting bison on foot was more difficult and uncertain than growing corn, gathering seeds, or hunting smaller animals.

Like other Plains Indians, those on the edges of the Rockies formed tribes, groups similar to the bands in which the Shoshoneans sometimes lived. Both tribes and bands were based on the extended family, both egalitarian, and neither supported full-time specialists like soldiers or priests. The tribe, however, was much larger than the band and controlled marriage between families more rigidly. A Shoshonean could marry anyone outside of his own family, but a Crow had to follow certain additional rules.

The tribes had little formal government. Different bands, or groups of families, moved as they pleased on the advice of chiefs who had proven their courage, skill, or wisdom. Spring and summer were the seasons for tribal congregation, but when winter approached, the bands packed their tipis on dog-drawn travois and scattered over the plains to hunt.

Nevertheless, only the foolhardy continually flouted tribal mores. To the intensely communal Plains Indian, the typical punishments for crime—public shaming or banishment—were extremely serious. The Cheyenne supplemented informal group pressure with a complicated system of tribal laws.

Most tribes, too, had warrior societies, which acted as police during the summer gatherings. Only men joined these societies, but women had their own craft guilds. Among the Crow, both men and women joined the tobacco society to raise and smoke the ceremonial

Another Catlin painting limns a war dance. In many tribal cultures combat was an essential element, with ceremony, ritual, and preparation as important as the actual battle.

crop. Since they were based on activities, not kinship, the societies were something like modern American fraternities, political parties, or religious organizations. Much of the Plains Indian's daily life was societal; members danced and feasted together, and sometimes shared common myths.

Though tribal rule and custom were exacting, and the penalty for a mistake was public condemnation, there were some escape valves. Among the Cheyenne, for instance, the bravest warriors were also privileged clowns who did everything by opposites. These "contraries" said "no" when they meant "yes," went away when called, and splashed each other with boiling water, complaining of the cold.

Among the Blackfoot Indians, there was still a place for youths who preferred a sedentary, protected life.

Unlike the other men, who counted coups and boasted of dangerous horse-stealing exploits, the *berdache* wore women's clothing, did women's work, and sometimes joined women's societies. He was not an outcast; people treated him with some pity and religious awe, for he was *wakan,* or sacred and unexplainable.

Plains Indians loved ceremony, and as the different peoples of the plains mingled and traded, they came to share one important ritual—the Sun Dance. Usually a person joined the Sun Dance to gain good luck in a dangerous enterprise such as the Plains Indians were fond of undertaking to win wealth and prestige. Before the dance, the participant sweated out his impurities in a sweathouse much like a Finnish sauna, and went without food and water. Then he danced around a sacred pole for days, sometimes torturing himself by

In this view of Fort Union, artist Charles Bodmer shows Indians breaking camp. Gathering to barter at military and fur trade outposts, the Indians acquired tools, firearms, alcohol, and disease.

staring at the sun or suspending himself from the pole by skewers thrust through his flesh. With luck, this self-mortification gave the dancer a vision that guided him in hunting or raiding.

Religion bolstered the Plains Indian's courage and stamina so that he could perform the daring exploits that kept him alive. Some magic was also intended to befriend the natural forces that gave him crops. Like the Shoshonean, he searched for his spiritual protector alone. But because his life depended on dangerous feats more than the Shoshonean's did, he prized visions more highly, eagerly seeking them out. Like Hindu yogis or medieval ascetics, Plains Indians had found that isolation, fasting, and self-mutilation made them more susceptible to hallucinations. Most members of the tribes—not just those who were called to be shamans—went on quests for visions during their lives. At

puberty, the Indian boy wandered into the wilderness without food or water, seeking a vision that would help him direct his adult life. With luck, a giant eagle with wings of thunder might swoop down, or a rabbit pursued by a hawk might call to the boy, promising him supernatural powers in exchange for help. This magic animal, which became his guardian, taught him magic songs and prayers, a personal ritual, and what materials to assemble for his private "medicine bundle," or protective charm.

Even before the horse, the gun, and the white man's incursions, the Plains Indians were warlike. Typically, though, they launched only swift raids with few, if any, casualties. Some tribes felt it dishonorable to lose a single man on these ventures; often the warrior who killed an enemy got less glory than the one who counted coups. Other tribes did take scalps, and some raided to

The apartmentlike ruins of Mesa Verde are all that remain of a highly organized tribe that practiced agriculture and irrigation here in the thirteenth century—then disappeared.

123

In a re-enactment of a centuries-old tradition, a modern Indian of the Taos Pueblo bakes her bread in an earthen oven.

steal goods from their neighbors. Anthropologists speculate that these small wars were essential to integrating Plains Indian society. They argue that since the Plains Indian founded his identity on individual daring, aggressiveness, and competition for status, rivalry and feuding often set band against band, family against family. Uniting against a common enemy was a sure way of overcoming these divisions and affirming tribal solidarity.

OF ALL THE ROCKY MOUNTAIN CULTURES, the Pueblo's was the most complex. Tribes on the mesas were much more cohesive than those on the plains; through many mutually reinforcing institutions, Pueblo society governed almost every moment of the individual's daily life. First of all, every Pueblo belonged to a clan—a group something like an extended family that showed its common relatedness by identifying itself with certain animals or natural forces, performing certain ceremonies, using the same name, and sharing a mythology. Although members might not know specifically how they were related, they were required to marry outside the clan, and they were expected to help each other in building houses and harvesting.

Everyone belonged to several other tribal institutions as well. Typically, the Pueblo man lived with his wife in her mother's household, belonged to his own clan, took part in a different religious society, frequented a kiva of that society, and perhaps belonged to the priesthood of that kiva. From that priesthood, he might be chosen to serve on the town's ruling council, which decided town policy, initiated ceremonies, and judged those accused of witchcraft and other crimes. Some men also belonged to a warrior society, which policed and defended their town.

Though members of the council decided Pueblo affairs, all the townspeople were their equals, since priesthood and council membership were temporary and part-time. Pueblo Indians made few distinctions in social status; wealth was distributed fairly evenly.

The Pueblo did not seek visions in the wilderness, fasting and torturing himself; his religion was an orderly and well-planned series of activities performed by priests for the whole town's benefit. While Plains shamans had to communicate personally with the supernatural, Pueblo priests needed only to be trained in conducting ritual. Each clan, priesthood, and society had its own dances and ceremonies, so that hardly a week passed without some religious or ceremonial activity that involved everyone.

Ceremonies began in the kivas, where cult leaders kept their painted *kachina* masks, symbolizing different deities and ancestral spirits. During designated seasons, priests put on the masks and roamed through the town, impersonating different spirits.

Too much solemnity can be oppressive, though, and Pueblo ritual had a place for clowning. While the kachinas paraded through town, clowns followed, cavorting and satirizing them. Clown societies gave much-needed relief to a repressed, religious people whose tensions often exploded otherwise in bickering, feuding, and accusations of witchcraft.

A LTHOUGH PREHISTORIC INDIAN LIFE included plenty of warfare, the white man's coming greatly increased rivalry for land and goods. Armed, mounted, and pushed off their original territories by whites, many Indians migrated westward in the eighteenth and nineteenth centuries, struggling in earnest for possession of the land. Today's picture of typical Indian culture—hard-riding, fast-shooting, and buffalo-hunting—was actually the product of white intrusion. The French, for instance, gave guns to the Ojibway of Minnesota, encouraging them to war with their neighbors the Sioux. The Ojibway displaced the Sioux, who wandered out onto the plains, pushing out tribes who in turn warred on the Cheyenne and other tribes of the Rockies region.

Forced to mingle and barter for white goods, Plains Indians at first made many positive cultural exchanges and rapidly grew rich. The wealth and flamboyance of the new life, however, had been created by whites and depended on whites for its continued existence. Plains Indians had come to live almost exclusively off the dwindling herds of buffalo and white trade. For tribes on the edges of the plains—the Apaches and some Shoshoneans, for instance—life changed similarly.

Even when white men lived or traveled in peace among the Indians, their presence could be deadly to the red man. Since traders found liquor a cheap exchange for furs, they encouraged the susceptible Indians to use it, and many became hopeless alcoholics. Diseases carried by whites, such as smallpox and measles, took a tremendous toll among the previously unexposed native populations.

Once whites began to expand westward in large numbers, Indian cultures of the Rockies—already profoundly altered by the white presence—were truly doomed. Frontier people had no notion of coexisting peacefully with the Indians, partly because they did not consider them people like themselves. To them, the Indians were just another natural obstacle, like rugged mountains, harsh weather, and lack of water. Just as he busily set about digging wells and clearing land, the frontiersman did his best to exterminate the Indian wherever he settled.

CHAPTER 10

PROBING THE BARRIER

*Official expeditions of the Spanish and American governments—
sorties into a mountain chain they always found inhospitable*

THE EARLY EXPLORATION of the Rockies is largely the story of other places and other events. For both the Spanish and the Americans, the mountains were a formidable obstacle, offering little of value, to be avoided if possible. Until the latter half of the nineteenth century, explorations sponsored by either government tended to penetrate the mountains only when they passed through in transit. Always there was another goal in mind—scouting an enemy, determining a boundary, or finding a pass to a greater Eden beyond the mountains—and therefore any information gathered about the mountains was essentially incidental to another objective.

The Spaniards who first moved north out of Mexico were motivated by their own fantasies and drawn by tales of wealth beyond measure—wealth that would bring the power and prestige that meant success in empire-building Spain. They followed rumor onto the arid plains, often further tempted rather than dismayed when their dreams dissolved before them like evaporating mirages on the horizon. Strangely, the retreating phantoms of their hopes never seemed to lead Spanish adventurers into the mountains. Coronado, striking north out of Mexico in search of the Seven Cities of Cíbola, extended his search across north central New Mexico and onto the plains of Texas and Kansas, tantalized by assurances from Indians eager to please (and be rid of him) that his goal lay only a short distance beyond the horizon. Unfortunately for Coronado, the land had more horizons than he had energy, time, and dreams. *Norteamerica* refused to mirror

Spanish dreams, and the prospect of another Mexico or Peru eluded the conquerors. But the route of Coronado, together with the routes of other wandering dreamers, leaves the impression that cities of gold and empires of dreams rose mainly where the walking was easy, for the early Spaniards made no serious attempts to breach the sanctity of the mountains.

For much of the eighteenth century, the Spanish avoided the rugged heart of the Rockies. From the northern outpost at Santa Fe, expeditions and adventurers went east and west, but no government parties ventured north. Juan de Ulíbarri, on a punitive expedition to catch runaway Pueblo Indians in 1706, skirted the mountains to the southeast and continued his pursuit on the plains; Governor Valverde of New Mexico, out to reconnoiter French advances toward his province in 1719, similarly shunned the mountains and stayed to the east of the Front Range foothills; Pedro de Villasur, on a similar expedition in 1720, stayed clear of the heart of the mountains and enjoyed comfortable progress on the plains—until some Pawnee caught him on the South Platte and made him eternally comfortable. These forays, and others like them, acquainted the Spanish with the southern and eastern rim of the cordillera, but the interior of the mountains remained a forbidding mystery to Spaniards who sought for over two centuries to hold and expand an empire in the southern shadow of the mountain chain.

But near the end of Spain's suzerainty in North America, the pattern of avoiding the mountains was broken. Between 1761 and 1765, Juan de Rivera, a

The earliest Spaniards, assured by Indians that the fabled riches of Cíbola or Quivira lay "just beyond," skirted the Rockies in favor of the plains. (Drawing by Maynard Dixon.)

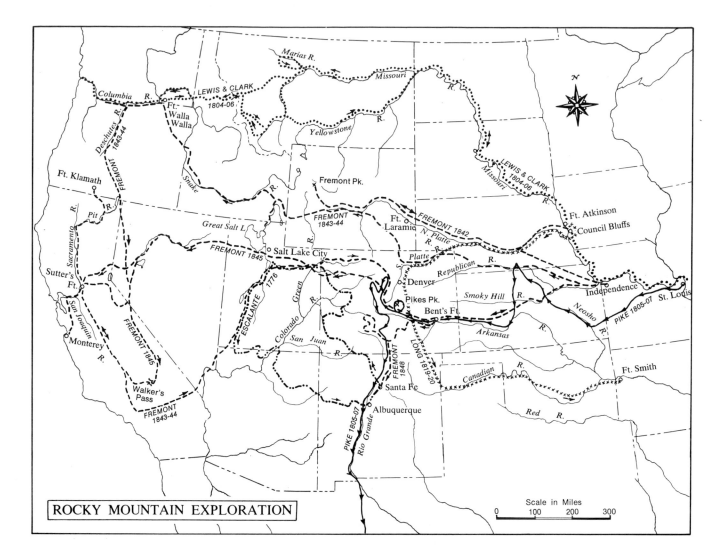

ROCKY MOUNTAIN EXPLORATION

tough Indian fighter of many years experience on the Spanish frontier, led three separate expeditions, into the San Juan Mountains, the Green River country of Utah, and the Wasatch Mountains. He ranged what is now central Colorado from the San Juan River, past the Uncompahgre, to the Gunnison. Rivera apparently did a lot of riding and looking, conducted a little trading with the natives, and supervised some proselytizing, but his exact purpose has been obscured by a dearth of surviving records. Like most Spanish expeditions, his party included traders, priests, and soldiers, and was therefore capable of commerce, conversion, settlement, or war (the Spanish usually traveled prepared for any eventuality), but Rivera apparently accomplished noth-

ing of permanent effect. No maps were made, no high-level interest in his discoveries developed, and officially Spain continued to content herself with the fringe of the mountains.

Over a decade after Rivera's final expedition, the last major Spanish *entrada* into the mountains was mounted—in an effort to find a quick and easy route through the barrier. When the soldier-adventurer Anza established colonists in California at Monterey and San Francisco, Fray Silvestre Vélez de Escalante was assigned the task of finding a supply route from Santa Fe to the new outposts. Hoping to avoid Hopi Indians, still hostile from Spanish attempts to save their souls, and further discouraged by the harsh desert expanses

Coronado's expedition never made a significant penetration of the mountains.

of the far Southwest, Escalante took his company north and west through the mountains. The course was slow and winding, bent and redirected more by the dictates of terrain than the goals of Escalante.

Despite the tediously convoluted course, the mounted party of ten moved through southwest Colorado, heading north until it crossed the Colorado River into wild and completely unfamiliar land. Turning west, the horsemen followed a valley of the Uinta Mountains to the Green River. Although by now Escalante probably realized that the route was not feasible for supply of the California outposts, he nevertheless continued to struggle westward, breaking through a pass in the Wasatch to Utah Lake. By then

it was December, supplies were very low, the animals were worn and broken down, and Escalante knew, if they were to survive, they had to start back for Santa Fe immediately.

The return through the stark and broken land of southern Utah and across the Colorado River was harrowing, but the party finally made its way back to Santa Fe. Although the expedition was technically a failure, Escalante had returned with a map and at least marginal impressions of the interior of the mountain region. Except for a few hardy Taos trappers, the Spanish never returned to the land Escalante had found so uncompromising.

The pageant of American conquest and occupation

Zebulon Pike, "The Lost Pathfinder," raised as many questions as he answered about the mountains.

in the Rockies and the Far West opened with the expedition of Lewis and Clark. An exciting adventure, laced with honorable men of courageous deeds, the journey was transcontinental in scope, leaving the impression of complete thoroughness (detailed journals survive, documenting every discovery and observation). Its enormous success opened the door to a century of expansion and acquisition.

Before Lewis and Clark, contact with the cordillera by men who kept records or reported what they saw was limited. The Rockies had been crossed once, by Alexander Mackenzie in 1793, but that had been far to the north. The Spanish had butted against the mountain chain often from the south, making little headway beyond the fringe, and consequently could shed only scant light on the scope and shape of the interior. The result was a vague notion of a mountain belt lying north and south along the continent. Where it ended, how wide it might be, and what it was like were unknown. Imaginary geography of French, Spanish, British, and American origins had accumulated over the years to suggest a low, narrow range lying

close to the Pacific shore. Popular notion, created more by desire than concrete information, allowed that the Missouri was navigable to within one hundred miles of the Pacific, and that a short portage to the headwaters of the Columbia River was the only obstacle the mountains presented.

Lewis and Clark corrected the illusion and in the process hinted at the enormous scale and potential of the new domain. Because their path was narrow, their reports on geography and mountain life-forms were limited, but to a nation that knew nothing of the interior of the continent, the information Lewis and Clark gathered seemed a treasure trove of detail.

But probably the greatest value of the exploration was the excitement it stirred in, and the land it promised to, a country hitherto preoccupied with securing the future and consolidating its gains as a new and weak member of the Atlantic community. The journey, which would provide the basis for a tenuous claim to the Oregon country, planted small suspicions in the American mind that the continent belonged to those strong enough to take it—suspicions that would germinate for thirty years, almost unnoticed, before flowering into the seemingly spontaneous demand for continental solidarity known as Manifest Destiny. But in the interim, the report of the expedition encouraged trappers, traders, hunters, and homeseekers to try their hand in uncharted but hinted-at utopias in the West.

In retrospect the expedition seems to have been inexorably tied to the Louisiana Purchase, but plans were under way and money appropriated before the purchase ever emerged as a rationalization. The purchase, Jefferson's motives for commissioning the exploration, and the objectives and results of the trek itself have become tangled in a complex web of international relations, eighteenth-century rationalism, and the Orient trade sweepstakes. Jefferson's original intent was a combined scientific expedition (to satisfy his own Enlightenment curiosity) and inland probe for a convenient Northwest Passage to the Orient. When Napoleon surprised Robert Livingston and James Monroe, the American envoys to France who were seeking a right of deposit at New Orleans, by offering to sell the whole of Louisiana to the United States, the scope of the expedition changed. Interest in finding a Northwest Passage began to diminish beside a developing passion to explore a new national domain; not incidentally, the extension of the trek to the mouth of the Columbia River offered support to the fragile American claim on Oregon made by Robert Gray in 1792 aboard the ship *Columbia*.

The expedition, commanded by the moody, cerebral Meriwether Lewis and the practical extrovert William Clark, was remarkable for its smooth and efficient progress. Although there were lean times and an abundance of hard drudging work, there were no disastrous Indian raids, no discouraging and aimless wandering, nor any starved and frozen bodies left behind to mark their route; the only death was the result of a ruptured appendix. The outbound journey was regular and free from an all-consuming struggle for survival; the number of observations made and specimens collected are adequate testament to a smooth operation that would permit such academic pursuits. The return, after wintering near the mouth of the Columbia, was more arduous, but nonetheless marked by scrupulous observation and annotation.

The seeming ease with which the two years of wilderness living and travel were accomplished was due not to incredible luck but rather to thoughtful preparation, careful management, and expert execution. A strong and experienced crew was selected—malingerers, weaklings and disciplinary problems were weeded out and sent downriver before the Mandan villages were reached—but the real strength of the expedition lay in its leadership.

Between them, Lewis and Clark shared a remarkable collection of talents and skills: Lewis was a consummate scientist and natural historian with a phenomenal ability for attending to and recording detail; Clark was a frontiersman, field engineer, and accomplished boatman—possessed with an intuitive sense of geography that was awesome in its accuracy. Because they excelled in different fields, leadership of the expedition was shared, each assuming responsibility for those tasks he knew best—without any of the rancor or jealousy that usually typifies a divided command. Their ability and willingness to share leadership probably contributed more to the success of the exploration than any other single factor.

The party of two officers, fourteen soldiers, seven Kentucky hunters, and Clark's black slave, York, was

This replica of Pike's winter stockade in the San Luis Valley stands on the original site.

gone three years on what was primarily a waterborne expedition. The first year was spent laboring up the Missouri, making notes and observations, hunting, and encountering Indians of varying degrees of hostility. Clark's great skill at negotiation with the Indians—knowing when to show force and when to conciliate—was largely responsible for keeping them out of serious trouble the first year. They wintered with the Mandans in North Dakota, where they were joined by a French trader, Charbonneau, and his Shoshoni wife, Sacajawea, who, while helpful, was not the dauntless guide and savior of the expedition that popular legend would have her be. She was most helpful in the Rockies, where she made friendly Indians even more cooperative.

The expedition reached the Rockies in the second traveling season, and the encounter marked an abrupt change in the pattern of exploration. The Great Falls of the Missouri forced a portage, and shortly thereafter the party found the Jefferson Fork to shallow for the boats. What had been a boating trip, with notes and observations on the immediate drainage basin, became an overland trek in search of a pass through an incon-

Stephen Long treats with the Indians—though Long, Indians, and landscape never looked so noble.

venient obstacle. Lewis moved ahead, crossing the Continental Divide at Lemhi Pass, and brought back horses from the Shoshoni. It was here that Sacajawea, reunited with her brother and her people, made her most valuable contributions as interpreter and agent of goodwill for the expedition. With a Shoshoni guide and Shoshoni mounts, the party traveled three hundred miles on horseback through the Rockies, seeking a suitable place to return to the more convenient and familiar mode of river travel.

The mountain hiatus was generally regarded as a distasteful, dangerous, and hungry interlude—to be endured but terminated as soon as possible. Interestingly enough, the only time the party divided was on the return trip when they reached the mountain barrier. In search of a better pass through the mountains, or a navigable river that penetrated deeper into the cordillera, Lewis went due east from the Bitter Root River while Clark started south along the original route and then turned east. Despite bouts with grizzlies, some heavy snows and dense forests, and a one-eyed French hunter who mistook Lewis for a bear and shot him in the leg, the party was reunited on the Missouri—neither group having found what it sought.

The captains had encountered the Rockies and

journeyed through them, interested not so much in what the mountains held as in how best to get through them to the other side. They didn't see all, or even very much, of the mountain chain—there was neither time nor energy for side trips. The expedition was preoccupied with river travel and finding a passage to the sea, and the mountains loomed most importantly as a barrier. But even though exposure to the Rockies was minimal, the journals bulged with information that would provide the beginnings of a library in Rocky Mountain natural history and ethnology.

As LEWIS AND CLARK were returning to the relative civilization of St. Louis, another government expedition was being launched across the plains to the southern Rockies, under the command of Zebulon M. Pike. Pike was assigned to the expedition by his friend and mentor, Gen. James Wilkinson, that enigmatic and treason-tainted warrior of the southern borderlands. It is fairly certain that Wilkinson was involved at the time with Aaron Burr in some jingoistic venture, but precisely what they were about may never be known; their affairs provide, at best, a speculative paragraph in the history of unsuccessful treason. Fur-

An illustration of the day commemorates Frémont's conquest of the "Highest Peak." (It wasn't.)

thermore, Wilkinson was known to have connived with the Spanish, although the extent of his services to them is also unknown. Because of Pike's long association with the general, and what seemed to be a persistent effort to be captured by the Spanish once he reached the mountains, Pike has been scrutinized for possible condemnation as an agent and advance scout for Wilkinson and Burr.

On the surface, Pike's exploration was important to the United States. The southwest boundary of the Louisiana Purchase was being contested by Spain. Although many Americans contended that the Red River formed the boundary, the government had no specifics, and they needed to have someone find out. Pike's official instructions warned him to be scrupulous in respecting boundaries, and although he might have received oral instructions to the contrary from Wilkinson, his sojourn into Spanish territory is understandable in light of faulty geography. His map, based on Alexander von Humboldt's, showed the Red River rising east of Taos, but this river was in fact the Canadian. Proceeding on this mistaken assumption, Pike traveled far west of the boundary, even as the United States regarded it.

In 1806, Pike began his journey up the Arkansas, continuing along the river until he arrived at the present site of Pueblo, Colorado. From a camp there, he set out to climb the peak that would later bear his name. The mountain, however, proved to be much farther away than the explorer, deceived by the rarefied air, had estimated. On November 27, 1806, Pike, the expedition's physician Dr. Robinson, and two privates stood on Cheyenne Peak and looked at their goal twelve miles away. Defeated by frigid weather, deep snows, depleted supplies, and exhaustion, Pike made his estimate of the mountain, which ultimately proved to be as inaccurate as his geography: "No human being could have ascended to its pinical [*sic*]."

Pike moved to the mouth of Royal Gorge (Grand Canyon of the Arkansas), detoured north, exploring the South Park region and the upper Arkansas, and then traveled south, in search of the source of the Red River, crossing the Sangre de Cristo Mountains. He erected a small fort on the present southern boundary of Colorado, and it was there that he was captured by the Spanish. He was taken to Santa Fe and finally to Chihuahua where, though honoring the diplomatic conventions of hospitality, restraint, and tact, the Spaniards regarded him as a spy. He was finally deported through Texas in July 1807.

John C. Frémont: "The Great Pathfinder."

His report, issued in 1810, left many questions unanswered. Due to inaccurate mapping, the extreme boundary of the Louisiana Purchase was still in doubt. Pike created the stuff of which myths are made when he noted that the "vast plains of the Western Hemisphere may become in time celebrated as the sandy deserts of Africa. . . ." This statement, partly the product of Pike's belief that it would be advantageous to limit the spread of the nation to manageable size, was repeated by Maj. Stephen Long in 1820, providing the "factual basis" for the myth of the "Great American Desert."

In terms of information and understanding gained, Pike's explorations in the Rockies were of questionable value. His actions indicate that he was lost, and if he did know where he was he concealed the fact well enough to encourage historical debate regarding his mission to this day. His cartographic contributions are suspect, inasmuch as Humboldt later complained that the map Pike published after the expedition was only a copy of his own. In the end, Pike's report did little to encourage or enlighten the American public about the mountain West.

FOR TWELVE YEARS after Pike's inconclusive explorations, the government refrained from official activity in the Far West. This hiatus was broken with the organization of the Yellowstone Expedition of 1819, an undertaking distinguished by its lack of success. River steamers built by private contractors to carry the combined scientific and military party into the Yellowstone country—to overawe the Indians, to explore and record scientific data, and possibly to frighten British traders back to their traditional trapping grounds on the Pacific side of the divide—proved unequal to the task of negotiating the currents of the Missouri. The venture finally died before it ever began, largely a victim of incompetence and indifference—but not without a wake on the floor of the Senate and a dirge sounded by an irate public. Interest in the neglected domain was rising, at least temporarily.

Out of the rubble of the Yellowstone undertaking, as a sop to a nation angry and disgusted with the failure, rose an expedition to the southern Rockies under the command of Maj. Stephen H. Long. Long's company was ably equipped with personnel to make scientific observations, classify flora and fauna, and record topographic information. Additionally, there remained the task of finding the headwaters of the Red and thereby completing the job Pike had begun in 1806.

In June of 1820, the party ascended the Missouri to the Platte, striking west from there for the mountains. They followed the great river of the plains, taking its south fork to the present site of Denver. From there they wended their way south, through small canyons and over minor divides with little difficulty, to Manitou Springs (Colorado Springs)—the settlement from which the expedition's physician, Dr. James, and a small party ascended the mountain that would become known as Pikes Peak. The expedition continued southward, collecting specimens, recording data, and plotting landforms and position, until they reached the Arkansas. There Long divided the company, sending Captain Bell with eleven men down the Arkansas to-

Confused from the beginning, Frémont's fourth expedition to the Rockies ended in disaster.

ward civilization and leading his own party south in search of the Red. Long repeated Pike's error, mistaking the Canadian for the Red, and exposed himself and his nine men to a purgatory of desert heat, violent storms, and encounters with Comanches, only to find the entire effort futile. The elusive head of the Red River was still unexplored.

Long's report indicated that the "country between the Missouri River and the Rocky Mountains . . . is wholly unfit for cultivation," reinforcing Pike's estimate of a Great American Desert. Even more important, he regarded this barrier-land as a boon—a protection against invaders and a natural limit for the expansion of the republic. Apparently, he found little in the high country to recommend it to a nation feeling the first stirrings of adolescent strength; he saw no empire in the mountains worth braving the plains.

The final great government expeditions came in the early 1840s, after most of the geography of the southern Rockies was well known to the fur trappers who called

the region home. The man in charge of these explorations, Capt. John Charles Frémont, was intent upon promoting himself and convincing the nation that it should disregard the nay-sayers, like Pike and Long, and take the continent for its own. The evidence is strong that he promoted Manifest Destiny because in conquest lay his own fame, but while promoting his plan and himself with elaborate published accounts of his travels in the Far West, he made that land *known* to a nation heretofore largely ignorant of what it held.

Frémont fancied the accolade "The Great Pathfinder," but he was guided by mountain men (including Kit Carson, "Old Bill" Williams, and Thomas Fitzpatrick); his real contribution was in publicizing the routes. In regard to the mountains, he was neither pathfinder nor explorer, but rather a pass-marker, seeking overland routes through the Rockies. He was an active agent of American continental design. After his second expedition had instilled faith in the importance of California to the Union, he regarded the Rockies as a barrier to be quickly hurdled. He made four expeditions to and through the mountains, publishing lavish reports on his explorations of existing and potential emigrant trails—and by implication, representing himself as a leading contributor to a continental empire.

His first expedition, undertaken in 1842, proposed to learn the nature of the "rivers and country between the frontier of Missouri and the base of the Rocky Mountains, and especially to examine the character, and ascertain the latitude and longitude of the South Pass, the great crossing-place of the mountains on the way to Oregon." This information, he hoped, would aid immigration to "the lower Columbia" and thereby secure Oregon against the British. He accomplished his purpose neatly, but the first intimations of the self-serving character, the judgments determined by pride, and the comedy of vanity that would mark his life emerged during this excursion. He appears as the hero and principal subject of his journals, and yet in a fool-hardy and unnecessary attempt to shoot the rapids of the upper Platte, he very nearly lost all of his men and equipment. In an effort to achieve distinction by climbing the loftiest peak in North America, he selected a mountain in the Wind River Range, named it for himself, and left an epic record of a rather ordinary climb—while five miles to the north stood the higher Gannett Peak, not to mention the thirty peaks in Colorado of even greater height.

His second expedition, in 1843, was a promotional tour to encourage migration, dispel any fear of the overland crossing, and show the wealth of the West, by mapping the entire Oregon Trail. While on the surface the purpose sounds commendable and Frémont appears as the architect of a grand design for empire, his own journal entries would seem to discredit these notions. He noted while resting one day that emigrant trains were already headed west, the plain before and behind dotted with white covers, and the number of emigrants in evidence large. Frémont had leapt on an already stable, rapid, and well-directed bandwagon. But he provided a most effective advertisement for Manifest Destiny, and perhaps therein lies his worth. Also, his observations on the Great Basin, made during the expedition, first piqued Brigham Young's interest and laid the groundwork for the empire in Zion.

By the time of his third expedition, Frémont had begun to heed his own words. He passed quickly up the Arkansas and through the heart of the Colorado Rockies, his only concern to find swift passage en route to the greater glory of conquest in California. Again in 1848—seeking to recoup his reputation and his fortune following a court-martial that grew out of bitterness and hostility with Kearny engendered during the California foray—Frémont sought another pass through the mountains. Hoping to establish a winter route to the Pacific, he took men and mules, despite warnings, into a disastrous debacle in the snow-choked San Juan Mountains. The pride and arrogance of a waning political luminary and tarnished tin soldier killed over half the men of the party and marked the end of Frémont's excursions.

Frémont's exploration of the Rockies, like those of most of the Spanish and earlier Americans, consisted primarily of finding a way to avoid exploring the mountains—either by skirting them entirely, or by finding quick passage through. Until after the fourth decade of the nineteenth century, private citizens generally tended to follow the example of their governments. They approached, they encountered, they retreated, they skirted, and even passed through, but with the notable exception of the fur trappers, efforts to live with—and profit from—the mountains were notable by their absence. For men with other options, the Rockies were a formidable bastion.

The Square Tower group at Hovenweep National Monument stands as a mute memorial to an Indian civilization that tried and failed in the arid lands.

A Sioux encampment, with a chief's elevated funeral scaffold to the right.

A mounted Blackfoot Indian, the nemesis of the mountain man.

Overleaf: "Coronado Before Hawikuh": Wolfinbarger's painting is accurate in costume and armament.

Crow Indians, who ultimately became staunch allies of the whites.

Albert Bierstadt's "The Oregon Trail" (1865) rendered the overland trek in glowing proportions.

A rare lithograph of John Charles Frémont, who took four expeditions through the Rockies and published lavish reports of his explorations.

Remington's painting of Captains Lewis and Clark. Charbonneau and Sacajawea stand behind.

Lt. Zebulon Pike and his party being escorted to Santa Fe as suspicious characters. Since they were not yet captives, artist Remington correctly shows them still in possession of their weapons.

CHAPTER 11

FUR TRADE ON THE FRONTIER

The brawling pageant that bred a new kind of folk hero and fostered
the first intimacy between the white man and the mountains

HEIR TIME WAS BRIEF, but their passage was marked by the violence and daring of which myths are made. They worked at a lonely trade far out on the cutting edge of the frontier, skimming off only the most accessible wealth. They mapped a wild and unknown land in their minds, and by their presence staked a tenuous claim to a land that would yield an enormous return. They are variously remembered as romantic Rousseauean men-in-nature, hardboiled Jacksonian entrepreneurs, rough-hewn agents of American imperialism, or boorish savages whose mindless rape of the land can never be undone. They were hard, cunning, profane men living in a land where the first order of business was survival. They were called mountain men; they were the men who trailed the beaver.

The business of gathering furs in the wilderness was not a new one. For hundreds of years the Russians and western Europeans had been invading virgin frontiers in search of furry wealth; indeed, this search had been one of the original motives behind the earliest English, French, and Russian explorations of the North American continent. The *terra incognita* of America's eastern woodlands frontier was explored and explained by men whose knowledge of the land was a by-product of their search for furs and skins.

That fur hunters would be the first to explore a region is logical and even necessary. They came to a region, like everyone after them, to extract the natural wealth; but, unlike the subsequent industries to which any region is susceptible, the fur trade cannot co-exist with settlement. Since the animals that constitute the wealth of the fur trade would flee the approaching annoyances of civilization, the trapper had by necessity to precede any settlement.

Although the fur trade was not a new one, the American experience in the Rockies wrought changes in the methods of fur-gathering that transformed the region into a stage for giant men of epic deeds. The fur trader would become a fur trapper, and within this subtle shift lay the seeds of drama and legend. The two hundred years of fur-gathering in North America previous to the empire in the Rockies was dominated by a system of barter between Indian and white: the Indian trapped and skinned the beaver, and then exchanged the pelts for the hardware and trinkets of an industrial society. This system normally bound the fur trader to a post or fort where his relatively civilized existence left little opportunity for danger or adventure. The American experience in the Rockies during the first half of the nineteenth century would change this by moving the white man into the wilderness to do the actual trapping, as well as trading. It was this changed role, bringing white men into intimate contact with nature—even to becoming a part of it—that distinguished the American fur trade in the Rockies.

AS THEY DESCENDED THE MISSOURI in 1806 following their transcontinental explorations, Lewis and Clark met no less than eleven separate parties of men bound upstream intent on exploiting a heretofore only

The mountain man (rendered here by Frederic Remington), was the picket-rider of
American civilization in the mountain West—an imperialist with the hair on.

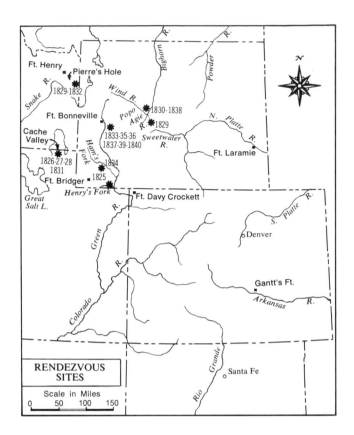

RENDEZVOUS SITES

Scale in Miles
0 50 100 150

his company to trap on their own. The Hudson's Bay Company had used trappers in a brigade, but they were virtually slaves, unlike Lisa's men who worked for high wages or on shares. Lisa's success in the fur trade was moderate, however, marred by skirmishes with Indians and a number of false starts and errors as he felt his way through a strange business in an even stranger country.

Lisa's endeavor, along with the entire Rocky Mountain fur business, was interrupted by the War of 1812, as Indians supplied and encouraged by the British began to exact a terrible toll in lives and goods. Their depredations forced a cessation of activity and a withdrawal to the protection of St. Louis.

Although Lisa's brief venture in the mountains never quite recovered from the depredations of war, and business reverses during the ensuing years left his dream unfulfilled and his empire incomplete, his contributions to the fur trade were important. He introduced white men into the mountains as highly mobile trappers who remained in the mountains year round. Also during his tenure a pattern of Indian hostility developed that colored and shaped events until the end of the era. Lisa had begun his trade on the Yellowstone with the Crows, hereditary enemies of the Blackfoot, supplying them with sophisticated weaponry that left many a Blackfoot squaw mourning.

Taking advantage of this natural hostility, the British (in the form of the Hudson's Bay Company)—for nationalistic or possibly just pecuniary reasons—encouraged and supplied the Blackfoot against the Americans. Such fighting created a traditional animosity, replete with acts of plundering to be returned in kind and old scalps to be avenged. Add to this John Colter's siding with the Crow while scouting for Lisa in 1807 in a battle that littered the Three Forks country with Blackfoot bodies, and it is small wonder that the Blackfoot would remain the nemesis of the American mountain man until the industry declined. Many an incipient entrepreneur, entering the mountains with high hopes and all of his capital invested in a single venture, would drag himself back to St. Louis while his goods adorned some Blackfoot tipi and the bodies of his operatives lay rotting and naked in the wilderness.

Lisa had laid the groundwork for a significant change in the approach to the fur trade in the Rockies,

hinted-at wealth in furs. Most of these men carried trade goods for commerce with the Indians, which was the traditional means for acquiring furs. One of the members of the homeward-bound expedition, John Colter, left his captains at the Mandan Indian villages (near present-day Bismarck), and turned back upstream with one of the trading parties to winter in the beaver country. The knowledge he gained there formed the foundation of his education in the Rocky Mountain fur trade and was put to good use one year later by Manuel Lisa.

In the spring of 1807, Colter was once again floating down the Missouri when he was intercepted by Lisa and persuaded to return to the Rockies and share his expertise and knowledge in another commercial venture. Establishing a fort and trading post on the Yellowstone River at the mouth of the Bighorn, Lisa began to pursue the business in traditional fashion. He sent emissaries to the Crow Indians nearby, persuading them to bring their furs to him, but added an innovative element when he dispatched other men of and by the time the overland Rocky Mountain trade revived after the war, another man would be ready to enter the mountains with a scheme for fur-gathering that would alter the trade still more.

TO ENTERPRISING YOUNG MEN. The subscriber wishes to engage one hundred young men to ascend the Missouri River to its source, there to be employed for one, two, or three years. For particulars inquire of Major Andrew Henry, near the lead mines in the county of Washington, who will ascend with, and command, the party; or of the subscriber near St. Louis.

/s/ William H. Ashley

The above announcement, appearing in the *Missouri Republican* (St. Louis) on March 20, 1822, heralded a new era in the Rocky Mountain fur trade. By the time Henry and Ashley retired to St. Louis as wealthy men only four short years later, they had developed and set in motion a system for fur-gathering that exhibited all of the salient features now associated with the drama of the fur trade: the brigade system, begun by Manuel Lisa, which under the hand of Ashley evolved into the systematic trapping (and consequent exploration) of most of the central Rockies; the rendezvous, which served as annual meeting ground and trade fair where bacchanalian diversions, brawling, and openhanded profligacy earned the mountain man the reputation as the most advanced and efficient degenerate of the western world; and the free trapper, the aristocrat of the mountains around whom the tales of the courageous man-in-nature grew and prospered.

Ashley's system introduced necessary innovations in the fur trade; necessary not because they were the only means for extracting the furs, but necessary because something different had to be tried to challenge the ascendency of the Hudson's Bay Company. The traditional methods of the Americans were modeled on those of the British company, with its permanent forts where Indians brought furs for barter. Unfortunately for the Americans, the Hudson's Bay Company was well established, possessed immense capital reserves, was supplied by sea via the Columbia River, thereby avoiding the expense of an arduous and dangerous overland trek to get their goods to the Indians, and

Each spring supply trains made their way across the plains to provision the annual summer rendezvous.

enjoyed the protection of a government monopoly. For the American neophytes to try to compete on the Hudson's Bay Company's own terms would have been economic suicide. Even the Montreal-based North West Company, possessed of thirty-four years of experience, money, and daring operatives skilled in the trade was beaten and absorbed by the Hudson's Bay juggernaut. Ashley's alternative method, though not triumphant, at least permitted the Americans to compete effectively for the mountain wealth.

Basic to Ashley's plan for fur-gathering was the elimination of the permanent fort. He intended to take his white trappers into the mountains in brigades, winter in the mountains, trapping in the fall and spring, and return to St. Louis with the catch during the summer; there to resupply and head back to the mountains before the fall hunt. Such a system cut expenses, increased mobility, and removed the dependence upon fickle Indians who might bankrupt him by

"The Trapper's Last Shot": Ultimately, a mountain man measured his success in survival, not furs.

taking all of their trade to the British. By 1825, Ashley found it even more economical to leave all of his trappers in the mountains. Taking a small group for protection, he undertook the trek to St. Louis, agreeing to meet the trappers after the spring hunt in 1826 on the Henry's Fork of the Green River. This prearranged meeting, subsequently reenacted at Cache Valley, Bear Lake, the Popo Agie, Pierre's Hole, Horse Creek, and Wind River, was the beginning of the rendezvous—a summer rite that reshaped an industry and provided the totem around which historians and old liars would gather to create a heroic American archetype.

The brigade freed the mountain man from the fort, and the rendezvous freed him from his employer. Anyone was free to attend these "Rocky Mountain Fairs" to trade his furs for goods and credit against the coin of the realm. Similarly, any trader was allowed the opportunity to bring his merchandise and bargain, with the elements and the aborigines the only real hindrance. From this situation evolved the "free trapper," a man not employed by a company, nor drawing wages, who bought all that he needed from the man who would pay the most for his furs, and who was totally dependent upon his own skills and strength for survival. The free trapper was the quintessence of the mountain man—a paragon of antisocial behavior whose wilderness skills and instinct for survival have remained a part of the Rockies' heritage in the stories about Jedediah Smith, Hugh Glass, William Sublette, Jim Bridger, Thomas Fitzpatrick, and "Black Jim" Beckwourth. These, and others like them, were the men who coursed the mountains and valleys, rivers and plains of the Rockies, learning the geography so important to subsequent settlement and challenging the British right of ownership to the Rockies and Northwest merely by their presence.

Smith, Glass, and Sublette were among the hundred-odd young men who responded to Ashley's *Missouri Republican* advertisement and journeyed upriver under Henry and Ashley in the spring of 1823. This was their introduction to the mountains, where they received their first instruction in survival, where they were blooded in combat, and where many did not survive the first lesson. They learned vigilance and preparedness the hard way when Ashley relaxed his guard and the Arikaras slaughtered fifteen of the company and stole all their horses; they learned when to fight and when to run, after Ashley left them stranded on a Missouri River sand spit surrounded by Indians and they had to do a little of each to survive; they learned contempt for the government when the army's punitive expedition, through sloth and timidity, allowed the Arikaras to escape; and they learned the value of appearances and a reputation when their Sioux allies saw the bungling of the army and assumed the Americans would be easy marks whenever they wanted equipment to steal or a scalp to lift.

But skill and courage came quickly, or they came not at all. The choices were few: either a man turned tail for civilization, or he stayed and learned quickly enough to survive. The third possibility was not really a choice, but enough neophytes died prematurely to make it a factor in the decision to run or to remain.

Those who remained and survived soon began to assume the characteristics of their surroundings. They dressed in animal skins, learned to trail and hunt like Indians, developed senses like the animals of their wilderness, and often began to smell like a buffalo carcass hung too long in the sun. The characteristic equipment and garb appear romantic today, but they were usually determined by the demands of survival and the availability of material, rather than vanity and fashion. The buckskin hunting shirt, leather breeches, and moccasins were durable and could be made by hand or purchased from a friendly squaw. Woolens were not unknown but available only at rendezvous, and they seldom lasted through a month of hard use; recourse to leather was mandatory, whether desirable or not. The pistol and tomahawk, skinning knife and whetstone, bullet pouch and powder horn, and stubby Hawken rifle were the instruments of survival and commerce in the mountains; a man's longevity was usually directly proportional to his skill with them. Around his neck dangled his "possibles sack," containing the comforts of pipe and tobacco and the

necessities of bullet mold and awl. When all this was combined with an incisive mind, it made a self-contained, self-supporting package fringed with long hair and whiskers, often sporting the scars and disfigurements of a hard life, that moved forward on legs arthritic or rheumatic from too many hours in cold streams.

The life of the free trapper in the mountains followed the cycle of the seasons. Early in the spring he emerged from winter's enforced hibernation to begin trapping for the beaver pelts still heavy with rich winter fur. He began low in the mountains where sun and chinook had very early thawed the ice and brought to life the streams around the beaver lodges. Working alone or in pairs, the beaver men followed the thaw upstream, seeking sign of beaver activity and trapping as they went.

The trapper moved in the shallow waters along the creek banks watching for sign, using the skills learned from hard experience to determine where to set his traps. He sacrificed the relative comfort of the dry banks for the painfully cold streams to insure that no "man scent" would frighten the beaver away from his trap. Finding a suitable site, he set the trap about four inches below the surface of the water, scraping away or building up the bottom to give the proper depth and free play to the jaws of the trap. Next, the trap chain was extended into deep water and secured by a stake driven into the streambed—a dead, dry stake that would prove unappetizing to beaver but would mark the trap's location, should trap, chain, and all be carried off by a persistent or unexpectedly powerful animal. Once set, the trap was baited with a succulent willow wand stabbed into the bank and arched out over the trap. Often the wand would be daubed with castoreum (the extract of beaver sexual glands that not only elicits the expected response in healthy male beaver but has also provided an ingredient in the perfumes of civilized humans). A beaver so enticed would lift his nose to test the wand, driving his foot onto the trip pan of the trap. The terrified animal, responding to instinct, would dive for the safety of deep water, dragging the trap along, where its weight would hold the struggling animal until it drowned.

When the trapper had retrieved the animal, he set about the task of preparing the skin, first removing it and then scraping the skin side of the pelt free of tissue and sinew. The skin was then stretched on a willow hoop and rough-cured in the sun for several days. When dry the pelt was folded, fur side in, and bundled into packs to await barter at the rendezvous. If he worked in a large company brigade, all of the preparation of the skins was done by camp tenders, and the trapper just drew his wages; if he was a free trapper, he did it himself, unless he was fortunate enough to have a squaw along. The work was hard and time-consuming, sufficient to keep the number of his traps down to about six.

Throughout the cautious search for likely beaver sites and the careful placement of traps, the bone-chilling wades through the water, and the laborious preparation of the skins, the beaver man had to be constantly vigilant. While he crouched in the pre-dawn chill carefully preparing his traps, he had to be listening and watching for Indians intent upon taking his horse, guns, traps, pelts, and hair. While coursing the streams seeking beaver sign, he had to watch for Indians and bear to avoid an unexpected meeting in terrain that might restrict combat or flight. His sleeping ground had to be changed nightly to reduce the chances of ambush, and the comfort of a small fire often had to be foregone to prevent detection by roving bands of hostile Blackfoot, or even ordinarily friendly Indians who might not be able to resist the temptation of booty easily taken from a man alone.

The hard work and vigilance continued through the spring, the trapper moving constantly higher into the mountains until, even there, the warmth of coming summer caused the beaver to shed the marketable winter fur, and trapping had to cease. With the end of the hunt, the trapper turned his steps to the Green or Wind rivers, Cache Valley, Pierre's Hole, or the Popo Agie to trade his furs and replenish supplies, renew old friendships and rivalries, and lift a cup to those who had "gone under" during the last winter.

The rendezvous was the most civilization a free trapper was likely to see all year, and he celebrated it with a robustness that defies present-day metaphor: there is nothing like it anymore. The trapper arrived at the site, selected the previous year, to find other free trappers, Mexicans, French-Canadians, Indians, and company trappers gathered sometimes six hundred strong waiting for the St. Louis packtrains to arrive.

James Beckwourth was a mulatto whose daring and violence were legendary even among his associates.

By the 1830s, competition for trade in the mountains had increased to the point where the traders raced to the rendezvous, lest they should arrive late to find the pelts all traded, their company brigades deserted to another outfit, and themselves stranded with thousands of dollars' worth of unnegotiable trade goods.

The risks to the trader were great, but when the trappers pushed up to the trade blanket to begin bargaining, the merchant was richly rewarded for his efforts. The trapper first settled past accounts—merchandise received on credit in leaner years or moments of carefree overextension—and then traded for the necessities of mountain life: blankets at $20 apiece, tobacco at $5 per plug, powder at $4 per pound, hatchets at $6 apiece, sugar for $3 per pint, and lead, rifles, flints, knives, and cloth at similarly inflated prices. The trapper traded for such items with beaver pelts valued at about $6 apiece. What would have cost him a dollar in St. Louis rose to a value of $10 in the mountains, and as a consequence the trader hauling from the East

Jedediah Smith, mountain man and geographer, was also distinguished by his piety and literacy.

usually made a 600 percent profit after expenses.

But it was not on necessities that the trader made his fortune or the trapper squandered his; the real profligacy followed the trading for staples. Raw alcohol was shipped from St. Louis in small casks, cut with water many times, and then sold at the rendezvous at $5 per pint. Even when considerably watered down, it provided the fuel for sustained celebration by men already primed to explode by a year of loneliness and wariness in the wilderness. Passions that had lain dormant behind the cool calculation and vigilant restraint of survival for three seasons erupted briefly but spectacularly in a summer orgy of self-indulgence. A year's pelts were thrown away on "busthead" and trinkets to entice any available female to dalliance on the trade blanket. What he could not spend to satiate his body and libido, the free trapper wagered on horse races, shooting matches, fights, and games of chance.

The scene, when viewed by literate contemporaries, usually evoked horror and disgust, but among those who saw and enjoyed the spectacle was Captain Bonneville, who recorded his reaction through Washington Irving:

This, then, is the trapper's holiday, when he is all for fun and frolic, and ready for saturnalia among the mountains. . . . The rich treat . . . was to see the 'chivalry' of the various encampments, engaged in contests of skill at running, jumping, wrestling, shooting with the rifle, and running horses. And then their rough hunters' feastings and carousels. They drank together, they sang, they laughed, they whooped; they tried to out-brag and out-lie each other in stories of their adventures and achievements. Here the free trappers were in all their glory; they considered themselves the 'cocks of the walk,' and always carried the highest crests. Now and then familiarity was pushed too far, and would effervesce into a brawl, and a 'rough and tumble' fight; but all ended in cordial reconciliation and maudlin endearment.

The caravans of supplies arrived at the valley just at this period of gallantry and good fellowship. Now commenced a scene of eager competition and wild prodigality at the different encampments. . . . The free trappers, especially, were extravagant in their purchases. For a free mountaineer to pause at a paltry consideration of dollars and cents, in the attainment of any object that might strike his fancy, would stamp him with the mark of the beast in the estimation of his comrades. For a trader to refuse one of these free and flourishing blades a credit, whatever unpaid scores might stare him in the face, would be a flagrant affront scarcely to be forgiven.

The revelry lasted until the pelts and booze were gone, often a week and sometimes longer, and the trapper was left amid the carnage to collect his senses and recuperate his strength. He often recovered to find that during his celebrations he had gambled away, not only his surplus, but also his necessities. When this happened, he turned to a trader for supplies and equipment on credit, pledging not only his debt, but sole

Jim Bridger survived the decline of the fur trade by serving as a guide for emigrants and the U.S. Army.

to compensate for the frenzied activity of the trapping seasons. With the spring thaw, the mountain man moved out again to the lower streams to begin the trapping cycle again.

THE FUR TRADE and the mountain man contributed substantially to the conquest and ultimate disposition of the Rockies. Under the onslaught of the white mountain man, the Indian fell back, beaten as much by the dependence upon the goods the white men brought as by the wilderness skill the mountain man learned from the Indian and then turned against him. The mountain trader also brought the Indian liquor that befuddled his brain, smallpox that killed him by the thousands, and venereal disease that confused and weakened him—any one of them a pestilence of tragic magnitude.

By their presence the mountain men challenged the British right to the Rockies, and their service as guides and advisors made it possible for Oregon-bound pilgrims to reach their destination and secure that region for the United States to the 49th parallel. Another byproduct of the fur trade was the trading centers—Fort Hall, Fort Laramie, Bent's Fort, and Fort Bridger—which remained as way stations and supply depots for the overland migration of the 1840s and 1850s. But the greatest contribution of the mountain men was nothing more than a tool of the trade that made all of the other contributions possible: they explored and understood a complex and trackless barrier land astraddle the course of a young nation's growth.

The government expeditions, though useful, revealed little about the Rockies beyond the narrow track of their traverse. A river basin or a series of canyons might be understood, but what lay between the routes of these exploring parties was known only to the mountain men. They alone of the white men knew where each pass led, what hazards a river might offer around the next bend, how far it was to the next palatable water and when during the year the sun would bake the water hole dry. It was a mountain man, Jedediah Smith, who recognized that South Pass was a gentle gradient to the Continental Divide, and therefore effectively discovered the only feasible wagon route over the Rockies, the gateway for settlement on

rights on the next year's catch. Such an arrangement gave the trapper what he needed and the trader some guarantee of furs for the following year, but for the trader it was a bad risk; a scalp dangling from a Blackfoot belt might be all that remained of the collateral on an otherwise unsecured loan by the time of the next rendezvous.

Accounts settled, the debauch over, and equipment in hand, the free trapper returned to the high country for the fall hunt. He reversed the pattern of the spring hunt, working his way down the streams ahead of the freeze, trapping beaver that had once again put on the valuable heavy winter fur. When snow and frozen streams ended the fall hunt, the free trapper holed up until spring in a valley protected from the winds and drifts of a Rockies winter, often finding companionship in other trappers or the family of his squaw. Winters usually passed quietly, the idle time spent repairing equipment, making clothes, hunting when the weather permitted, and collecting a backlog of sleep the Pacific. John Colter scouted the Jackson Hole–Yellowstone country, only to find himself branded a liar—although other mountain men listened intently when he told them how to find it. Jim Bridger knew southern Wyoming and northern Utah and Colorado so well that he was repeatedly called upon by the army and emigrant parties to show them the way. Unfortunately for the mountain man and the fur trade, their knowledge made the region less awesome, and it pointed up the potential for wealth other than furs that the Rockies offered to anyone willing to settle and civilize the country.

But even before the encroachment of civilization could drive the beaver from the mountains and end the fur business, the fur traders and trappers themselves began to destroy their livelihood through their own zeal and unbridled competition. Prior to 1830, the pattern of trapping had been designed for sustained yield; trapping in one area only lightly, leaving enough beaver for procreation to insure a harvest in subsequent years. But beginning in 1830, the Hudson's Bay Company and the Americans challenged one another in the Snake River country, and the frenzied competition resulted in a "fur desert."

The Americans, principally the Rocky Mountain Fur Company under the control of Jedediah Smith and William Sublette, and the monolithic British concern, each set out to eliminate the other by trapping off all the beaver. Although never specified, the implicit hope of each was to deprive the competitor of an income and force him out of business. Others, notably the American Fur Company, also entered the fray, and in the heat of competition the judicious trapping policy that left breeding stock in every stream was abandoned. Within three years, the unrelenting pressure on the beaver proved too great, and the region was virtually trapped out. But the Americans did not confine the practice to international competition: re-

peatedly rival brigades working the same area overtrapped the streams in an effort to cut off the opposition entirely. The cumulative effect could only be disastrous for the entire industry.

Also at this time, more American companies entered the mountains trying to garner a share in what appeared to be a fantastically profitable business. At the 1832 rendezvous in Pierre's Hole, the number of participating companies and trappers had grown enormously; in addition to the usual Rocky Mountain Fur Company and the American Fur Company, there were the wealthy Boston merchant Nathaniel J. Wyeth, the St. Louis firm of Gantt and Blackwell, an Arkansas group, some Taos trappers, and the quasi-government operation of Captain Bonneville. In subsequent years, this large number of participants took a tremendous toll among the beaver. Also during the thirties, the winds of fashion changed, and silk top hats began to replace beaver felt hats in popularity. This trend brought a declining price for beaver, forcing increased trapping to show the same profit; no longer were beaver left to multiply, and it would be only a matter of time before there was nothing left to trap.

By the summer of the 1839 rendezvous at the Green River, the effects of this self-destructive course were obvious and visible. There were few packs of beaver pelts and only desultory trading for necessities; the scene was subdued as there was no money left over for alcohol or gambling. By 1841 it was all over. The end of the companies and the rendezvous meant that the "free trapper" was now truly free: free to scratch out a meager and precarious existence hunting indiscriminantly for pelt and bounty, guiding government scientific and military expeditions, and leading settlers through and into his former hunting ground. In short, the mountain man brought the civilization he had so determinedly escaped and defied during his reign as monarch of the Rockies.

CHAPTER 12

MAPPERS OF THE WILDERNESS

The government surveys of Hayden, King, Wheeler, and Powell, who put benchmarks on an empire and offered a plan for living in it

THE DECADE between 1870 and 1880 in the Rockies marked an era of tremendous activity, and not unselfish motives. Cities grew and civilization matured almost in spite of the twin mottoes that dictated mountain behavior: Survive, and Get Rich—the assumed corollary being Get Out. Into this turmoil of promotion, development, and random energy came scientists, selfless by comparison, to map the land, probe its composition, gauge its potential, and even chart its future. They had the same rough exterior as everyone else—a few weeks living on horseback did that to even the most carefully gilt scions of the best eastern families—but they were genuine eccentrics; for they came not for money, but for knowledge.

While others burrowed in the ground, scraped gradings for right-of-way, or felled the big trees for mine-shoring, crossties, smelting furnaces, and rude dwellings—doing anything that would net a profit— it was strange to see the introspective geologist tapping with his hammer for samples, or the cartographer taking transit sightings on a mountaintop, swaying in the wind and dodging lightning, for little more than an army private's pay. Even the Indians found them a little peculiar: the Sioux left Ferdinand Hayden alone, even avoided him, figuring that whatever made a man run all over the badlands by himself, pecking at the hillsides, might be catching.

These men who came west proposed surveys for the scientific examination of the land: they would map the land, investigate the geology, and record the plants and animals. Within the relatively new disciplines of geology, paleontology, paleobotany, zoology, botany, entomology, and ornithology, they would record the face of the Rocky Mountains and lay substantial foundations for understanding in the various fields of study. In short, they would provide the first systematic information on the West for the government and its citizens.

The four great surveys of the Rockies were largely products of individual initiative. Four men—Ferdinand Vandeveer Hayden, Clarence King, Lt. George M. Wheeler, and John Wesley Powell—assumed leadership, promoted their respective surveys, and accepted responsibility for the results in the face of a government that could be described at best as indifferent. With the exception of Wheeler's survey, which was largely a military mapping enterprise, the leaders of the surveys annually had to coax small grants from a reluctant Congress. Congress, suffused with the warm glow of self-righteousness that overwhelmed the country in the wake of the Grant administration graft scandals, was particularly parsimonious and suspicious. Each year the survey directors had to show their results and try to convince the guardians of the public trust that there were practical and tangible rewards from the effort and money expended.

Complicating the problems of these men, who each year organized expeditions, found talent, spent months in the field gathering data, prepared reports, and begged money, was the necessity to compete against one another for the money Congress made available. Competing for money meant competing for attention,

A member of Lt. George Wheeler's survey sketches the ruins of Canyon de Chelly in 1873. Artists and archaeologists had a place in all the surveys.

Bringing the amenities of scholarly life to the field, Hayden (left), wife, and friends brunch near Ogden.

and often sound scientific reporting was sacrificed in the rush to present an attractive and impressive record of the year's activities. The bickering and backbiting involved in the contest often necessitated demeaning a rival survey; when everyone was indulging in such behavior, the result could only be counterproductive.

Additionally, there was always the suspicion that, in an effort to garner attention and favor from congressmen who liked to hear good things about their districts, the proponents might make their reports unduly optimistic. Cyrus Thomas, an agronomist with Hayden's survey, noted increased rainfall along the semiarid Front Range of Colorado in the seven years prior to 1869, leading him to surmise that rainfall had increased in direct proportion to population growth. It was a flattering and optimistic proposal, picturing an Eden through sheer numbers, but one that hurt the credibility of the surveys when farmers, with soil tilled and seed planted, waited vainly for the rains until the

wind blew the dirt, the seed, and most of the farmers into insolvency. At the same time, the scientists had to be cautious lest they say anything too derogatory or pessimistic. The most dangerous animal the surveyors faced was the legislator who found his district maligned at government expense—and an actively hostile congressman could cripple or kill a survey through a petulant holdout at budget time.

Forced to compete with one another, and annually to court an indifferent Congress, the surveyors often found themselves short-changing science. Too much effort was distracted from the gathering of field data; reports were often shoddy as the leaders hurried to make a presentation to Congress; energy and thought that should have produced important data on soil and rainfall often went into colorful maps instead, because they made better ammunition for the cloakroom guerrilla warfare that characterized the scramble for survey funds. These distractions hurt the surveys, rendering their results less complete and informative, but they did not make the surveys totally ineffectual.

I F SUCCESS WERE TO BE MEASURED in terms of longevity, growth, funding, and popular acclaim, then the reputation of Ferdinand V. Hayden and his survey would be secure. Cruelly, Hayden was involved in a scientific endeavor that demanded accuracy and attention to detail, something he often sacrificed in the course of courting the public and Congress. Ultimately his crowd-pleasing accomplishments tarnished somewhat alongside the more pedestrian, though more accurate, efforts of the other surveys.

Hayden began his career modestly enough conducting a minor survey of Nebraska in 1867, using leftover funds from the General Land Office. He immediately began efforts to convince Congress of the need for an extensive survey of all the territories, and 1869 found him the head of an independent agency with the Department of Interior, assembling a caravan of paleontologists, entomologists, botanists, artists, cooks, packers, and reluctant army surplus mules. The 1869 Geological Survey of Colorado and New Mexico was swift and superficial, and Hayden's hastily prepared report, complete with Thomas's observations on rainfall and population, was understandably shallow. It

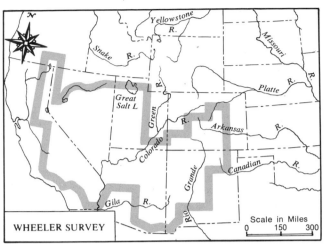

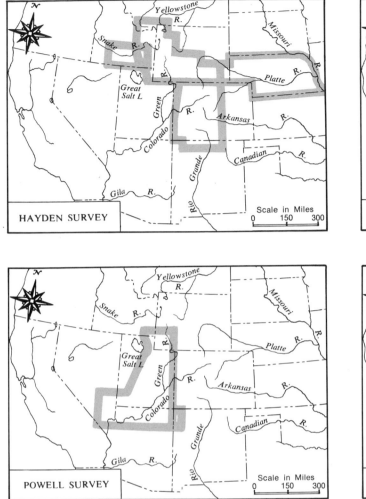

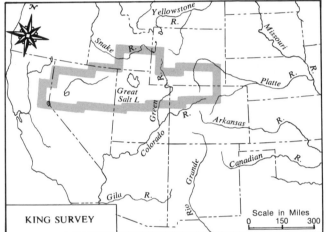

impressed Congress, however, and the following year Hayden was assigned the same task in Wyoming—for over twice the money. But Hayden's fame was largely local and official; it was during the next four years, 1871–74, that he would make the "discoveries" and file the reports that would net him public acclaim and an expanded survey.

In 1871 and 1872 Hayden led expeditions to the Yellowstone region to verify what a lot of people already knew. The phenomena that mountain men like Colter, Fitzpatrick, and Bridger had been branded liars for describing were seen in the early 1860s by Montana gold-seekers, mapped by Walter DeLacey in 1865, and surveyed and described by the Washburn-Doane Expedition of 1870. Hayden, however, captured

the public imagination through the publication of photographs taken by young William Henry Jackson, who had joined the party the year before. His photographs, supplemented by Thomas Moran's paintings made in the course of the 1872 expedition, made a public figure of Hayden and provided a powerful lever for prying funds loose from Congress. Hayden's fortunes would soar even higher in the following year, when Jackson's photograph of the almost legendary Mount of the Holy Cross struck a responsive spiritual chord, and the nation went crazy for copies. The following year archeological findings at Mesa Verde elicited a similar response, and Hayden's public reputation was secure.

Attractive paintings and exciting photographs, how-

W. H. Jackson's famous photograph of Mount of the Holy Cross, taken on the Hayden expedition, capitalized on a national religious fervor and brought public attention to the survey.

ever, were only part of Hayden's formula for success; his alchemy also included telling congressmen and the public what they wanted to hear. His reports were laced with glowing predictions and favorable assessments that were easily translated into the "facts" of western promotional literature. While his conclusions were not necessarily lies, neither were they always the truth; as Richard Bartlett noted, Hayden "worked with a telescope instead of with a microscope."

Despite shortcomings, Hayden's passion for topography, developed during the Yellowstone expeditions, bore fruit in a splendid, systematic atlas of Colorado that occupied the last four years of the survey. And despite a lack of precision in all things scientific, Hayden's publicity probably reflected well on all the surveys—a not inconsequential contribution when all of them were struggling for survival.

As HAYDEN SET ABOUT HIS SURVEY of Nebraska in 1867, Clarence King was launching an active but brief career from the Pacific side of the divide. A brilliant student, writer, and conversationalist, King was a self-made man who combined intellect and brawn in a package that, judged by all who met him, was irre-

sistibly charming. Despite his flamboyance, he was as meticulous as Hayden was haphazard, a thorough-going scientist. But what made him exciting and intriguing evidently also made him unstable; not only did he lack the tenacity to bring the schemes of his later life to fruition, he was fissionable, burning himself out even as he pursued life.

When King was yet a green graduate of Yale's Sheffield Scientific School, he joined Josiah Whitney's survey of California. From 1863 to 1867, he fed a venturesome spirit and learned his trade firsthand in the mountains and valleys of the Sierra, ultimately conceiving his own survey. In 1867 he took his proposal for a survey of the 40th parallel to Washington, lobbied an appropriation, and hastily set about collecting equipment and qualified personnel.

It was a motley group that finally gathered on the California-Nevada border: in addition to the rough packers and camp help, there was a contingent of soldiers, none too happy that their commander was a civilian; as a counterpoint to the soldiers and packers were Arnold and James Hague, Samuel F. Emmons, and King, all well-educated, European-traveled young gentlemen with impeccable family connections; and completing the group, Sereno Watson, an aging botanist, and Robert Bailey, a sixteen-year-old ornithologist. All of the professional personnel would ultimately rise to the top of their respective fields, adequate testimony to King's good judgment in selecting his staff. The soldiers, on the other hand, distinguished themselves by a fanatical devotion to desertion that threatened to wreck the expedition—until King pursued a private for a hundred miles, capturing him in what the intrepid scientist described as a "desperate hand to hand struggle." While King's sense of drama may have been a little too acute, his action nonetheless put an end to disobedience and desertion.

King had before him the task of mapping, examining, and evaluating a strip 100 miles wide along the 40th parallel from the eastern slope of the Sierra, across the Great Basin, over the Rockies, to the western edge of the Great Plains. The land he had chosen to survey was arid and uncompromising, hard on men and animals alike, and on its western half a land that still defies dense settlement. After two long seasons in the field, the survey party reached the Great Salt Lake, the next year moved into Wyoming, and after a brief hiatus, completed to the the east of Cheyenne. The care and discipline that King and his associates lavished on their examinations and collecting became apparent when the multivolume *Report* began to appear. James Hague's *Mining Industry,* Sereno Watson's *Botany,* and King's own *Systematic Geology* are methodical, complete, reasoned documents that laid the foundation for science and civilization at mid-continent. But it was neither careful research nor the literate and scholarly *Reports* that brought King the public recognition he sought—but rather two wily entrepreneurs, Philip Arnold and John Slack, who told the nation about some diamonds they had found.

King's passion was geology—along with its more practical and lucrative relative, mining—and the report that diamonds had been found in northwestern Colorado wounded him; he had examined that country, found nothing to indicate the presence of diamonds, and was disturbed that he might have missed a discovery of great importance. Arnold and Slack had convinced some San Francisco investors of the worth of their find, and the country was rapidly building up the momentum borne of rumor that would line their pockets with speculative dollars. It was a region preg-

Clarence King (right) got his start with Whitney's party, three years before heading his own survey.

nant with potential for quick gains, and people were willing to believe that diamonds, emeralds, and even pearls (!) were there, along with the gold of a decade before. King responded to the reports with characteristic deliberation. After his thorough examination of the site revealed the hoax, the press and the public couldn't shower enough attention on King.

AMONG THE SURVEYS, only one never had to scratch for the funds to continue: the United States Geological Surveys West of the 100th meridian, commanded by Lt. George Montague Wheeler and conducted under the auspices of the War Department. In an effort to provide systematic maps of the Far West, the Wheeler survey covered more ground than any of the others, but to slightly different ends.

The army and Wheeler were not particularly interested in geology or any of the other natural sciences, but rather in maps and information an army would use. The focus was twofold: the routes, dry stretches, and canyons that would hinder or help an army; and the settlements, roads, and other artificial features that marked man's passage and presence. The emphasis was on the practical rather than the theoretical; not so much what *was*, but rather what *resulted* from what was, and how best to use it.

The survey group annually included a number of scientists, but outstanding contributions were usually lost in the welter of bickering that invariably seemed to arise between Wheeler and his civilians. The lieutenant was often cruel and brutal to his men, his animals, and the Indians—and abrupt with the scientists who chastized him for his actions—and neither army nor science became reconciled to the other's methods. While the Wheeler survey was no means a failure, neither was it a success, and when consolidation of the surveys occurred in 1878, the animosity Wheeler had engendered within the scientific community resulted in the cancellation of his project. Wheeler's systematic map was never completed, and despite a partial report published in 1889, the work of eight years and a half million dollars was for all practical purposes thrown away.

John Wesley Powell, head of the Geographical and Geological Survey of the Rocky Mountain Region, had neither the personal magnetism of Clarence King, the press-agent mentality of Ferdinand Hayden nor the vast military resources that supported Wheeler; what he had was a self-administered education, an acute, scientific mind that was as penetrating and comprehensive in the conclusions it drew as it was meticulous and thorough in the observations it made, and an unnerving energy and talent for battling (and occasionally subduing) government bureaucracy. The pragmatic, one-armed major's survey was the smallest of the four efforts, but in the course of two trips down the Grand Canyon of the Colorado and a precise appraisal of the surrounding region, Powell and his aides saw beyond the confines of the region and a simple analysis of the land, to propose a means for man to live compatibly and profitably with the arid West. What he conceived was quite possibly the most insightful and prophetic document of the American experience in the West; had it been heeded at the time it was written, it would have been the most influential as well.

Powell's *Report on the Lands of the Arid Region,* which provided the substance of a report to Congress by the Academy of Sciences in 1878, was a caveat. Because with few exceptions the lands of the mountains

John Wesley Powell took on the Colorado River, bureaucracy, and an occasional photographer.

and Far West receive less than twenty inches of rain per year (the minimum for agriculture without irrigation), Powell argued that it was folly to use the square-grid, 160-acre homestead as the basic unit. He recommended adapting a unit whose size in respect to utility would be determined through information on water, rainfall, soils, and terrain accumulated by the surveys.

The 160-acre rectangular allotment was an anachronism from a humid woodland frontier. It made sense where rainfall was adequate, but in the arid regions it was too little land to support a family, either raising cattle (about four on 160 acres) or growing crops. If the land was irrigated, which increased the number of hours per acre required to prepare, tend, and harvest the land, 160 acres was more than one man needed, or could handle. Conversely, because water was at a premium and land useless without it, a man could preempt an empire by taking several small holdings that controlled all the water in a drainage basin.

Powell suggested dividing the land into 80-acre irrigated farms and 2,560-acre pasture farms. The plots would have irregular shapes, allowing maximum benefit to the greatest number from a drainage system; there would be no monopoly of water, and therefore no monopoly of land. Mineral lands would be set aside, and provisions made for closing to preemption lands that were good to no one.

The largest obstacle to the plan came from the government. The plan called for a complete survey of all lands west of the 100th meridian, and then a careful analysis of the land features for the purpose of dividing it into usable units. This required not only time, money, and considerable effort from the federal government but also closing of the land to settlement until the survey was complete—thereby incurring the wrath of settler and speculator alike. Congress, attacked and pressured from all sides, abdicated its responsibility; in effect defeating a rational plan because it was difficult, expensive, and unpopular.

In addition to the government, Powell's *Report on the Arid Lands* was opposed by an assortment of western interests. Some western legislators opposed the abandonment of the old rectangular survey 160-acre freehold—and its attendant Pre-emption, Homestead, Swamp Lands, Desert Lands, and Timber and Stone acts—because of a misplaced sense of order and tradition; some citizens feared their holdings might be lost if the status quo was upset, and many speculators and empire-builders regarded any change as anathema to the bonanza in land theft they were enjoying under the prevailing system. But the greatest opposition was ideological: it was heresy to assume that the land was less than a garden; were they trying to talk the Great American Desert back into existence?

The misapprehension at work at the time—and even today to some extent—was that all of the land could be made to bloom. When it was realized that precipitation wouldn't provide enough moisture, the assumption developed that irrigation would. (The fact remains that there is enough water in the West for only one-sixteenth of the dry land—in Utah only 3 percent—and until man accepts this actuality, and accommodates himself to it, all the irrigation projects in the world will not solve his problems.) Symptomatic of the confusion, and the optimism, that surrounded the subject of irrigation in the arid West was an incident that occurred at the Irrigation Convention in Denver in 1873. An English engineer, Frederick Stanton, proposed that 1.5 million acres of heretofore dry land could be reclaimed for agriculture in Colorado by building a canal 100 miles long, 12 feet wide, and 3 feet deep. Enthusiasm was rampant until a canny old farmer, a veteran of more than one encounter with the arid lands, pointed out that to achieve this end the water would have to flow down the canal at approximately 420 miles per hour; not to mention the incapability of the mountains to muster enough water even to fill the ditch during the dry season.

On February 18, 1879, a measure passed Congress providing for the classification of lands, but with no change in land law. Nor was any provision made for closing the land to settlement while the region was surveyed, evaluated, and divided, rendering classification a gesture similar to closing the barn door after the cows have left. A basic assumption of democracy holds that a majority will know how to achieve the greatest good for the greatest number; unfortunately, that majority may discover it only after the barn is empty.

The bill that devastated Powell's program also provided for the consolidation of all the ongoing surveys as the U.S. Geological Survey. Although the reorganization cut off some of the excitement of the individual surveys, it also ended the bickering, duplication, and waste that marked the experience of the seventies. The resultant solidarity and unity of opinion supplied the necessary strength for prodding Congress into passage of the Newlands Act and the Taylor Grazing Act, both measures that resurrect the legacy of Powell in accommodating man to the mountain West.

PART FOUR

THE SHAPING
OF
CIVILIZATION

Cities that transcended the arcadian simplicity of the trapper's frontier, civilization lent permanence by the gentling hand of family life—these were the dream of those who came to stay. Building on the crude and often shaky foundations of the mining industry, tying their efforts together with steel rails, eliminating natural obstacles like Indians with ruthless ingenuity, learning to farm an arid land or adding a new dimension with ranching, the newcomers fashioned a rough reflection of the world their fathers had built in the East.

Denver Station, 1870.

163

CHAPTER 13

DIVIDING THE WATERS IN ZION

*The Mormon experience, unique in the West, which provided the nation
with a prototype for survival in a remote and arid land*

ALTHOUGH OTHER WESTERNERS eventually found many lessons for frontier survival in the Mormon experience, it was at first an anomaly in the history of the Rocky Mountains. It began with the choice of a place no one else wanted.

Amid early nineteenth-century exploration and pioneering, Salt Lake Valley remained an isolated spot, blocked from the east by the Rockies and from the west by the Great Salt Lake Desert—"the paradise of the lizard, the cricket, and the rattlesnake." Most settlers stayed away. But for members of the Church of Latter-Day Saints, persecuted wherever they moved, from the East to Missouri to Illinois, this inhospitable wilderness seemed a possible shelter from human inhospitality.

The first 149 Saints reached the valley in 1847; in a few years they and the thousands of Mormons who joined them from the Midwest and Europe had transformed the desert into a thriving agricultural city and were soon to settle throughout the Great Basin, even extending their influence into parts of Colorado, Idaho, and the West Coast. In the arid West, where so many ventures failed, their success was another striking anomaly, intimately related to a combination of the Protestant Ethic with strict church rule based on adapting society to the requirements of the land.

The reasons for the trek to Utah and for the unique and successful experiments there were not obscure; they lay in the religious and social message of Mormonism, in the temper of the people it attracted, and in the turbulent early history of the group.

Since 1827, when Mormonism's tenets had been revealed to founder Joseph Smith, the Mormons had always considered themselves a people set apart. The Book of Mormon told Smith and his six original followers that they had been chosen to bring Christ's word to a fallen world. They began preaching and selling copies of the new Word to the people of upper New York State, but found them unprepared to accept the new dispensation. The small group of Saints moved to Kirtland, Ohio, to escape resentment and find more receptive souls. But here again the Mormons faced increasing hostility, especially when the Panic of 1837 stirred envy of their comparative prosperity. Once more Smith took his followers west, to Missouri, only to be branded as a public enemy who should be "exterminated or driven from the State."

The Mormons moved to Nauvoo, Illinois. There, in spite of prejudice and some persecution, their numbers continued to grow. Mormonism had many attractions, especially for Protestants of mainly English, Scottish, and Danish origin—all thrifty, industrious people. Converts from the industrial slums of England and over-settled agricultural areas in America flocked to the town, attracted by Mormon evangelism and material success alike. As an English arrival wrote, "In this place, there is a prospect of receiving every good thing both of this world and that which is to come." Nauvoo soon contained about two thousand brick homes watched over by an enormous stone and gilt temple. Mormonism's ability to satisfy both body and soul helped unify the new community; Gentile persecu-

*A young Brigham Young, whose iron-handed control and foresight during the early years
in Deseret contributed more than any other factor to the Saints' survival.*

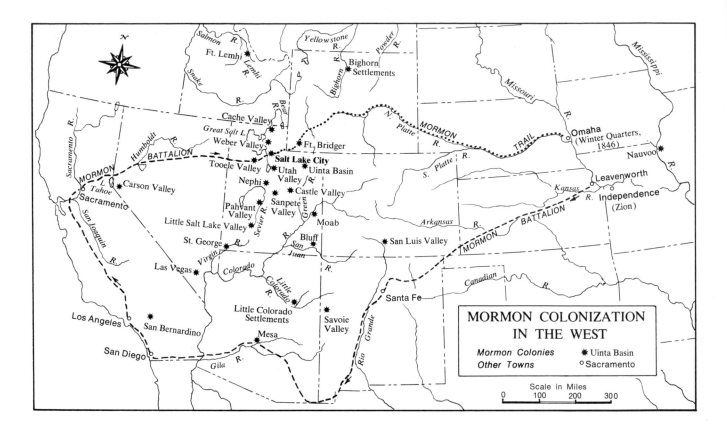

tions resumed in 1844 and solidified it even more.

Ironically, oppression from without was invited by unrest within Mormon ranks. When Joseph Smith announced the doctrine of polygamy in 1844, some Saints protested and denounced him. Smith promptly sent the Nauvoo marshal to destroy the presses of the apostates, and Gentile authorities in turn arrested him. A mob of anti-Mormons stormed the jail and assassinated the Mormon prophet. Faced with a mass outbreak of persecutions, the Saints quickly rallied around a new leader, Brigham Young.

According to most accounts, Young was well suited for the job. "A practical and puritanical Vermonter," he combined religious zeal with incisive expression and remarkable administrative powers. He may have been a prophet, but it was said of him that "he did not listen to the spirits; he commanded them." Most important at this critical juncture, he had a plan for the embattled Mormons: they were to migrate to Salt Lake in Utah, a place he had researched in John C. Frémont's exploration journal.

L IKE ITS GENESIS, the difficult exodus of the Mormon community into the promised land was to leave a strong imprint upon the Zion which later sprang up in Utah. The mixture of pragmatism, efficient organization, obedience to the church hierarchy, and religious fervor with which the Saints confronted their tribulations was to become a hallmark of Mormonism.

During the move, which began in February 1846, all Young's organizing abilities were needed. Fifteen thousand men, women, and children had to be moved across the Great Plains as quickly and safely as possible. Young appointed an advance party which moved ahead of the mass throughout the migration, setting up camps and, as the spring wore on, planting crops for the next arrivals. According to Young's plan, the people traveled in small, tightly organized bands under the strict supervision of captains and lieutenants.

Though at first blizzards and later driving rain and knee-deep mud caused great physical hardship, Mormon hopes remained high, boosted by religious fervor and the security of rigid planning. As one Saint was

Joseph Smith, the visionary whose teachings founded the Church of the Latter-Day Saints.

In later years, Brigham Young led his people in conflicts with nature and the U.S. Army.

able to recall, "We were happy and contented, and the songs of Zion resounded from wagon to wagon, reverberating through the woods while the echo returned from the distant hill."

When all were safe in winter quarters on the Missouri, however, Young had to recognize that their progress had been too slow; it had taken them almost a year to cross Iowa. The tightest organization could not completely overcome nature, nor could the Saints always deal with some members' lack of supplies and shelter. The majority must wait in the bleak winter camp while a "Pioneer Band" composed mainly of men pressed forward to their goal.

Their usual efficiency characterized the Mormons' travel, and the Pioneer Band reached Salt Lake on July 14, 1847. By the next fall, 1,800 people were living on the shores of the lake. Building Zion, however, proved even harder than getting to it. The winter was harsher than they had expected, and some Saints had not planned enough to ensure themselves adequate provender and shelter. In the spring, a late frost struck

parts of the valley, and a swarm of grasshoppers devoured half the crops. Worse yet, many Mormons had trusted to God rather than to irrigation for their water, and most of their crops dried up. As 1,891 new pioneers arrived and a lean winter approached, even the Saints began to doubt their venture. Only a firm hand could keep some persons from leaving for more inviting lands in California and Oregon.

Young's solution was to extend church control to all aspects of Mormon life, especially those in which individual failure or self-interest could threaten the livelihood of all. Land use, irrigation, and city planning were to be strictly cooperative, he told his followers on September 30, 1848. The church assigned each head of family a plot of land according to his need and supervised the construction of irrigation ditches and the allotment of water. No individual could sell land or own the streams so crucial to everyone's life. The irrigation system instituted at this time was so efficient that it might have been designed by modern engineers, and it set an example—largely un-

*In response to the problem of limited funds and equipment, the Saints organized "handcart brigades,"
in which new converts walked as much as 1,400 miles to Salt Lake pulling a few possessions.*

noticed for many years—of the kind of adaptation needed to survive in the arid West.

At the same time, Young set up a system of government intended to keep the water and land under tight surveillance. He called it a "theo-democracy," but it was actually an oligarchy. Young, who communicated the word of God to his people, was the supreme authority; the Quorum of the Twelve Apostles and the Presiding Bishopric, which supervised spiritual and practical matters, answered to Young. Though the lower officials were elected by the people, Young controlled the nominations.

The 1848 measures established a government that was antithetical to most American tradition, especially that of the West. Ironically, the frontier, which so beckoned individualists, proved the ruin of many, for most non-Mormons balked at such cooperative effort and tight community control of resources.

In the late 1840s and 1850s, Mormon land-use policy and hierarchical government spread throughout Utah and even to parts of Nevada and California, as Young and his followers attempted to carve out a kingdom in the West. The Saints hoped to make themselves totally independent of a Gentile world that again and again had proved hostile to them. Even if Gentiles should eventually settle among them, the Mormons intended to play the authoritative role of "old settlers" —no longer the minority newcomers in their chosen homeland, but the majority. Their first goal was to occupy and farm all the land between the Rockies and the Sierra Nevada that could be irrigated; they hoped also to use the mineral resources of the land and establish their own industries.

Mormon irrigation and unity of purpose produced such successful agricultural communities as Ogden, Provo, and Parowan in Utah, San Bernardino in California, and Carson City and Las Vegas in Nevada. Mormons' wheat production tripled between 1850 and 1860, and their cattle and orchards flourished. Only 3 percent of Utah land was ever farmed, but by means

Some didn't make it, like those depicted in this contemporary engraving of late arrivals caught in an early storm. Despite the hazards and hardships, thousands undertook this trek on foot.

of efficient irrigation, the fields that were cultivated provided enough food, and no outstanding failures.

These decades, however, gave indications that the Saints' dream of separatism was not completely realistic. While their agricultural efforts blossomed, industrial development required more than determination and organization: it called for capital and manpower that the Mormons could not yet command. More important, the Gentile world was expanding westward.

THE FIRST DRAMATIC HINT that Zion could not isolate itself came with the 1849 gold rush to California. The Salt Lake became a stopping place for all kinds of Gentiles who had been swept up in the gold frenzy. The forty-niners posed critical problems for the Mormons, because the lure of rapid wealth made some of the Saints dissatisfied with the steady toil of farming. Even those who resisted temptation had to endure a large and "motley brigade of individualists"

in their midst. The easy morals and "get rich quick" mentality of many of these new arrivals clashed with every Mormon tenet, and relations between the opportunists and the old settlers were tense.

But the Gentile presence had some advantages, and once again a combination of church control and Protestant Ethic produced prosperity from possible disaster. The miners and other emigrants came at the right time for the Mormons; a severe winter had killed off much of their stock, and the harvest of 1848 had not lived up to their expectations. As one Mormon said wryly, "It looked like there was a splendid chance for going naked." Though price controls had been instituted by the church, the exceptional privations induced many to hoard food and set blackmarket prices. The Mormons found a booming market among the "Winter Saints," who arrived in Zion exhausted and hungry for fresh produce, their oxen staggering and their wagons overloaded. The travelers were happy to barter goods and pay high prices for whatever vegetables,

169

The Mountain Meadows Massacre, re-created in an anti-Mormon engraving, shows Saints murdering women and children (far right). Shrouded in confusion and bias, the truth of the event remains a phantom.

dairy goods, and draft animals the Mormons had on hand. The coming of the gold-diggers stirred up trouble, but more important, it provided material security that lessened unrest among the Mormons themselves. Young's assertion that wealth was to be found at home rather than in the goldfields farther west kept the Mormons to their husbandry. The church's analysis of the situation proved correct, as "busted" returnees from California soon began to demonstrate.

Having survived the first Gentile onslaught, Zion found itself embroiled in a jurisdictional conflict with the federal government. Young had hoped that Zion would become a state in 1849 and thus continue its home rule undisturbed, but the federal government ruled in 1850 that it must become a territory instead. Fearing more direct federal intervention if he did not comply, Young reluctantly agreed. The Mormon Church managed to continue its local rule by electing Young governor, but Utah's territorial government, like any other, consisted mainly of Gentile officials from Washington. Many of these officials saw Mormon independence as undesirable for national economics and politics, and attacked Utah's "twin relics of barbarism" —theocracy and polygamy.

During the next decade, a series of inflammatory events led finally to a crisis between the Mormons and the government. In 1855, Mormons began refusing to take cases to federal courts, preferring the county courts

*In a rare early photograph, Mormon emigrants are shown struggling through Echo Canyon. To ease
the passage through the muck, brush had to be laid in the wheel ruts (foreground).*

controlled by the church. Disgruntled federal judges
returned to Washington in 1857 to lobby against
Young's rule and the alleged persecution of Gentiles
in the territory. Hitherto a local issue, Mormonism
was becoming a federal problem.

To make matters worse, a fanatical religious revival
swept Zion in 1856; zealous Mormons turned on other
Mormons they thought unfaithful, and violence occurred. Anti-Mormonism in the outside world became
even more intense as newspapers carried lurid accounts
of the unrest. Calling the disorders a "rebellion," President Buchanan ordered 2,500 soldiers to Utah to establish law and order. The Mormons prepared for guerrilla
warfare, sending out small forces to raid the army's

supply trains, drive off its stock, and burn everything
in its path.

Events had paved the way for the major crisis—the
Mountain Meadows Massacre of 1857. A combined
force of Indians and Mormons, angered by the insults
and minor depredations of an emigrant group, over-
reacted and attacked the Gentiles, murdering almost
all of them. Hysteria grew in Utah and the outside
world. Only careful mediation persuaded Young to
accept a new Gentile territorial governor and, when
the president pardoned the "hostiles," to agree to the
army's entering Utah. The army remained there peacefully until the Civil War.

The new agreement looked like a big concession from

Carefully planned with broad thoroughfares and deep lots for kitchen gardens,
Salt Lake City in the late 1840s was an attractive and growing community.

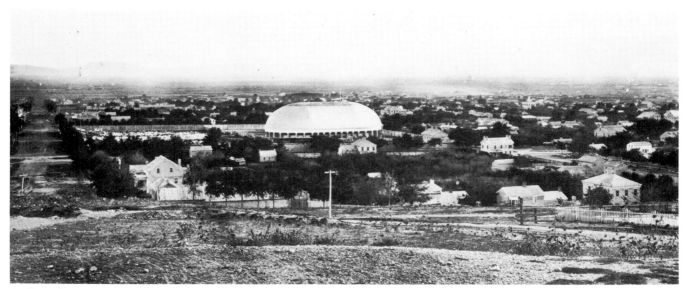

In less than two decades the town was assuming the proportions of a city, as shown in this photograph
taken in the 1860s. The tabernacle, a recent addition to the skyline, is in the center foreground.

Young, but the Mormons reorganized their local institutions so that most important matters still came under church rather than territorial jurisdiction. They abolished territorial taxes, so that "all public works were to be done on labor tithing and under the control of the bishops" and retained their own military force.

FOR THE NEXT GENERATION, two problems—self-preservation and statehood—dominated Mormon life. Both were related to their unique adaptation to the West. Though the Gentile influence grew around and even among them, the Mormons still hoped for economic security in isolation. In the 1870s, Brigham Young revived an old notion of Joseph Smith's—the United Order of Enoch. At that time, there was a growing wage class in Utah, and the Panic of 1873 provoked concern that Mormon workmen might begin striking like their Gentile counterparts. The United Order was intended to promote cooperative and home industry efforts in Zion, under the continuing leadership of the church. The new system was even more strictly cooperative than the old: rather than work his own plot with his own tools, each person was to pool his land with the rest and use community tools to work it communally. The tithes that had been paid individually were now paid by the community. Many new towns, like Orderville and Bunkerville in Utah and Sunset in Arizona, were founded under the order, and some established communities were reorganized.

The order was a more extreme form of the religious, social, and political organization that had always characterized Mormonism, and that had worked so well in a frontier environment, where man had to husband land and water carefully if he and his community were to survive. Nevertheless, the United Order was short-lived. By 1880 there was grumbling and confusion at most of the communities; because some Mormons looked out for themselves more than for the community, others began to object that the order gave "equal credit for unequal labor." Apparently the limits of Mormon tolerance for cooperative effort had been reached under the old system; perhaps now that bare survival was secure, a greater cooperation than before seemed unnecessary.

Statehood remained a problem for Zion until a generation after the Mormon "war." Gentile opposition to Mormon polygamy kept Congress from voting Utah into the Union. Polygamy was originally a way of assuring economic security to many women who would have been poor or spinsters, and of boosting Mormon population, thus guaranteeing that a sea of Gentiles would not swamp them in their own territory. But by the 1880s, the Mormons were ready to make some concessions, especially after the Edmunds Act of 1882 banned plural marriage and some of the most prominent Mormons went to jail as "cohabs." In 1890, the church gave up polygamy, though the institution continued underground for some time—some say, even up to the present. In 1896, Utah received its statehood, official recognition of its relation to the Gentile world.

The Mormon experience—especially its cooperative irrigation and land-use policies—ultimately became an integral part of American tradition, as more and more western communities followed its example by setting up local cooperative irrigation districts and state agencies to control natural resources, and finally courted federal aid and supervision in these matters.

CHAPTER 14

BONANZA IN THE HIGH COUNTRY

*The gold and silver that built cities, ushered in civilization, and
created a mercuric prosperity for nearly half a century*

IVILIZATION had avoided the mountains with
what seemed a studied caution, intimidated
perhaps by imposing ridges, ragged gorges, and
extreme winters. It was a remote land, bounded on
one side by the desert of Pike and Long, and on the
other by a basin so formidable even the Mormons
hesitated to venture beyond one corner of it. Explorers
had either skirted the apron of the cordillera, convinced
that nothing worthwhile lay within, or moved quickly
through available passes in search of lands beyond.
Mountain men followed every stream and ridge of the
mountain citadel and probably came to regard it as
home, but their very lives were the antithesis of civilization, and the beaver an automatic casualty of permanent settlement. The mountains were a barrier to
be hurdled by the thousands who passed through between 1840 and 1860 en route to the greener meadows
and golden streambeds of California and Oregon. It
was to take that unlikely candidate, the miner, to
provide the purpose and the means for cities and
civilization in the Rockies.

It was a shard of hope—the prospect of gold and
silver—that brought men *to* the Rockies; first the prospectors and miners, later the engineers and investors—
men often as unreliable as the veins they followed and
unstable as the powder they set, but they found the
wealth and built the camps that grew into cities and
civilization. The foothold they gained was slippery,
but by relying on precious and base metals to broaden
the base of wealth, by calling on outside technology
and capital, and because of the timely arrival of rail

transport, mining survived the problems of recalcitrant
ores and isolation long enough to build a permanent
population in the mountains.

The mining bonanza that struck the Rockies first
in Colorado, sending shock waves up and down the
mountain spine to periodically shake loose other ex-
citements, was the product of humbug. In 1858 a party
of Cherokee Indians and Georgia miners headed by
John Beck and Green Russell, remembering a smat-
tering of "color" found in Colorado streams by Cherokees bound for the California goldfields in 1850,
worked their way along the Front Range sampling
the streams for potential placer sites. Although their
efforts were largely unrewarded, they did manage a
small return of gold from the gravels of Cherry Creek,
near the present site of Denver. In the same year,
another party, out of Lawrence, Kansas, was working
the same region to much the same effect. These two
small yields, magnified by boosters, outfitters, and merchants in the Missouri valley and on the plains who
saw a mercantile bonanza in supplying prospectors,
touched off a rush that had little basis in reality. Augmented by yet-hopeful losers in the financial collapse
of 1857 who would chase any rainbow to recoup their
fortunes, the rush took on avalanche proportions by
the spring of 1859. Misplaced geography and a sardonic
sense of prophecy combined to provide a banner for
the ill-timed argonauts that read, "Pikes Peak or Bust."

Founded on hyperbole, the rush had to collapse.
Many of the men, ill equipped or inadequately pro-
visioned, started back immediately; others milled

*While a few found fortune in Colorado's goldfields, all found hard work. Here four hopefuls
cooperate on a sluice, sharing the work, the investment, and perhaps the bounty.*

When the placers gave out, the miner, if he stayed, had a choice of digging a hole or washing the mountain down. The latter—hydraulicking—left ugly scars still visible today.

around in the foothill streams confirming the lie and plotting diabolical revenges against the perpetrators of the hoax. But even as disillusion at Cherry Creek worsened, a savvy old prospector named John Gregory was exposing the outcropping of a fabulously rich lode, on North Clear Creek. Almost immediately, similar strikes at Idaho Springs and Gold Hill buttressed Gregory's discovery, and the shambling retreat across the plains reversed itself. Encouraged by successes in the remote, rugged high mountain country, the prospectors invaded the tangled interior of the mountains as no one had since the era of the mountain man. Once again an extractive industry had brought men to the mountains—transients indifferent to the land and the region's future—but this time the mountains offered treasure enough to coax more out of man.

Gregory Gulch, as the find on North Clear Creek came to be called, didn't last long; the quartz lodes drifted into the bowels of the earth, and the surface placers played out quickly under the onslaught of hundreds of exuberant miners. None of the surface diggings lasted very long in the Rockies—there were always too many men and not enough gold—but every stream seemed to yield a find that justified staying on, until towns and cities arose to supply the needs and cater to the pleasures of men who intended to get rich and get out. Russell Gulch and Spanish Diggings, Twelve Mile Gulch and Jefferson Diggings, Tarryall and Fairplay creeks—all took their turns to keep the men in the mountains. When the placers were gone,

A dream ended and a business begun: Shaft mining, like hydraulicking, was too expensive for individual miners, who often had to abandon their hopes of a strike to work for wages in the mines.

lodes that promised wealth sufficient to justify deep-hole mining conspired to hold a population. With the help of enthusiastic journalists like Horace Greeley and Henry Villard, there began to develop the first vestiges of a metropolis in the mountain belt.

The cities largely responsible for promoting the original rush—Kansas City, Independence, Leaven-worth, and Council Bluffs—continued to profit by pro-visioning the miners and prospectors, but a supply depot in or adjacent to the mountains was necessary. John Beck and Green Russell had precipitously laid out St. Charles Town on the South Platte as a specu-lative venture in 1858, when their small find touched off the false rush, but with the debacle that ensued, their hope for overnight growth had faded. William

Larimer, a Kansan caught in the early enthusiasm, still saw promise, lured the remaining residents of St. Charles Town into getting drunk, appropriated the townsite, and renamed it Denver. His chicanery paid off with Gregory's strike, and by October 1859 Denver was beginning to assume the trappings of civilization with the arrival of a schoolteacher and a theatrical company. The rowdyism and lawlessness of a rough mining camp passed quickly for Denver, and by 1860 the teacher and the theater had been joined by a library, two newspapers, and a debating club.

Other towns arose as quickly—not just mining camps where men slept, ate, and drank together, but genuine supply centers with the appearance of permanence—at Pueblo and Boulder. The nesting instinct of the Amer-

*The smelters of **Gilpin County**, which revived Colorado mining. The furnaces digested not only whole mountains of ore, but whole forests of wood as well. Note cords stacked between the buildings.*

H. A. W. Tabor, the eccentric Leadville merchant who parlayed grubstakes into millions.

John Gregory, whose find on North Clear Creek saved the Colorado rush of '59.

ican in a frontier situation, that compelling desire to adopt a constitution, elect officials, and clear out the riffraff and undesirables as soon as three people had a saloon and a stable they could call a town, asserted itself immediately in an abortive move in 1859 to establish the "State of Jefferson." Left to languish as a neglected satellite of Kansas Territory until 1861, the residents of mining camp and incipient city alike extemporized with the extralegal expedient of the mining district: by common agreement, laws were established to protect claims, keep order, provide for officials, mete out punishment, and collect taxes.

Fortunately for the Rockies, along with the miner came the less exciting, though more permanent and stable farmer. Near Golden, as early as 1859, David Wall was turning water onto a truck garden of rare vegetables: peas, onions, watermelons, cabbages, and squashes. With freight moving across the plains at $4 to $6 per hundredweight, it was a profitable undertaking; more importantly, it was the precursor of an industry that would provide a measure of independence

for the region that all of the bright mineral treasure and promising cities could never provide.

The tentative civilization that began with placer mining grew into permanence with the establishment of lode mining, but not without trauma. By 1863 the placers had played out, and it was obvious that deep-hole mining was going to require large outlays of capital. Sinking a shaft was expensive, requiring pumps to keep the water down, and wood to fire the pumps and shore the shafts; scarce labor and high shipping costs to remote mines added to the expense. But Colorado mining's greatest obstacle lay in the ores: the gold and silver were locked in a sulfide matrix that resisted the standard quicksilver amalgamation process. These reluctant "sulphurets," or pyritic ores, took anywhere from 50 to 90 percent of the gold in the ore right across the riffles, through the mercury, and into the tailings to be lost for good. Such ores ran costs very high, breeding a series of events that had tragic consequences for the mountain states and plagues them even today.

In an effort to improve the efficiency of refining tech-

Leadville in the late 1870s: The first surge of prosperity brought with it the hasty, haphazard erection of rude dwellings to house a suddenly burgeoning population.

niques, Colorado mineowners invested heavily in machinery and experts, neither of which appreciably increased profits. In large measure, these "improvements" were financed with eastern capital, and when the ores remained intractable and mortgages came due, ownership of the mines passed into eastern hands. Absentee ownership became common and ultimately meant that, while the mines brought jobs and prosperity for a time, the majority of the profits left the region. Faced with impossible ores, but plenty of eager capital, Colorado mine operators and engineers found it easier, to quote Rodman W. Paul, "to work the 'suckers' than the Colorado ores." Easterners ventured more money and operators spent it more rashly, the resultant overextension bringing collapse in 1864–65. Many eastern investors foreclosed on temporarily worthless mines; but when prosperity returned, the Rocky Mountain residents—the people who had come to work the wealth of the mountains—were little more than tenants.

Colorado mining experienced a revival by 1870 that was the result of hard work, improved methods, and lower costs. The arrival of the railroad during the decade of the seventies greatly reduced costs, both of manufactured goods brought in and intramontane movement of ores. The use of Cornish and Irish miners who brought advanced skills in hard-rock mining also helped, but it was improvement in the technology and chemistry of reducing the refractory ores that made the most significant difference. Nathaniel P. Hill, a Brown University chemist, studied European techniques, hired a German metallurgist, and set out to make the Gilpin County ores pay. Hill built a smel-

Creede, Colorado, winter 1892: A town notorious for violence and sordid pleasures, it spilled out of the canyon that spawned it in a curious admixture of brick, wood, and tent dwellings.

ter at Black Hawk, and by 1873 his methods were sufficiently advanced to make reduction of the ores truly profitable. His developments in smelting were critical to Colorado, because they made possible the extraction of base metals as well as precious. Coupled with the railroads, which made transportation of base metals profitable, smelting marked the beginning of an era of prosperity for Colorado.

These improvements probably paid off in their most impressive fashion with the discoveries at Leadville. For over a decade, miners washing placer gold had been plagued by "the damned blue stuff" that clogged their riffles, but in 1877 August Meyer built a smelter at Leadville to extract the accursed material—a silver-rich lead carbonate. Meyer's efforts were an unqualified success. The boomers crowded in, and in three

years the town grew to a population of 15,000, second largest in the state. Around a nucleus of thirty mines and fourteen smelters blossomed a town with gaslights and a waterworks, thirteen schools, five churches, three hospitals, and enough saloons to earn the town a reputation for round-the-clock bacchanalia. Rails arrived in 1880, and by then it was obvious that Leadville was the bonanza needed to restore the mining economy to its former glory; between 1878 and 1880, the smelters ladled out over $23,000,000 worth of silver and almost $5,000,000 worth of lead.

Another product of Leadville's flamboyant years, and probably as memorable a part of the city's legacy to Colorado as the silver, was a portly merchant named Tabor, who had a remarkable affinity for profitable holes in the ground—and apparently a devastating ef-

*South Pass City, Wyoming, was founded on fat rumors and thin evidence. The gold played out quickly
—but not before man could erect this sagging monument to his precipitous enthusiasm.*

fect on women. Horace Austin Warner Tabor spent
over twenty years pursuing an obscure destiny as a
grocer and drygoodsman in one small mining town
after another, until he grubstaked two Leadville prospectors in 1878. What they found eventually became
the Little Pittsburgh Mine; for less than one hundred
dollars' worth of food and tools, Tabor netted one-
third of a multimillion-dollar operation. He branched
out, sinking the Chrysolite and Matchless mines to a
chorus of guffaws from local mining engineers; both
paid enormous returns.

His fortune secure, Tabor began to diversify, spreading his millions through real estate, insurance, and
banking. He built the Tabor Opera House in Leadville
and then went himself one better, building the Tabor
Grand Opera House in Denver. He went to Denver as

lieutenant governor, cut a wide swath with the ladies,
unloaded his wife of many decades, married his mis-
tress Baby Doe before his divorce was final, poured
enough money into the Republican political machinery to earn a thirty-day interim appointment as U.S.
senator, and generally left a trail of clinquant opu-
lence and shattered propriety wherever he went—not
to mention a daughter he demurely named Rose Mary
Echo Silver Dollar Tabor.

But the health and vitality of Colorado's economy
depended upon a continuing supply of silver, not on
the antics of the rare individuals who amassed enough
to subsidize a sideshow for the industry. Since Leadville's rise, gold had diminished in importance, and
despite the railroads and developing farming and
grazing industries, the region was primarily dependent

*Main Street, Helena, in 1869 reflected the haste, the crowded activity, the ebullient optimism,
and the often squalid waste that characterized civilization on the mining frontier.*

upon how much silver was taken out of the ground. The boom that began in the seventies and carried through the eighties was accompanied by gradually rising production costs and the inflation that accompanies any boom. But in 1893 the Sherman Silver Purchase Act, which guaranteed the price of silver, became a casualty of a mercurial world money market and a collapsing American economy. The price of silver plummeted, and the fortunes of the mountains with it. The discovery of gold at Cripple Creek buoyed Colorado's sagging economy temporarily, but the devastation was so complete that it was only a short time before miners and owners began to squabble over wages and working conditions, only to breed further economic hardships (see chapter 18).

The mineral industry that saw Montana through its

frontier stages was largely a by-product of the Colorado rush. Although gold in substantial amounts had been washed by Francois Finley in the Deer Lodge Valley as early as 1852, no one noticed or cared until 1862 when John White made a find on Grasshopper Creek while en route from the Colorado mines to the Idaho diggings. The strike, at what would become Bannack, set off a flurry of prospecting that ran its course in only a few years.

Stragglers from a prospecting expedition to the Yellowstone made the next major gold strike in Montana, at Alder Gulch. Barney Hughes, a member of the party sent to Bannack for supplies, was followed on his return by three to four hundred enthusiastic miners. Unable to elude the caravan and fearing that he would lose his claim, Hughes agreed to show them the way in exchange for a larger claim for himself and his partners—and then sneaked away under the cover of darkness. The avaricious horde found the gulch anyway and quickly fanned out over the area, staking almost contiguous claims for its entire seventeen-mile length. Although preoccupied with the pursuit of treasure, they stopped rooting in the streambed long enough to bicker over whether to name their staked-out city for Lincoln's wife or for Jefferson Davis's, finally settling on the politically neuter and hopefully pristine Virginia City.

In 1864 small strikes hit all over Montana, spawning a mining industry that was erratic but rich. The gold excitement that took men to the Gallatin River, Wisconsin Creek, and Emigrant Gulch passed quickly, but some of the camps survived to become cities, as, for instance, Last Chance Gulch, which grew into Helena. Probably the most important camp to survive, and the one that rules Montana even today, was Butte. Founded as a gold camp in 1864, it declined as the accessible placer and shallow-lode gold diminished. In 1875 the discovery of rich silver ores revived the town, maintaining the operation of the mines until 1893, when the waning price of silver hit Montana even harder that it had Colorado. While Colorado staggered into the twentieth century still trying to produce silver and gold, Butte gave up completely, switched to copper, and struck that state's biggest bonanza.

The metals produced by Montana mines have yielded something in excess of three billion dollars, fully two-thirds of that amount coming from copper. Copper kept Montana's economy healthy in an era of mining depression, but fiscal health came at a high price. Because the copper was so rich, and because there was only grazing to diversify the economy, the state's fortunes and its future became inexorably tied to Anaconda, the company that controlled Butte's copper. In the rare instances when the company (or copper) suffered in the marketplace, almost the entire economy of the state was adversely affected immediately. At the same time, because copper and the money

it earned were so important, Anaconda gained almost total control of Montana's machinery of government; what it couldn't direct, it could influence enormously. While prevailing policy dictated benevolence, things went the company's way, and it wasn't until midway into the twentieth century that irrigation and agriculture would diversify the economy sufficiently to erode the feeling that Montana was, indeed, a company state. In the final reckoning, Montana's interest on her debt to copper broached on usury.

MINING HAD LAID THE CORNERSTONE for civilization in the Rockies, bringing with it a kind of prosperity. Unfortunately, along with the bonanza contradictions sprouted that plague the region to today. Men came to the mountains because of the precious metals, and gold and silver built most of the towns and raised most of the families before the turn of the century; but because it took money to make money, the ownership of the mines passed out of local hands. Although money had been everywhere, it never seemed to build anything but mines. When the economy collapsed with the repeal of the Sherman Silver Purchase Act, the region lacked the resilience that might have come from diversification. Profits from mining had instead gone East to owners, leaving little real money in the mountains to build a cushion of alternate industries.

To get at the metals, men had to cut down the forests for shoring and fuel. For a while it was questionable whether the wood could last long enough to get all the metal—and in Colorado, especially, one resource was nearly devastated to extract another. Had the gold and silver held out, or the prices stayed up, one wonders what would have been left. It was a demonic cycle, only a part of the impact of mining on the mountains. Mining, like any other extractive industry, was generating its own destruction even as it flourished—the more prosperous it became, the closer loomed its debilitation. Yet without the metals to extract and the forests to exploit, there would have been nothing at all.

Weathered remnants of the prophetically named Ghost Mine are all that remain of the once dynamic prosperity in Yankee Boy Basin near Ouray, Colorado.

Main Street of Silverton, Colorado, basking here in the afternoon sun. Although long since the victim of collapsed

A decaying mill and mine tailings, arrested in their once inexorable movement across the valley, remind travelers

silver prices, the town now mines the tourists as effectively as it once did the mountains.

near Silverton of the San Juan Mountains' frenetic past.

*The remains of a concentrating mill at Leavick,
Colorado, framed by Horseshoe Mountain.*

*The ghost town of South Park was shifted intact
to entertain tourists at Fairplay, Colorado.*

*Overleaf: Perched on a mountain shelf in Red Mountain Pass, the Idarado Treasure Tunnel Mine waits
for the day when rising gold prices will stimulate a return to full production.*

Dilapidated buildings and a head-frame (center) that once clattered men and ore between the surface and subterranean treasure of the Oreville Mine sit quietly before Mount Massive in Leadville.

CHAPTER 15

RAILS ACROSS THE DIVIDE

*Transcontinental lines that tied the West to the rest of the nation,
and shorter roads that bound the mountain region together*

HE MOUNTAIN WEST that awaited the attentions of a war-weary nation in 1865 was still a frontier. Although the province of the white man for almost a half-century, and already sustaining little knots of civilization connected by a spiderweb of trails, roads, and traces, the mountains still tolerated only those men who were tenacious and able enough to grapple the wilderness to some kind of compromise. It was a remote land, isolated by long distances and a dearth of navigable rivers, dictating a civilization that neither consumed nor produced in bulk—and it was not until the coming of the railroad made both possible that the West experienced the growth and development that marked the last three decades of the century.

It was a palatable bromide of the era, that railroads were an economic panacea. According to the formula, land values would spiral out of sight, crops would be marketable at a fraction of the cost, and if one were to believe the promotional literature that advertised land along the right-of-way, the rainfall would increase tenfold and the land would bloom in a crosstie-and-rail-nurtured cornucopia. Because everyone believed it, that was precisely what happened—for a while, at least. Paradoxically, the railroads later became too important. Their presence created farms and towns that depended entirely on rail service, with the lives of entire communities inexorably tied to the vacillating fortunes of the railroads. Before the century had run its course, the railroads would not only be credited with creating an empire but would be charged with destroying it as well. Both statements bear modification.

The Indians knew that the steam-belching juggernaut that laid footprints ahead of itself portended their demise, just as surely as the white man knew that his own brand of civilization would follow the rails. The railroad tied the mountain West to the rest of the nation, revived a waning mining industry, and started and sustained grazing and agriculture on the high plains and in the mountains. Small cities—tiny facsimiles of eastern metropolises, it was hoped—began to grow up, as families brought west the institutions and artifacts of a pre-rail life-style they had left behind. Sodbusters and merchants began to arrive in numbers —men who built and perpetuated society by demanding stability and order, men who represented, not the cutting edge of the frontier, but the steamroller of civilization.

WHEN GRENVILLE DODGE took his Union Pacific construction crews out on the plains west of Omaha in the spring of 1866 and pointed them toward the sunset, he set in motion an old and often delayed dream. Behind Dodge and his gandy dancers lay two decades of sectional bickering and financial maneuvering. A transcontinental railroad, the Industrial Revolution's contribution to Manifest Destiny, began to receive serious consideration in 1848, when the Treaty of Guadalupe Hidalgo provided the final act in a three-year drama of acquisition that roughed in the outlines of the nation.

It was agreed that the railroad was necessary to tie

*The narrow gauge Denver & Rio Grande, resurrected more by sentiment than need,
now carries tourists along the Animas River between Silverton and Durango.*

193

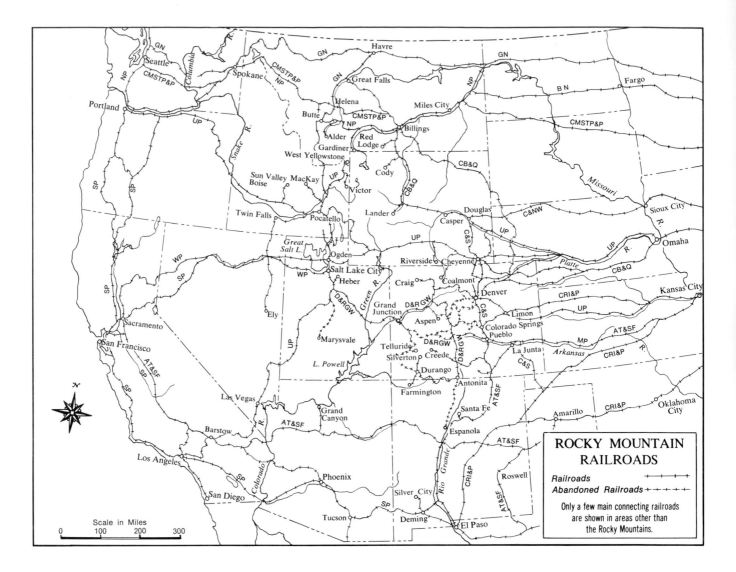

the new domain in the West to the East, but the project withered in the heat of the approaching sectional crisis; partisans of the northern and southern routes, determined to insure their respective regions the wealth and influence that would accrue from the line, argued the project to a standstill throughout the fifties. The coming of the Civil War, while settling the question of route, distracted the men and money needed for construction. By the time the problem of financing had been solved—with land grants that totalled 12,800 acres per mile and government loans for each mile of track laid of $16,000 on the flatlands, $32,000 in the foothills, and $48,000 in the mountains —the war was over, and a depression in the East had

provided a ready pool of labor. The problem of finding immediate cash was solved by the creation of the *Credit Mobilier,* an ingenious economic institution that was only a little bit crooked.

Despite decidedly inauspicious beginnings, the railroad built deliberately up the wide valley of the Platte through two summers, reaching the eastern apron of the Rockies in the fall of 1867, there establishing an end-of-track winter camp at Cheyenne. Like the earliest explorers, immigrants, and gold-seekers, the Union Pacific was interested not in the mountains but, rather, in what lay beyond them; with the coming of spring a dash for the other side of the barrier was launched that was not even slowed by the following winter. Preoccupied with acquiring as much of the lucrative federal land and cash subsidy as possible, and disinterested in a land of apparent limited potential value, construction hurried across Wyoming, indifferently scattering the seeds of statehood along the roadbed.

The activity that built the Union Pacific also built Wyoming. The ever-moving end-of-track carried with it a little town to serve the needs of the construction gangs: a motley group of gambling dens, saloons, and bordellos, collectively known as Hell-On-Wheels, that leap-frogged along the right-of-way always staying invitingly close to the workers. Many of the little towns thus born were begun with great expectation, as streets were laid out and buildings thrown up, and speculation in city lots built paper fortunes; but as the railhead passed by, taking with it the ready cash, booze, gamblers, and whores, most of the hopeful little towns dried up in the high, dry winds of the Wyoming shortgrass country. Some, like Cheyenne, survived as division points or junctions; others, like Laramie, remained as tie camps, providing the materials of construction. Even those that survived depended entirely on the railroad; until the development of the range cattle industry gave Wyoming the tools to create its own wealth, railside service to traffic bound for other regions provided the only livelihood.

But before the excitement waned and the population dwindled with the passing of construction, a small—and, it turned out, unwarranted—gold rush near the Continental Divide created South Pass City, Atlantic City, and Miner's Delight. Between the gold and the apparent, though short-lived, vitality brought by the Union Pacific, enough enthusiasm was generated to create Wyoming Territory in 1868—the federal officials arriving just in time to watch most of the money and population, and all of the vigor, leave the territory on what had become a through track.

As Wyoming enjoyed a year of eager optimism before prosperity closed down, the Saints to the west in the valley of the Salt Lake evinced some uncharacteristic ambivalence regarding the approaching rails. Although eager at the prospect of a railroad to import industrial machinery and additional converts, the Mormons recognized that the railroad would break down the insularity that had protected their religion, built local industry, and encouraged self-sufficiency. Fears of

Gen. Grenville Dodge, shortly before taking charge of construction on the Union Pacific.

a powerful Gentile merchant class or a mining boom with its attendant aliens arriving with the railroad were very real, and Brigham Young prepared with propaganda and pressure to de-emphasize mining prospects and insure that everyone would "buy Mormon."

In an effort to reap a worldly dollar—and to avoid the mobile Sodom and Gomorrah that had accompanied track construction across the continent—the trustees of the church took bids on 150 miles of grading, tie-laying, and tunneling for both the eastward-building Central Pacific and the westbound Union Pacific worth $2,000,000. The Union Pacific, avoiding the tangled canyons east of Salt Lake City, ran the line instead to the north through Ogden, forcing the church to build thirty-seven miles of Utah Central Railroad to connect Salt Lake with the outside world. The coming of the railroad had bred fears among the Saints of subjugation to, or infection by, an imperfect outside civilization, but while the rails increased contact, Gentile inroads were modest. The most devas-

tating result of the transcontinental line on Zion resulted from the construction contract: the Central Pacific and the Union Pacific both defaulted on payment of over half the contract, leaving the church with over $1,200,000 in debts. Given the experiences of a long history of contact with their fellow countrymen, they really shouldn't have been surprised.

THE TRANSCONTINENTAL LINE, although essential to the development of the mountain West, had been built principally to tie the two coasts of the nation together. Building along the geographic line of least resistance, the railroad made no effort to connect with Denver and Salt Lake City, the two largest existing population centers in the mountains, thereby condemning both to a quick demise, as population, business, and commerce relocated along the right-of-way—or so experience and frontier economic axiom dictated. But the Mormons, characteristically atypical, used the singular advantage of religious solidarity to marshal the money and muscle necessary to build the connecting Utah Central. Denver, lacking any special advantages, should have faded away and died—and, indeed, almost did.

Denver's troubles began when Grenville Dodge elected to avoid the city after it became apparent that the mountains to the west presented too many obstacles to construction. As the railhead neared the mountains in 1867, a sense of futility settled deeply over the town, and the more realistic merchants and speculators decamped for the promising settlement at Cheyenne. Early in 1868 a traveler noted of the town that, "The old mining excitement has ceased. The old overland stage has stopped and its business rushes past on a railroad one hundred miles to the north. Business is dull; the town is quiet. . . ." What the traveler failed to notice was the quixotic optimism loose in the town.

Almost immediately upon hearing the Union Pacific's verdict, the business leaders of Denver began looking for an alternative. What they found was the Kansas Pacific Railroad—in 1867 an economic derelict wandering west from St. Louis under the guise of the "Union Pacific, Eastern Division"—subsisting on a series of railhead cattle towns. Denver appealed to the Kansas Pacific and lobbied in Washington, limning

William J. Palmer built the Denver & Rio Grande, Colorado Springs, and an enduring legend.

rosy pictures of a venture profitable for all—so successfully, in fact, that the Kansas Pacific decided that with such an obviously lucrative future it would ignore Denver and strike far south of the city, heading for an eventual connection with the Central Pacific. Convinced of the perfidy of all outsiders, Denverites determined that their only salvation lay in building their own connecting line to Cheyenne.

Grading on what would become the Denver Pacific Railroad was begun in the summer of 1868, even as the town peddled $2,000,000 worth of construction bonds to skeptical eastern markets. As the work moved north, news arrived that the Kansas Pacific had been forced to curb its ambitions after being denied federal construction loans and land grants, and once again was building toward Denver. Prosperity began to return as the work on both lines proceeded apace, employing graders, gandy dancers, tie cutters, and teamsters—who in turn helped to rejuvenate the economy

Cornish miners, brought west to work the lodes, often sold the railroads their expertise on tunneling projects. This group posed with their handiwork on the Colorado Midland in 1886.

A group of passengers on the Silverton Railroad transfer to wagons at Red Mountain Pass. The bearded gentleman (fourth from right) is Otto Mears, the line's determined founder.

by magnificent consumption of food, beverage, and sundry other excesses of the flesh. Merchants started to return, real estate rose, and the city launched on a boom that transcended the placer gold days. The disastrous news of 1867 had been turned to triumph in just three years; the arrival in June 1870 of the first train from Cheyenne was followed in August by the initial rail traffic from St. Louis. Denver was suddenly the junction through which flowed all the goods, services, and produce of a booming Colorado mining industry. The warm sense of security and accomplishment was short-lived, however, as a new threat to the town's commercial ascendency became apparent.

The Atchison, Topeka, and Santa Fe began construction in 1870, prospering on the growing cattle trade in Kansas and Colorado and cornering the Texas beef market by intersecting the cattle trails farther south than any other line. The line headed straight for Pueblo, Colorado, threatening to divert the lucrative markets of southern Colorado that Denver had so carefully cultivated. The threat was real; if Denver was to maintain dominance as a distribution center,

it had to find a way to draw the traffic of the south directly north away from the Atchison, Topeka, and Santa Fe.

Even as the AT&SF nosed out onto the plains in 1870, Denver's salvation was being organized in the form of the narrow-gauge Denver and Rio Grande Railroad. The line was the pet of Gen. William J. Palmer, construction engineer from the Kansas Pacific, for whom railroading was more an obsession than a business. Palmer's line, which ran south from Denver to Pueblo en route to tapping the transcontinental lines being built along the southern route, guaranteed a competitive mercantile position for Denver; incidentally, it marked the beginning of an escalating struggle that Palmer and his privately owned line waged against the corporate and federally subsidized AT&SF for control of transportation in Colorado and the Southwest. For ten years the two lines competed in construction and in court, culminating in two years of litigation that gave control of the Royal Gorge of the Arkansas, and consequently a monopoly on service to the rich silver camp of Leadville, to the Denver and

End of the line for the Denver & Rio Grande in Creede, Colorado—another of those brief cooperations between town and railroad for mutual benefit and survival.

Rio Grande. With that decision, the AT&SF ceased further building in the Colorado Rockies, and began to focus their attention on building an empire in the Southwest.

The profits that were realized from the line to Leadville were immense, but rather than retiring with his fortune, Palmer immediately sank it into continued construction, which ultimately laced up both sides of the Continental Divide. Working without government subsidy, Palmer pushed his three-foot wide tracks (which permitted steeper grades, tighter turns, lower construction costs, and cheaper rolling stock) west through Gunnison to Grand Junction and south into northern New Mexico. Hoping to imitate the success at Leadville, his rails followed the miners to Silverton and Creede in the San Juans.

Palmer's enthusiasm had a price, however. In 1882 his stockholders, angry after years of construction that gobbled up profits and a little frightened that the line might have overextended itself, forced Palmer out of the presidency of the Denver and Rio Grande. In time, as the silver played out and towns began to shrivel,

the empire that Palmer had conceived and nurtured began to die from disuse. Pursuing scraps of civilization high in the mountains, he had expended more effort and capital than the region could return without its precious metals. Like the prospectors two decades earlier, Palmer and the Denver and Rio Grande had followed a dream that was prompted as much by a passion for the act as the profit to be realized, finally enjoying the chase more than the accomplishment.

But Palmer was not alone in his passion. It was as if men were smitten by the challenge of twisted canyons, narrow gorges, steep grades, and high passes. The Colorado Rockies were probably the most difficult place to lay track in the United States, and yet for over half a century little lines kept appearing, many fading with the passage of time and mining excitement. Lines long and short, standard and narrow gauge, reached west to Utah, south to New Mexico, and deep into the mountains—all seeking cities and population to sustain them. Many were risky ventures, of so much more value to the towns they reached than the towns could ever be to them, that from present

Jolly excursionists on the Colorado Midland Railroad, detraining for a picnic, pause to mug for the photographer. Tourist hauls out of Colorado Springs were common in the 1890s.

perspective the builders begin to look like selfless philanthropists. The railroads were named to express every kind of hope—Denver, South Park and Pacific, the Colorado Central and Pacific, the Colorado Midland, the Northwest and Pacific, the Rio Grande Western—and whether or not remnants remain today, they were names to conjure with in the experience of several generations of high country life.

But the obsession for building mountain-climbing railroads probably reached its zenith with a turnpike owner-operator named Otto Mears, who decided that what Colorado needed most was a rail connection between Silverton and Ouray. His project, which involved twenty-six miles of track, came within eight miles of completion before it was stopped cold by the narrow Uncompahgre Canyon. But exemplary of the class of mountain magnate he had chosen to join, Mears sought a way around his dilemma: he backtracked to Durango, looped northwest to Rico through the San Miguel Range, through Ophir and Telluride, and curved back down onto his goal from the north. Rails finally joined Silverton and Ouray; the eight miles had been circumvented, and it took only 217 miles of

track to accomplish the fact. There could be no doubt that Mears had joined the inner circle of the railroading fraternity.

THE CONSTRUCTION OF RAILROADS in the mountains was typically met with great expectations—justifiably. Railroads meant progress: cities that grew and prospered in a nascent industrial age; schools and churches, women and children, who lent a reassuring permanence; and prosperity that evolved from fully developed grazing and mining. But more than anything else, the railroads made possible the pursuit of the national passion for agriculture onto the high plains and mountains.

The small, independent family farm was a fixture of the American scene. Essential to Jefferson's concept of the Republic, it had somehow become a fact of the national consciousness that land had escaped the furrows of the yeoman farmer was not realizing its fullest potential. For the railroads, this mania spelled bonanza; not only did many of the lines, as a result of federal grants, own a great deal of the land that the

200

hopeful farmers would have to buy, but they would be assured of continuous paying customers who needed the line to move themselves along with their possessions, produce, and acquisitions. For the railroads, the greatest profits lay not in land sales, but in an established population that needed the rail service.

Establishing that population meant promoting the land's potential, and enthusiasm routinely outstripped probability. Jay Cook's Northern Pacific Railroad, before it collapsed in 1873, taking his bank and the American economy with it, proposed a garden so complete that it was derided in the press as "Jay Cook's Banana Belt." Every line that built west dabbled in superlatives to promote farming settlements along its lines—whether feasible or not—but none so grandly as J. J. Hill and the Great Northern Railroad.

James J. Hill took a defunct railroad, built it up with Canadian capital, and by 1890 was building a dream that was both visionary and quixotic. Working without government subsidies or land grants, Hill built his railroad across Montana and the Northwest on borrowed money and the faith that he could encourage people to settle along his right-of-way. Using all the promotional techniques of the era, buttressed with unfettered enthusiasm, Hill succeeded in enticing farmers onto the grasslands of eastern Montana and taught them to turn the sod upside down. By freely dispensing information, material, and low freight rates, the Great Northern built a market that helped the line to prosper at a time when railroads like the Northern Pacific (graced with government aid, and land grants that amounted to a land grab—25,600 acres per mile) were going bankrupt. Hill, capitalizing on the American fetish for farming, had done it all on advertising.

But unfortunately for Hill and his farmers, a railroad and rampant optimism won't grow crops. It became increasingly apparent during the nineties that rainfall that had sustained grass for cattle was inadequate for any kind of farming. Thousands realized this fact only after the sod was turned wrong side up

for grazing. Hill, in his exuberance, had created a wasteland in Montana—fit neither for farming nor grazing—and left a legacy of frustration and anger for a generation of farmers who had only been following an American dream.

RAILROADS CHANGED LIFE in the mountains, creating a civilization that depended on rail service for continued prosperity and existence. Everyone's fortunes were tied to them. The fiscal dry rot that began amid the chicanery of construction financing before long threatened the stability of most lines, and the periodic flux of America's boom-or-bust economics invariably seemed to shake loose some railroad that was barely hanging on to solvency. And when a western railroad was hurt, the people it served and sustained were usually devastated. What had been a beneficent agent of Progress, accelerating growth to such an extent that it created booms everywhere it went, would become the chief agent of economic debility in a region. The railroads were blamed for higher costs on goods, lower prices for produce, rising freight rates, falling property values, depressions, inflations, and sundry pestilences and dry spells—with justification in many instances, although occasionally the lines were as much victims themselves.

They had created a civilization that then demanded to be sustained, and when the task proved too great, the failure registered not only on the financial balance sheets, but in very human frustration and suffering. And although the railroads were found to have the frailties that man imparts to most of his institutions, there is always the suspicion that when farms failed or cities and citizens suffered depressions, the railroads were only part of a larger human error of expecting something more, or different, from the land than the mountain West had to offer. Rails had brought the mountains into a modern era, making it possible—for better or worse—for the Rockies to pursue life just like the rest of the nation.

CHAPTER 16

RED MAN'S LAST STAND

Threescore years of tragic struggle between Yankee farmers and
Indian nomads for a land that could never serve both

IN 1879 at the height of difficulties with the Ute Indians, Governor Pitkin of Colorado issued a statement: "My idea is that, unless removed by the government, they [the Utes] must necessarily be exterminated. I could raise 25,000 men to protect the settlers in twenty-four hours. The state would be willing to settle the Indian trouble at its own expense. The advantages that would accrue from the throwing open of 12,000,000 acres of land to miners and settlers would more than compensate all the expenses incurred."

Pitkin's attitude and appraisal of the situation was characteristic of most mountain folk; because they were a threat to the lives and property of the citizens of Colorado, and because they chose not to farm, mine, or cut timber, the Utes were wasting land a white man could use. As with any other natural phenomenon that stood in a man's way, it was only a matter of technology and grit to crush or circumvent the obstacle. The Indians were a nuisance, a problem to be solved by the most expeditious means available. If that meant packing them up bag and baggage—or failing that, annihilating them—then it had to be done. Unfortunately for the Indian, the white man's medicine was strong.

Before mid-century the Indians along the cordillera were sovereign, although they were forced to trade with whites for hardware; and despite a marked susceptibility to the white man's disease, booze, and cannon, the Indians of the mountain West nonetheless commanded the respect and fear of any who trespassed on their hunting grounds. Products of a warrior society —in which fulfillment and success were not sought in honest toil and good works, but rather were measured in terms of the individual's ability to smite his neighbor and steal his goods—the Indian of the high Plains and mountains acquired a well-deserved reputation for ferocity and skill in the martial arts. During the first four decades of contact, when an Indian stole a white man's horse or his hair, he seldom felt any personal animosity—he was simply a man fulfilling a cultural heritage. But as the white man's presence in the mountain region increased, this would change—the conflict would become, eventually, a war for survival.

The conflict began not because men came to the mountains, but because they passed through, following the lure of Oregon and California. There had been minor depredations along the North Platte River (the Oregon Trail) during the 1840s, consisting mostly of small Sioux raids, but they never really grew to concerted warfare against the emigrant groups. The federal government nonetheless sought a solution by calling a general peace conference. Thomas Fitzpatrick, the United States' agent for the high Plains Indians, and D. D. Mitchell, the superintendent for Indian affairs at St. Louis, assembled some ten thousand Sioux, Cheyennes, Arapahos, Crows, Assinboines, Gros Ventres, and Shoshonis at Fort Laramie in September of 1851 to seek a solution. The entire group was forced immediately to decamp for Horse Creek, thirty-five miles down the North Platte, to find enough graze to pasture the tens of thousands of horses.

After several days of eloquent speech-making, an agreement was reached and a "treaty" signed, which

Cultural counterpoint: Sioux of the Pine Ridge Reservation reflect the dilemma of a defeated
people—forbidden the old life, not assimilated into the new, living with shreds of each.

The principals of the Camp Weld Council, September 1864. The Indians, given assurances of safety, returned to their camp on Sand Creek—only to be slaughtered by Chivington. Agent Wynkoop kneels, left.

stated that the Indians would not fight among themselves, that they would confine themselves to specific territories, that the Americans could build roads and mountain forts through these lands, and that the Indians would be compensated for grass, buffalo, and timber lost to emigrants in the amount of $50,000 in goods per annum for fifty years. This Treaty of Fort Laramie, remarkable primarily as the first major document of U.S.-Indian relations in the mountain West, had some other notable features: for one thing, the Shoshonis, though present, were ignored, and their traditional hunting ground given (by the United States!) to the Crows; the individual tribes, though agreeing to boundaries on their lands, relinquished no rights for hunting, fishing, or trespass on any lands they had ever used; the U.S. Senate (without ever informing the

Col. John M. Chivington, the one-time preacher who led the pre-dawn massacre at Sand Creek.

This engraving from an eastern tabloid of the day attempted to depict the defeat of Captain Fetterman and his hapless troop of eighty-one along the Bozeman Trail in 1866.

Indians) unilaterally changed the treaty to provide the annuity for only ten years; and finally, the Indians never had any intention of allowing the treaty to alter their lives in any way save for the annual collection of goods.

The treaty, though conciliatory and well-intentioned, had little real effect on Indian-white relations in the mountain region. The most remarkable aspect of the meeting was the fact that 200 soldiers managed to keep 10,000 Indians—most of whom shared intertribal rivalries of ancestral proportions—from turning Horse Creek into a slaughterhouse.

The treaty temporarily curbed raiding along the Oregon Trail, but by 1854 the Indians—unhappy over emigrants and traders who cheated them; the rising incidence of smallpox, measles, and cholora; and the depletion of grass and game along the Platte—were becoming restive. One band of Cheyennes threatened to begin raiding unless (1) the wagon trains stopped, (2) they received their entire annuity in cash and guns,

and (3) a thousand white women were handed over for wives. But before the Cheyennes could really press their demand, a very ordinary incident occurred which, because of the pent-up tensions, touched off almost three years of bloody reprisals.

It began with a Mormon cow that wandered away from its wagon and into a Brulé Sioux cook-pot. Because it happened near Fort Laramie, Bear-That-Scatters, the head of the band, came in to make amends and settle up. Unfortunately, an impetuous young lieutenant named Grattan, dissatisfied with the arrangement and bent on making an example of the offender, was permitted to go to the Brulé camp to arrest the guilty Indian. Although accounts of what transpired vary somewhat, in the end Grattan found himself trying to pick a fight in the middle of fifteen hundred Sioux. An official report on the incident would later state that "no doubt Lieutenant Grattan's want of knowledge of the Indian character, and the rash language used by a drunken interpreter, was the cause of the

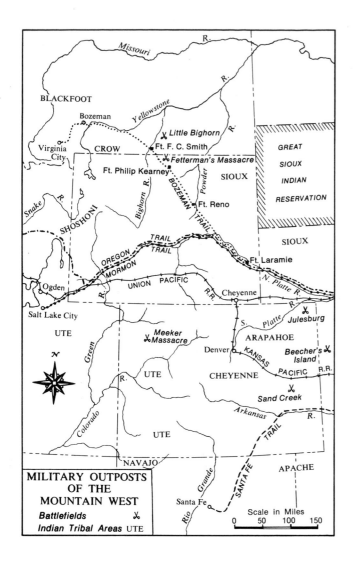

MILITARY OUTPOSTS
OF THE
MOUNTAIN WEST
Battlefields ✘
Indian Tribal Areas UTE

Relations were deteriorating elsewhere, as well. During 1856, in isolated incidents, the army killed several Indians near Casper, Wyoming; Indians and freight teamsters staged a shoot-out along the Platte in Nebraska; a Platte River emigrant train was attacked, a woman killed, and a child taken captive; and A. W. Babbitt, secretary for Utah Territory, was ambushed and killed en route to his post. This kind of conflict, occasionally flaring into full-scale war, would mark Indian-white relations for thirty years.

In 1857 the Cheyennes had grown sufficiently pesky to warrant a campaign. Col. Edwin Sumner, like Harney with the Sioux, chased any Cheyennes he found—regardless of guilt—until he managed to corner a band, kill a few Indians, and destroy their winter supplies. At the campaign's conclusion, as with Harney's, the Indians agreed to behave, the government promised to send goods, and neither lived up to the arrangement.

T HE COMING OF THE CIVIL WAR diverted national attention and garrison troops from the mountain West. The Indians continued their raiding along the emigrant road, but an undermanned army was hard-pressed to retaliate. By the spring of 1862 the Indians were striking all across Wyoming, from Fort Bridger to Fort Laramie, pursued largely by green troops composed of Californians and Mormon volunteers. Along the Continental Divide in Wyoming and westward, the Bannock* and Shoshonis harassed travelers and the Mormon missions until Gen. Patrick Conner (who also had harassed the Mormon missions) caught a large encampment on the Bear River in southern Idaho and enthusiastically slaughtered 250 Indians. But for the most part, the army fought a holding action against isolated raiders—except along the Front Range in Colorado.

The Arapahos and Cheyennes, preemptively pushed

unfortunate affair." Whatever the cause, the lieutenant, his troop of twenty-nine men, and a drunken interpreter managed to fire a volley that killed one Indian before they were killed to a man.

Responding to the "Grattan Massacre," as it came to be known, the government sent Col. William S. Harney on a punitive expedition against the Sioux. As the column embarked, Harney remarked, "By God, I'm for battle—no peace"; and true to his word, he trapped a Sioux band at Ash Hollow on the North Platte, refused two offers of armistice, and killed 86 men, women, and children, while losing four of his own men. The cost of one Mormon cow, so far, was 122 lives.

---

*The spelling of this name—whether in reference to a mining camp in Idaho, a city in Montana, or, as here, a distinct group of northern Paiutes—never fails to stir passions among local and regional writers. Rather than enter the fray, suffice it to say that the Indians could spell neither "Bannock" nor "Bannack," and early semi-literate whites evinced remarkable ingenuity in rendering the name ("Banek," "Banick," etc.). Lacking a personal bias, "Bannock" was arbitrarily selected for use here.

into a small reserve in southeast Colorado after the Pikes Peak mining rush, began raiding prairie commerce as western military forces diminished during the early 1860s. As the raiding increased, supplies became scarce and prices rose; the citizens of Denver convinced themselves that an Indian war was in the offing, and in early 1864 Governor John Evans raised a regiment of cavalry under the command of Col. John M. Chivington. Chivington, an amateur soldier and former preacher, was eager to sustain a military reputation recently acquired when he led a flanking action by Colorado volunteers that destroyed an invading Confederate Army at Glorieta Pass in 1862. Unfortunately, Chivington regarded his current assignment as a holy war of extermination.

Chivington led his troop of a thousand horsemen to an encampment of Cheyennes and Arapahos gathered on Sand Creek under the protection of Indian Agent E. W. Wynkoop. Despite obvious evidences of the Indians' peaceful intent—including an American flag flying in the village—the colonel attacked at dawn, killing indiscriminately. Estimates of the dead ranged as high as six-hundred men, women, and children—although the regiment only bothered to bring back a hundred souvenir scalps.

Chivington was censured and castigated for his role in the Sand Creek Massacre, though not by very many of his high country neighbors. A storm of protest raged in Congress and the eastern press for a time—largely to no effect. The Cheyennes, however, did more than talk: in January 1865 they killed nine veterans of Chivington's army; shortly thereafter they overran and looted Julesberg, Colorado.

WITH THE END OF THE WAR in the East, attention once again focused on the mountains and far West. Railroads gained speed, emigration increased, and the pressure of miners and ranchers for traditionally Indian land in the Rockies pushed the army once more into conflict with the aborigines. A typical instance involved the Bozeman Road.

John Bozeman had blazed a trail northwestward from Fort Laramie to the goldfields in Montana, a direct and popular route. Unfortunately, it ran through traditional Sioux hunting grounds. The Sioux began

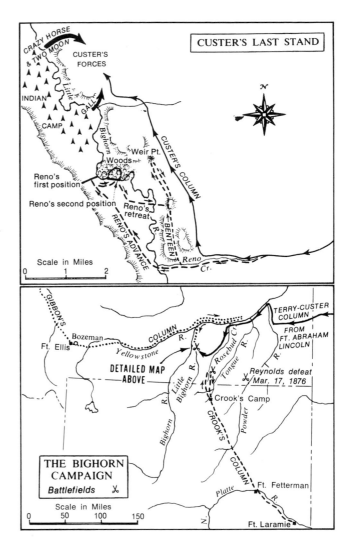

raiding along the road immediately, and the army moved to fortify the route. Col. Henry Carrington built Fort Phil Kearny, in direct violation of an agreement with the Sioux, who responded by luring one of Carrington's officers, Col. Wm. J. Fetterman, into an ambush. The Sioux snuffed out eighty-two officers and men, and the government began to re-evaluate its position on the Bozeman Road. With the Laramie Treaty of 1868 the army agreed to stay out of Sioux territory, and the Sioux in turn promised not to annihilate any more inexperienced officers. But the demands of Americans for access to land and minerals in the Rockies would soon overcome fear of the Indians and any governmental policy.

Officers and ladies of the Seventh Cavalry pose at Fort Abraham Lincoln. The rakish fellow third from the left is their commander, Gen. George Armstrong Custer.

The Black Hills, part of the Indian territory declared inviolate by the Laramie Treaty of 1868, were coveted by prospectors who, having exhausted the placers of Colorado, Montana, and Idaho, speculated that fortune waited in the narrow canyons. By 1874 interest had grown so keen that Lt. Col. George A. Custer led a reconnaissance through the region—in direct violation of the treaty. His report confirmed the suspicions, and the government decided the land was too valuable for Indians. An embarrassingly small offer was made in an effort to buy the land, and when the Indians refused, President Grant ordered them off the land and onto reservations by January of 1876. Any Indians remaining outside the agencies were declared hostile, and in May of the same year a three-pronged expedition was launched into an area between the Bighorn Mountains and the Yellowstone River to round them up.

Gen. George Crook marched from the south, Gen. John Gibbon from the west, and Gen. Alfred Terry from the east. With Terry was a lieutenant colonel, then breveted to brigadier general, named Custer—the same who had led the treaty-defying summer excursion of 1874. Custer, the "boy general" of the Civil War, had led a checkered career in the West. After a winter campaign against the Cheyennes in which he began to build a reputation by a surprise assault on a large band on the Washita, he was nearly cashiered out of the service for criticizing the army before a congressional committee. Motivated by ambition and pride, he rode in the vanguard of Terry's troops, intent on

Sitting Bull, Sioux medicine man who organized the attack on Custer at the Little Big Horn.

Ouray, the Ute leader who practiced conciliation and coexistence with the whites—and lost his homeland.

restoring his reputation and emerging a national hero. Immortality, of a sort, was to be his.

Crook, riding north from Fort Fetterman, made the first contact of the campaign, fighting a day-long battle to a draw with some 2,000 Sioux and Cheyennes. His soldiers were resting along Goose Creek in the Bighorn Mountains on June 25, even as Custer and the Seventh Cavalry, scouting for Terry, advanced on the Little Bighorn River.

Custer commanded a force of 630, with which he was to scout the enemy and prepare for a general attack by Gibbon and Terry. Seeking a victory for himself, he refused to believe his Crow scouts, who warned of 2,000 hostiles ready for battle, and divided his command into four units for a surprise attack on the vil-

lage. In actuality, there were at least 3,000 Sioux and Cheyennes, led by Sitting Bull, Crazy Horse, Gall, and others—all better armed than Indians had ever been before. Blinded by ambition, Custer, a normally brilliant tactician, threw caution to the wind and led 220 men into a short, swift massacre. By the time reinforcements arrived, the Indians had worked their destruction and departed.

The Custer massacre, ignominious and unnecessary, led nonetheless to the Indians' final defeat. Concerted retaliatory campaigns were mounted throughout the summer and winter of 1876 by Crook and Gen. Nelson Miles, destroying lodges, food stores, and horses. The Indians, having expended most of their ammunition in killing Custer's regiment, could only scatter before

*Council at the Pine Ridge Reservation in 1890, during which the Indians squabbled over
their future course of action, shortly prior to the massacre at Wounded Knee.*

the advancing troops. By the end of winter most of the hostiles, facing starvation, returned to the agencies. Barring some escapes from the reservation and the final spasm of resistance at Wounded Knee, the "Indian problem" on the high Plains had been solved.

The Utes of western Colorado had lived largely unmolested since the American acquisition of their territory after the Mexican War. It was not until 1868 that anyone even bothered to establish a reservation; even afterward, they enjoyed isolation and most of their traditional hunting grounds. But in 1873 they lost a large section of the San Juan Mountains, and from then on their holdings were whittled away by mining interests and land-hungry farmers.

Guided most of this time by a gentle, conciliatory headman called Ouray, the Utes had retreated amicably before the greed of whites who failed to keep one agreement after another. Trouble erupted when Americans grew tired of merely taking their land and began telling them how to live. Nathan Meeker, founder of the agricultural colony at Greeley, was by 1879 the agent of the White River Reservation in western Colorado. He forced the Utes to give up their tipis, plowed their pastures, and threatened to starve those who would not take up farming. Most Utes remained stubbornly uncooperative until Meeker plowed up their racetrack, symbol of their national pastime. A band of young hotheads then killed Meeker and his staff, and carried off the women and children. Maj. T. T. Thornburg, sent to the rescue, was ambushed and killed along with eleven troopers, and Coloradans hysterically demanded the complete removal of the Utes to prevent a recurrence of the incident. Besides, that was pretty good farmland they were sitting on. By June of 1880 the Utes had been tossed over the line into Utah and New Mexico, and another "Indian problem" solved.

THE INDIANS of the mountain West had been an obstacle to emigration, exploration, and settlement; like all of the other physical obstacles—isolation, aridity, and geography—they had been swept before an overpowering and inexorable white tide of technology, ingenuity, and population. The two societies could not coexist, conflicting in concepts of ownership, land use, wealth, success, and the myriad mores and values that guide a man's life. If one occupied the land, the other, of necessity, must leave entirely. Indians on land whites wanted to use were a nuisance, a stumbling block in the march of Progress, and the government solved the "Indian problem" by removing them entirely, squeezing them onto progressively smaller and more remote reserves.

The "final solution" was to reeducate the Indians, to transform them into white men. Agents worked actively to break down tribal leadership, destroy native religions, and make their charges completely dependent upon the government for food. They forbade traditional feasts and dances, polygamy, purchase of wives, and the destruction of property as an expression of grief. Indians like the Sioux and Cheyennes, and even the Utes and Shoshonis, grew angry as their families starved and their pride was progressively eroded. Thus it was that they snatched at faint hopes of solution, and in the case of the Sioux especially, realized tragic consequences.

In the late 1880s word spread among the Indians of a new Messiah in the West, a Paiute who promised a millennium to the Indian. The whites would be buried under an avalanche of mud, he predicted, and the grass would again grow for their ponies, and the Indian would return to his former glory. It was a nostalgic prophesy, a revival, and as such the final futile hope of a people unwilling or unable to adjust to the new conditions that existed. The teachings of the Paiutes were passive, even pacifistic—just keep the faith and the Deity would do the rest—but when a warrior society like the Sioux interpreted the new religion it emerged that Wakantanka might need a little temporal assistance. As historian Robert Utley notes, "Each tribe shaped the religion to the framework of its own mythology, and each individual adherent added further embellishments of his own."

The Sioux ascribed supernatural powers to the ceremonial shirt the Paiutes prescribed—claiming it rendered them invulnerable to soldiers' bullets—and prepared for the day of reckoning. The army and Indian agents, seeking to suppress the new religion at the Pine Ridge Agency, herded over a hundred of the Ghost Dancers (as followers of the ritual were then being called) together at Wounded Knee to disarm them. With very little to lose, and the hope of restoring the past in the offing, the Sioux lashed out. Surrounded and outnumbered, at least 84 men and boys, 44 women, and 18 small children fell under the fire of Hotchkiss guns. In its desperate hope, futile challenge, and the utter finality of outcome, the massacre at Wounded Knee climaxed a half century of conflict and convinced even skeptics and prophets that life as the high country Indian had known it had come to an end.

CHAPTER 17

AN EMPIRE OF GRASS

The cattle business, from free range to fenced ranches—three decades
of a pursuit that stirred the imagination of the nation

OR OVER TWO HUNDRED YEARS of colonial and national life, the husbandry of cows was a routine part of American life. Cattle-raising during those years was usually a subsidiary operation to farming, or a task conducted just beyond the edge of the agricultural frontier by men who hoped someday to improve their station. But as stock-raising developed on the high plains of the mountain West, it took on a new demeanor. It adopted pretentions to empire, ceasing to be farming's poor relation, and became a dynamic industry that caught the public fancy.

The cattle business in the mountain West began routinely as an adjunct of overland migration, satisfying travelers' demands for dray stock, and continued to grow and prosper by providing beef to the mining industry. When the growing demands of an increasingly urbanized East were combined with the technology for reaching that market, the business evolved into an enterprise that no cowherd from the eastern woodland frontier would have recognized.

The open-range cattle industry excited both young men seeking adventure and cautious capitalists seeking investments, and in the course of less than a quarter of a century, it rose to a pitch scarcely exceeded by the mineral rush. Stock-raising on the open range built empires where only grass could grow; it roused rail towns like Cheyenne and Miles City from the torpor that followed construction; and it absorbed some of the shock of the often violent vacillations of the mining economy. It created the cowboy, the keystone figure of the American pantheon of heroes, and provided the

rationale for an action genre that has dominated popular literature and film ever since. And while its demise was almost foreordained—a victim of both progress and its own growth—it helped to nourish and sustain the mountain West for twenty-five years, and was the predecessor of a ranching industry that has ultimately proved to be a stable and permanent contributor to the high-country economy.

The range cattle industry that developed on the northern plains had its beginnings in Texas, where a beef bonanza had begun unnoticed and virtually unattended. In the verdant river valleys south of San Antonio, wild Mexican stock and an occasional settler's cow had multiplied and flourished. Markets were remote, prices low, and except for a random hide-and-tallow hunter, the Texans had ignored the increasing herds. But the end of the Civil War provided the conditions for change.

The burgeoning industrial centers of the East and Old Northwest created a demand for meat that pushed the price of beef to $30 to $40 a head. Texans, financially prostrated by the war and seeking an alternative for a temporarily devastated cotton industry, had a surplus of beeves, usually figured to be worth $3 to $4 a head. This figure was a concession to Lone Star pride, as it was the rare Texan who had $3 in cash to spend on a cow; initially, they were free for the price of a man's sweat and the wear-and-tear on his horse. Obviously, there was a fortune waiting for anyone willing to run the stock down and able to figure a way to get the $3 cow to the $30 market. The answer lay

Evoking fragile memories of longhorns and mustangs, this latter-day cowhand in the
Jemez Mountains herds registered herefords from his blooded quarterhorse.

Roundups meant long hours and hard work. This action shot of calf-branding in Wyoming was caught by Charlie Belden, probably the best of the old-time cowboy photographers.

in the animal itself. The tall, rangy, slab-sided, more-horn-than-meat critters that had evolved in the brush country—the longhorns, revered by everyone who never had to chase or eat one—were fast and durable, and therefore able to walk themselves to market. But while the concept was simple, carrying it out was another matter.

Although the long drive was not an entirely new idea—Ed Piper had driven a thousand head from Texas to Ohio as early as 1846—when Texans began driving in earnest in the late 1860s the techniques they tried for handling several thousand head of cattle were quickly refined through experience.

In the spring, herds began heading north out of Texas as soon as the grasses greened up enough for feeding, and they continued to leave into the summer, until the threat of being caught on the trail by winter stopped the exodus for another year. Herds usually numbered from 2,500 to 3,000 head, a size generally conceded to be both manageable and profitable. A

herd that size required a crew of eight to ten drovers, and a crew that size required a cook; a *remuda* sufficient to provide five to eight mounts per drover was tended by a wrangler. Commanding it all was a trail boss—euphemistically known as "God on a Horse."

A day began early, well before first light, with the cook building breakfast; activity increased with the light, as men rose, the *remuda* was brought in, and the herd began to move off the bed-ground, feeding slowly up the trail. The tempo increased further as men finished eating, horses were caught up inside a rope corral, and a lone jughead worked the stiffness of a cold night out of himself and his rider with a few jumps around his tail—for both, a minor ritual in celebration of a new day.

A herd moved slowly through the morning, often grazing only a few miles; pausing during the heat of midday, it would then push on again in the late afternoon. Progress was deliberate, even slow, usually averaging fifteen miles a day, for with judicious handling

J. G. McCoy, the man who brought the Texas drive and the railroad together at Abilene.

John Iliff, Colorado rancher-butcher whose holdings included most of the South Platte range.

and a little luck, cattle could finish a drive heavier than they began it. With nightfall the cattle were herded onto a bed-ground, night horses staked close to beds, drovers were fed, and bedrolls sought out for a short night's sleep—made even shorter by the two hours of night guard that every drover stood.

The daily cycle was tedious, the pay poor, the diet dull, and the dust thick. Between stampedes, flooded river crossings, homicidal horses, occasional Indians, and droughts—which could leave a herd with neither water nor grass—trail-driving emerged as an unpleasant business. And it was almost ended before it really got started.

When Texans in 1866 began moving stock across Kansas and Missouri seeking markets, they ran into an advancing agricultural frontier that was decidedly hostile. Farmers who objected to longhorns trampling their fields and infecting their own stock with Texas fever, scattered herds and beat drovers; some even stole or shot the Texas stock. By 1867 both Kansas and Mis-

souri had passed quarantine laws designed to keep Texas cattle out. Such laws would plague the Texas cattle industry for the next twenty years, and it was only a combination of indifferent enforcement, the railroads, and a man named McCoy that kept the long drive alive.

From 1867 on, the railroads, the trail herds, and the farmers played an elaborate game of tag across the middle border, which began when Joseph G. McCoy invited the Kansas-Pacific Railroad and some Texas trail herders to meet under his auspices at Abilene, Kansas. Abilene, a railhead town in 1867, was still west of the leading edge of the agricultural frontier and therefore beyond farmer and local stock grazer demands for enforcement of the quarantine law. Abilene would lose its isolation and therefore its value as a railhead, but a pattern had been established that would be repeated for twenty years: cattlemen avoiding the law by skirting the fringe of civilization, railroads jousting for position as they reached out to the

The rope corral, a jerry-rigged affair to hold horses just long enough for hands to catch the morning's mount. The wagon stacked with bedrolls was moved daily with the chuck wagon.

herds moving north, and the farming frontier creeping inexorably forward in the wake of the railroads, forcing the drovers farther west once again.

The Atchison, Topeka and Santa Fe quickly preempted the Kansas-Pacific's role in transporting stock by following a more southerly route and establishing railhead towns successively at Newton, Ellsworth, and Dodge City. Competition between towns and railroads seeking to be more convenient to the trail drivers resulted in Hays and Wichita. Even if it wasn't outflanked by a competing railroad, each railhead cowtown carried the seeds of its own destruction, because farmers follow railroads. Finally, even Dodge City closed as a cowtown, not because of competition, but because a growing number of local farmers and stockmen demanded that the quarantine laws be enforced. The drives were eventually squeezed into a narrow corridor running up the eastern border of Colorado —and that remained open only because authorities chose to wink at the law.

BUT EVEN AS THE DROVERS began twenty years of cat-and-mouse with farmers and quarantines, a change began to develop when the Texas men made two discoveries: first, that the market for their cattle was not infinite, and shortly thereafter, that longhorns wintered on the grama and buffalo grass of the northern plains got slick, put on weight, and brought a lot more money in eastern markets. What developed from these two realizations was a cattle business on the northern plains and in the mountain states that would eventually rival that in Texas.

Within two years after McCoy's first shipment of cattle to Chicago had demonstrated that transactions in Texas cattle could be profitable, the number of cattle moving north out of Texas had reached flood stage with surpluses constantly building up at railhead and packinghouse. An immediate outlet was found for the excess on the ranges of Colorado, Wyoming, and Montana. In 1871, an additional 300,000 head of unsold stock were thrown onto the northern

A roundup crew takes its noon meal at the chuck wagon near Trinidad, Colorado. These boyish faces would age quickly under the influence of long hours, limited diet, and bone-busting labor.

grasslands, and an empire was begun.

The northern grasslands had demonstrated an ability to sustain livestock years before the longhorn deluge. During the early years of the overland migration, such points along the route as Forts Laramie and Bridger and the Mormon settlements, made phenomenal profits trading fresh cattle and oxen for starving and sore-footed stock. These they fed up on the native grasses and passed off the next year at equally usurious rates. Pursuing this practice, a number of "road ranches" developed on both the east and west sides of the Rockies during the 1840s and 1850s. These small, anonymous enterprises provided meals, repairs, or goods, depending upon what the passing traffic wanted, but for the most part they traded in stock, sometimes building large herds.

These inauspicious beginnings were augmented by ranching operations that developed in both Colorado and Montana to supply the mining towns. Sam Hartsel, who joined the rush of fifty-nine only to find hard work and crowded placers, began herding stock in South Park for men preoccupied with mining. He gradually built his own herd, sold beef to miners, and by the time the mining excitement had run its course, had acquired a fortune in cattle and horses. Similarly, John Iliff, a butcher serving Denver's mining boom, began collecting his own herd to insure a steady supply of beef. Eventually, he amassed ranching interests along the Platte River that grew to dominate Colorado's range industry.

Although some of these small operations did grow to considerable size, they did not create the boom—they only demonstrated that the ingredients of success were there. The industry that erupted on the northern plains was due instead to the presence of a ready market, the construction of railroads to reach it, diminishing competition for the range from the Indian and the buffalo, and a large supply of inexpensive, hardy cattle that required little care or attention.

The ranching system that developed at the fringe

Its main street dotted with the trademark of the town's major source of income, Dodge City was born to serve the cattle trade—and languished before, after, and between the arrival of Texas herds.

of the mountains was simple and natural, a perfect accommodation of man to an environment. Initially, all that was needed to begin ranching were some cattle, a few cowboys to provide minimal care and handling, and a small piece of property for a home-site and ranch buildings; the grass was free. Taking advantage of a government that was as indifferent as it was remote, ranchmen ran their stock on the public domain free of charge. Since water was the essential ingredient, it was possible—and customary—for a rancher to buy, preempt, or homestead land along a stream and, by controlling the water, to control the land back to the divide—or at least halfway to the next water. With a lot of careful planning, and a little bit of larceny, a rancher could acquire miles of stream front, making himself in effect owner of thousands of acres of public land. What was created for a time was a business that ran more on hard work and presumption than on capital and legal sanction.

While it was free grass that made the range cattle industry profitable, it was cooperation that made it work; cooperation not only in respecting another man's right to the range he had preempted, but in virtually every aspect of the business. The working season on a ranch lasted as long as the good weather, and ranchers learned very early that they had to work together to make the most of the summer months. Normally cattle had to be gathered twice a year, for spring and fall shipping, and, in the process, branded, castrated, de-horned, and doctored. Because there were no fences, stock wandered and mixed to the point where a man couldn't possibly work just his own stock; similarly, if each rancher worked all the surrounding area individually, by fall all the stock would have been run to skin and bones.

The solution was the roundup, in which all the stockmen in a district anted-up men and equipment to a communal pool to gather the stock, separate by owner, brand and castrate as necessary, and turn stock back to its accustomed range. Spring or fall, it oper-

This roundup scene recorded in Johnson County, Wyoming, in 1884 depicts the range cattle business in its heyday—only two years before overstocking and a hard winter would ruin the industry.

ated about the same: daily the roundup foreman assigned the area to be worked, and long before sunup men rode out on "circle," a cordon of men thrown around an area, working the coulees and draws, ridges, and timber stands, pushing all the area's cattle toward a central location. By noon the circle was completed and the stock bunched, ready for cutting. It was here that a cowboy earned his pay (and quelled errant notions about the romance of his profession). Several cuts might be made: first, by owner; later, to separate stock for shipment; and again, to brand. The days were long and hot, the dust thick, and the stench of burnt hair and blood almost overpowering. A man might cut, or rope and drag, steers and calves while exhausting three horses; when he himself became too tired, he took a turn on the ground, wrestling animals into position to burn in a brand and cut earmarks. At day's end, the stock would be thrown back on the proper range (or held until it was convenient to do so), or moved for shipment. This process was repeated every

day, often for weeks, until the whole of a district had been searched. Although time, numbers involved, and more sophisticated organization would introduce modification in the system, the cooperative roundup would remain viable until the open range was cut up by fences, and the entire operation became unnecessary.

The summer between the two roundups was given over to long days of herding and loading cattle for shipment, tending range stock, and preparing for winter—for when winter came, everything stopped. It was common range lore that a cowboy got by on three hours' sleep a night during the summer because he did his sleeping during the winter. Some hands were kept on over the winter to live in the small line shacks, riding the divides when weather permitted to push stock back, occasionally putting out salt and chopping drinking holes through the ice for the cattle, but otherwise practicing the quasi-hibernation the long summer days had promised. Those with money saved loafed in town; others, lacking both money and jobs,

The winter of 1886–87, re-created in a contemporary engraving. Drifting before the storm, cattle were often trapped against the new barbed wire fences, where they huddled until they starved or froze.

rode the chuck line, sampling the hospitality of various ranches, being fed in exchange for news of the outside world.

Regardless of how the winter was spent, the annual cycle of the cowboy was one of extremes: intense monotony and boredom during the winter, juxtaposed to the dangerous, dirty hours of summer that tried both physical and psychological stamina.

FOR LARGELY INEXPLICABLE REASONS, the range cattle industry became the idyll of two continents, attracting young men who fancied cattle-raising on the plains to be one continuous adventure. Not far behind the young men, who for the most part found ranching a lot of hard work, came their fathers' money, seeking profitable investments. With low overhead by virtue of the free grass, the open-range industry enjoyed phenomenal profits. It became an axiom of the financial world that money invested in western cattle would readily net a 25 percent annual dividend. By the early

1880s Americans and Europeans alike, impressed by both the potential for profit and, no doubt, the prospect of participating at the conception of empire, sank lavish sums into the business. Huge investment companies were formed in England and Scotland, making possible multimillion-dollar ranches like the Swan Land and Cattle Company. Cattle-raising had reached bonanza proportions, but ominous indications were already beginning to appear.

Open-range methods were wasteful and extravagant: losses due to straying and weather were expected; loose supervision encouraged overgrazing; proper care was difficult and controlled breed improvement impossible. The introduction into the business of men who were largely inexperienced and primarily interested in immediate profit only aggravated these problems; managers and foremen suddenly faced with plenty of money lost their sense of proportion and began overstocking the range. The cooperation that had characterized the earlier years broke down. "Range pirates"—men who turned more stock loose on the open range than their range and water rights warranted—emerged in even greater numbers.

While some recognized that the carrying capacity of the range was finite, too many clung to a collective fantasy that the Baron von Richthoven gave voice to in his 1885 promotional monograph, *Cattle Raising on the Plains of North America:* "There is not the slightest element of uncertainty in cattle raising." Teutonic platitudes notwithstanding, the range was overstocked, and it was only a matter of time before disaster struck; in 1885 events began that conspired to create that disaster.

The summer of 1885 was dry in Texas, and large numbers of stock were moved north to better grass. At the same time, grazing permits for 300,000 head running in the Indian Territory were canceled, adding even more stock to the already overburdened grasslands. The summer of 1886 was again dry, keeping the northern graze down; complicating the situation was the problem of low prices, which kept the ranchers from selling off excess stock. By the end of the summer, the cattle were lean and ill-prepared for winter, and no hay had been stored for winter feed.

In November, heavy snows came, covering the meager feed. A chinook in January temporarily melted drifts and offered some hope, but a devastating blizzard followed, freezing the plains for weeks. Starving cattle drifted before the storm until they came up against drift fences, or wire, or wandered into coulees, where they huddled to die. Spring found only a few critters left per hundred, and those were all ribs, skin, and frozen feet and tails—gaunt and staggering monuments to a callous stupidity. Granville Stuart wrote their epitaph, and that of the open-range industry, when he said, "a business that had been fascinating to me before, suddenly became distasteful. I never want to own again an animal that I could not feed and shelter."

But even before the "Big Die" of the winter of 1886–87, sounded the death knell of this expansive industry, the business had begun to undergo a transition. Some mountain cattlemen had begun to breed up their stock, finding greater profits in improved breeding than in fattening Texas stock. The open range was disappearing, as ranchers increasingly bought and fenced their range, rather than just their water. Barbed wire, used by both rancher and granger to foil each other, began to lace across the empire, marking boundaries closer than the horizon. The kingdom was subdivided into boroughs—holdings that neither sustained nor inspired monarchs.

THE CATTLE BUSINESS in the mountain West staggered through to the turn of the century, squabbling with itself and the sheepherders over rights to a rapidly diminishing range. Squeezed further by the advancing agricultural frontier, ranching succumbed to the economics and technology of close herding, irrigated pastures, hay-feeding, selective breeding, and feed lots. Though resulting in a more prosaic business, the net effect has been to double the carrying capacity the range had during the "boom years" of the 1880s.

It hasn't all gone yet—Wyoming is still legally an open-range state—but the industry has learned to compromise. Cowboys who disdained any work that couldn't be done from a horse had to learn to run hay mowers and spend summers digging postholes and building barns—or find a new line of work. Cattle had to be carefully bred and tended, or a rancher couldn't compete in the marketplace. In a thousand small ways the cattlemen have retreated from the day when men and cattle ran free and no one threatened either's suzerainty. But it was a natural system, like the one enjoyed by the Indian and the buffalo, delicately balanced and susceptible to pressure from within and without. It was a system that demanded cooperation and moderation from its participants, that had to pass because it could not coexist with any other.

PART FIVE

THE CHALLENGE
AND
THE PROMISE

It is finally the mountains which endure, with their essential isolation and resistance to man's urban clutter providing the raw materials for a growing boom in tourism and outdoor recreation. But the land is finite, susceptible to man's excesses. For the mountains to yield a long term bounty— in wilderness, just as in oil, ranching, or agriculture—restraint and intelligent management must replace the greedy euphoria of the nineteenth century—and perhaps they have.

Garden of the Gods and Pikes Peak.

223

CHAPTER 18

UNHEALTHY YOUNG GIANT

*Economic collapse in mining, farming, and ranching that plunged
the West into a decade of agony at the turn of the century*

FOR DECADES the mountain West had been part
of the frontier that promised success to everyone. But in a brief span of years, beginning in
the late 1880s and extending through the turn of the
century, the three major elements of the high-country
economy—mining, farming, and ranching—either declined or collapsed. Nationally, the era was typified by
a faltering economy, but in the Rockies the condition
was complicated by an event that had sneaked past
almost unnoticed: the passing of the frontier.

The frontier—a moving, changing, always-relative
condition that was as much concept as fact—had offered
abundance. Whether fortunes were sought in furs,
mining, timber, transportation, livestock, or farming,
the land not only seemed rich but, if returns were less
than anticipated, provided an unlimited number of
chances to try again. The land was broad, and for a
time abundance did not have to run very deep to
satisfy demands.

But the early bonanzas built a large population,
which filled the land and consumed its resources. When
finally too many had asked too much of the land and
some prepared to move on, they found there was no
place to go. The frontier was gone, taking with it easy
opportunity and bonanza. The land was filling up, the
choice sites were taken, and men had to settle down to
making a profit on less promising land.

But sometimes not even hard work could guarantee
success. For many, the land had grown too stingy and
the methods too complex for frontier techniques to
work: the farmers, coaxed by the railroads, deceived
by uncharacteristic wet cycles, and equipped with the
kamikaze optimism that forms the spiritual cornerstone of the sodbuster mentality, had broken marginal
land that periodically dried up and refused to yield;
mining, though annually measuring success in ever-
increasing millions, had ceased to be the province of
the individual miner, becoming instead an organized,
capitalized, industrialized, and unionized effort to
wring a return from increasingly truculent ores; the
cattlemen, already devastated by the Big Die of 1886–
87, watched their rangeland shrink before an advancing agricultural horde, and felt the squeeze of increasing competition from within. The days were definitely past when individuals could build fortunes on
low overhead and luck.

The frontier had conditioned Americans to expect
success (or at least another opportunity to try), and
the economic blight at the end of the century was a
particularly bitter experience. For most of the high-
country folk, frustration with the failing economy
found angry outlets: seeking someone to blame besides
themselves, the farmers fixed on the railroads, fought
them with the political tools available, and created a
coalition that, for a time, seemed to offer hope of relief
from their predicament; the mining industry, although
momentarily joining cause with the agrarians against
an outside enemy, vented its frustration in a self-destructive warfare between management and labor—
which saw each blaming the other for ills neither could
control; the cattle ranchers, too independent for politics and conditioned by a heritage of self-sufficiency and

*Cripple Creek, Colorado—1893: The jarring incongruity of armed militia patrolling mining towns
in the Rockies would become all too common during the troubled decade of the 1890s.*

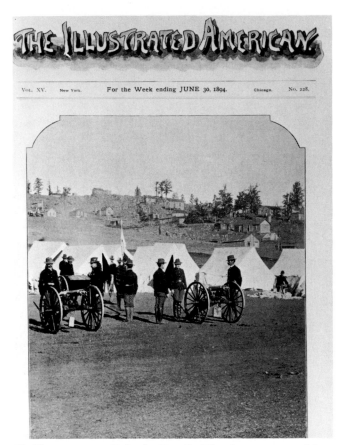

THE ILLUSTRATED AMERICAN.

VOL. XV.   New York.   For the Week ending JUNE 30, 1894.   Chicago.   NO. 228.

Gatling guns at Cripple Creek: The ferment would boil over again within ten years.

violence, lashed out at everyone who competed for their range—sodbusters, sheepmen, and one another. For the Rockies, the American Dream had collapsed, leaving the residents to rummage amongst the rubble, fighting for scraps and looking for someone to blame.

THE AGRARIAN-INSPIRED political revolt that helped to churn up turmoil in the Rockies during the 1890s had its beginnings two decades earlier. In the early 1870s, farmers began moving tentatively onto the high grasslands that stretched eastward from the mountains, meeting with moderate success and gradually discrediting Pike's and Long's pronouncement of desert a half-century earlier. Abetted by rainfall that increased through the late 1870s and early 1880s, optimism mounted, and a horde of sodbusters cut first furrows

across the Dakotas, eastern Montana, and along the apron of the eastern slopes.

The enthusiasm was encouraged, advertised, and in part created by the railroads. Often burdened with construction subsidy land grants that couldn't be sold and that sapped capital for tax payments, and seeking someone both to buy the land and to provide steady clientele for rail service, the railroads seized upon the new agricultural enterprise as salvation. They advertised the bounty of the land in Europe and America, offered low excursion rates to potential buyers, lowered rates to farmers moving in their families and household goods, published advice on farming, and, like J. J. Hill, even gave stock, grain, and equipment to new arrivals. For ten years the rains continued and the farmers expanded; encouraged by good prices and easy money from a booming mortgage market in the East, they broke even more marginal lands.

The small farmer who pioneered on the plains immediately found the experience different from that faced by his earlier, eastern woodland brethren; being determined, adaptable, and blinded to caution by the habit of success, he plunged ahead. Even with the uncharacteristically high rainfall, the land yielded sparsely; the answer of the farmers was to plant more acreage. This in turn required equipment and capital, which forced the farmer to concentrate on raising one cash crop, abandoning the safety of subsistence farming. Those who sought to supplement the meager rains with irrigation or windmills faced added expenses and multiplying mortgages. In every aspect, from fencing to planting seasons, it was different from the farming of their fathers—but they naïvely continued to expect the same things of it.

But despite all the new methods and the wet cycle, the land was still essentially arid, and much of it turned to the plow was marginal, producing only during the best years. The best years ended abruptly with the drought of 1886—the same that set the stage for the collapse of the cattle industry. Thinking the drought unusual, the farmers tightened their belts, extended the mortgages, borrowed a little extra, and stoically dug in to wait out the year. But there is nothing unusual about aridity on the plains, and one year stretched to seven with no relief. By 1893 the farmers were running short on hope and beginning to get desperate, when the gradual process of being burned out by sun and blown down by the wind was cut mercifully short by the nationwide panic of that year. Prices for the few crops grown plummeted, costs for goods rose, mortgages were recalled, credit dried up, and farmers who didn't lose their homes outright were completely devastated. The trauma provided a catalyst for revolt.

Since the first drought year, the farmers had lamented their condition, demanded action (of what kind and from whom was often obscured by the rhetoric), and looked for a villian—and they liked to do it in groups. The Grange, a post–Civil War phenomenon that was primarily social and informational, became a national clarion for agrarian complaints; the Farmer's Alliance emerged in the 1880s, serving a similar function; and gradually developing as the effective political arm of the small farmer, absorbing members and motives with every year of the drought, was the Populist Party.

Initially the western Populists directed most of their energies to attacking what had rapidly become a traditional enemy—the railroads. Such action was understandable and, to a degree, justified. Unwilling, or unable, to recognize their own role in their predicament, the farmers lashed out at what was both symbol and substance of their problems: the railroads, they reasoned, had not only maliciously deceived them about the weather and then sold them worthless land but were also the agents of the East, which sold them high-priced goods, held their mortgages, controlled the economy, and was getting rich while they starved. In fact, the railroads were occasionally abusive—often controlling grain prices, or raising rates—but usually because they, too, were struggling for solvency in the midst of a fluctuating economy. It was, after all, to the advantage of the railroads to keep the farmers producing; if the sodbusters were starved out, people and freight would cease to roll. Caught in this vicious cycle, and often part of its cause, the railroads were nonetheless found bellowing from the front pew when the prayers went up for rain and high grain prices.

When the Populists achieved national stature in 1892, demands for government regulation of the railroads were a central issue. The agrarians made substantial gains that year in both state and national legis-latures, only to face setbacks two years later. But by 1896, building on the discontent left by the Panic of 1893, and adding other westerners to their cause by advocating the free coinage of silver, the Populists built a potent political force. "Free Silver," a proposal that came to be regarded as a panacea for all western ills, promised to have the effect of easing credit (which farmers and ranchers wanted), and raising the price and amount of silver purchased (which a waning mining industry desperately needed); quite incidentally, it gave the Populists the ingredients for a powerful coalition.

The Populist Movement created a sectional identity; for the first time the people of the plains, the mountains, and the Far West saw themselves as a unit, with unique problems and different needs from the rest of the country. But these gains fell victim to a political error, when the Populists joined the Democratic Party in nominating William Jennings Bryan in the 1896 presidential election. Win or lose, they lost their identity; when Bryan lost, they lost their programs as well.

During their brief bid for reform, the Populists accomplished very little. They had prodded the federal government to make some changes in railroad regulation, pushed pieces of "agrarian" legislation through some state legislatures, but they had failed to effect any change in the standard of living or the condition of high-country agriculture. Even after ten years of drought, the farmers still had not realized what their problem was. Chasing the phantoms of railroads and corrupt capital, seeking government controls and laws to alleviate their suffering, they hadn't realized that the trouble lay with arid, marginal lands, and not with laws; they hadn't yet discovered that you can't legislate the rain to fall.

The mining industry in the mountains, although it was invariably affected by national and world financial fluctuations, and despite its brief courtship with Populism, was essentially self-centered. When something went wrong, it looked within itself for the culprit—and always managed to find one. For this reason, the management-labor relationship was convenient: no matter what happened, each had a handy scapegoat on which to hang the blame. It also provided someone to beat up, shoot, dynamite, or run out of town when the frustration ran too deep for words.

The slaughter and senseless brutality of the range wars profited no one. (From Leslie's Weekly.)

Mining evolved quickly from the individual prospector with pick and pan to a corporate hole in the ground operated by gangs of hired employees. Once the placers were gone, extracting the ores became an operation that required machinery to dig, move, process, and smelt. The rugged individualists of the mining frontier were replaced by owners or managers, and laborers working for wages.

By 1870 silver was king in Colorado, but despite an ever-increasing output, it was gradually becoming a tattered monarch—for reasons both internal and external. Internally, production was rising, but they were moving more earth to do it. The cost of getting silver out of the ground rose as shafts probed deeper; complicating matters were obdurant ores that defied conventional smelting to separate the silver. Externally, the price of silver was dropping on the world market. As early as 1878, the United States had passed the Bland-Allison Act, providing for government purchase of silver. The amount was inconsequential, the act largely a political sop, but it reflected a growing federal concern. By 1890 the situation had grown worse, and the legislation was replaced by the stronger, more substantial Sherman Silver Purchase Act.

As costs climbed and silver prices fell, the miners found that their wages were inadequate for the high cost of mountain living. With minor variation, wages of $3 per day were standard—had been for twenty years—on a job where men daily faced maiming and death from runaway lifts, "widow makers" (pneumatic drills that could kill in a single errant thrash), explosion, flood, cave-in, and fire. In the face of these low wages and bad conditions, the miners very early began to agitate for a bigger share of the treasure they worked so hard to uncover.

In 1880, in an effort to improve their situation, the miners of Leadville formed the Miner's Cooperative Union, requested an increase of one dollar per day over the prevailing wage of $3.00 to $3.50 per day, and walked out on strike when they were ignored. Governor R. W. Pitkin of Colorado, responding to owners' pleas, declared martial law, deported all "undesirables" (the union officials), and the strike was broken almost before it began. Despite these inauspicious beginnings, a decade later the miners would organize again, challenging the owners, and touching off an era of violence second only to the Indian Wars.

By 1893 the mining industry was moving toward a crisis: the buying power of a miner's wages had dropped so low that to miss a single day's work could mean financial disaster, and many men worked in a kind of deep-hole serfdom, in hock to the company stores; the mine owners continued to be plagued by descending silver prices, as the nation's economy teetered precariously. As the miners met in Butte, Montana, to organize the Western Federation of Miners and plan action against the owners, the economy was beginning to collapse. Within months after their meeting, the Sherman Silver Purchase Act was repealed, and silver mines and smelters closed all over the mountain West. Owner and employee alike were devastated, marking the beginning of a decade of squabbling over shares in a diminishing return.

As the silver mines closed, thousands of men decamped for Cripple Creek, seeking work in the burgeoning gold mines that continued unaffected by the general collapse. The Cripple Creek owners, capitalizing on the glutted labor market, cut wages; the federation struck, but the owners remembered Leadville of fourteen years earlier and settled back to wait for the troops. But in 1894 the governor was Davis H. Waite, a Populist sympathetic to the federation, who not only restored wages but adjudicated an eight-hour day, and established the W.F.M. as the bargaining agent for all the miners. It was a victory for the miners and the federation, but the owners were already grouping for the next clash.

Still flushed with the Cripple Creek success, the W.F.M. set out two years later to wring the same concessions from the mines in Leadville. Unfortunately for the federation, in the two-year interim Governor Waite had been replaced by the very conservative A. W. McIntire. The owners ordered a lockout, and at the first rumble of violence the governor declared martial law—ending the strike as summarily as had been done in 1880. The pattern was repeated elsewhere in the mountains—on the Coeur d'Alene in 1899, and in Telluride in 1901—as the federation uniformly found management organized to resist and supported by militia.

It was in a rematch at Cripple Creek in 1903–04 that the conflict reached its climax—and conclusion. To counter a strike called over wages, the owners brought in strikebreakers. To protect the scabs from intimidation by the union miners, Governor Peabody called out the militia—unfortunately commanded by a martinet named Bell. General Bell needlessly harassed the federation men, provoking tempers and almost daring the union men to retaliate. They did, with a spate of violence that culminated in the bombing of the Vindicator Mine, which killed the superintendent and a shift boss. Martial law was declared, leaders were locked up or deported, and by January 1904 it was obvious the owners had won. But the union remained, and six months later someone blew up thirteen scabs as they waited on a railway platform. It was all the excuse Bell needed, and he broke the federation completely, jailing those he could and scattering those he could not. The W.F.M. was finished, and most everyone else had had enough; it remained to bind the wounds and wonder if it had been worth the fight.

In over ten years of strife, nothing had really been accomplished: while maintaining the status quo might be regarded as a victory for the owners, the economy had not recovered and their mines continued to teeter on a narrow profit margin; for the miners, the unions had been destroyed, any gains negated, and their wages and working conditions remained just as unenviable. It had not been a pleasant time. Not only had everyone been broke and the local economy a sagging wreck, but terrorism and retaliation became so routine that, depending upon his persuasion, a citizen ran the risk of being either vaporized by a terrorist bomb or rousted by the military—or both, if he wasn't sufficiently fanatical one way or the other.

The collapse of the industry was a situation neither group had created but each found convenient to blame on the other. The economy, a nebulous target at best, was neither tangible nor handy, and an altogether inadequate target for the dynamite or deportation that made a person feel as if he had accomplished something. The violence was a result of the protracted disputes—a manifestation of the frustration that fermented among miners who knew that to work was to starve slowly, to strike was to hasten the process; and managers who faced financial collapse with a fortune just beneath their feet.

THE CATTLEMEN, like the mine owners who found themselves squabbling over shares in a diminishing return, discovered that their industry, too, was a victim of too-many-asking-too-much-of-too-little. Devastated by the winter of 1886–87, the cattle business found its recovery complicated by sodbusters who usurped the grasslands with their plows and reduced the available rangeland, sheepmen who competed for the remaining grass, and new, smaller ranchers eager to prove they had as much right to Uncle Sam's grass as anyone else. The cattlemen, once legendary in their power and independence, escaped neither the blight nor the strife of the century's last decade.

Like everyone else, the cattleman found his costs mounting and the price of his product falling. As the range grew more crowded, it became necessary for him to buy land and fence it so as to protect the grazing space that custom had once dictated was his. Expensive brood stock had to be bought and herds managed

Agents of reform, cattle country style: "The Invaders" of the Johnson County War, many of them hired Texas guns, who sought to solve problems of range management by a process of elimination.

closely to insure the best prices in a contested market; hay had to be grown, harvested, and stored to prevent a debacle like the winter of the Big Die. And as costs rose, he found that not only could he not expand to make up the difference, but he had to fight to keep from being squeezed even smaller. Frustrated by constrictions, confused by the disappearance of a way of life that once worked so well, and maybe a little frightened, the old ranchers fought their neighbors as the days of their suzerainty had taught them—with a desperation that precluded moderation.

Against the farmer, the cattleman was virtually helpless; once the grass was turned, it was useless for grazing, and therefore skirmishes with sodbusters were usually short-lived. But against his fellow graziers the cattleman could, and did, wage protracted warfare.

The sheepmen who came to the cattle country in the Rockies arrived after most of the range had already been claimed by cattlemen and moved into direct competition for grass the cattlemen were already overworking. Despite vociferous arguments that sheep and cattle were incompatible, that sheep fouled water holes, cropped rangeland too short, secreted an odor from glands in their hooves that prevented cattle from

ever eating the grass again, and smelled bad besides (all untrue, save the last statement), these rationalizations hardly disguised what was basically a concern for overcrowding—by whatever kind of creature. The sheep were just the easiest and most obvious target.

The cattlemen worked themselves into a fervor of spiritual proportions, to wage a holy war of extermination. The attacks on sheep by cattlemen cover almost half a century, from 1875 to 1920, but they reached a singular intensity during the lean and crowded years between the winter of the Big Die and the turn of the century. In 1887, 2,600 sheep were burned to death as they huddled in corrals at Tie Siding, near Laramie, Wyoming. In Montana, 2,500 sheep were clubbed to death by night riders. Sheep were rimrocked (driven over cliffs) by the thousands in Colorado, and herders and their dogs were killed almost as routinely. It has been conservatively estimated that between 1893 and 1903, 25,000 sheep and 50 herders were killed. The slaughter only began to abate after 1905, when the Forest Service undertook the regulation of grazing on public lands. After that time, killing the sheep didn't help much, if the sheepman held the lease on the grazing rights.

The cattle barons who had watched the open-range industry collapse, seen their empires shrink, and felt the squeeze of competition, did not confine their retaliations to sheepmen; they just as readily sought to eliminate one another. Typical of the cow-country fratricide that could erupt when competition for grass became too keen, was what happened in Johnson County, Wyoming, in 1892.

The rolling, unbroken grasslands of northeastern Wyoming were ideal cattle country, and until the crippling winter of 1886–87 it had been an unchallenged bastion for the open-range industry. An occasional cowboy working for one of the larger spreads, or even a new arrival, took a homestead on a river bend, threw a few head of cattle onto the range, put up some hay, and quietly worked his little operation. But in large measure the big outfits, all members of the Wyoming Stock Growers Association, held complete control of the range. As the large ranchers struggled to rebuild after the Big Die, more cowboys and settlers turned to grazing in Johnson County, trying their hand at ranching on a small scale. The members of the association began to feel the pinch, and struck back to eliminate the competition.

Once the Stock Growers Association had been all-powerful, dictating to the legislature and the courts, directing and controlling the roundups, and manipulating such regulations as the Maverick Law of 1884 to impede competition. But by 1890, the strength of the association had begun to slip in Johnson County: when association ranchers began blackballing small ranchers, and cowboys who kept a few head, to keep them from participating in the roundups, the populace turned against the large owners; when the association tried to jail their smaller competitors for violating a maverick law that served only the association, juries refused to convict. Convictions or not, the large ranchers had convinced themselves that their smaller neighbors were rustlers. Frustrated, angry, harried by diminishing profits and rangeland, the ranchers fell back on the simplest expedient.

The association members hired twenty-odd Texas gunmen, three teamsters, two newspapermen (evi-

dently to record the heroic event), and a surgeon. The group, numbering almost fifty, loaded a special train with wagons, horses, men, and supplies in Cheyenne and headed for Casper, Wyoming. There they detrained, cut the telegraph lines into Johnson County, and headed northeast to wipe out the men who had defied the association—rustlers, as the cattle barons had dubbed them.

Poorly led and plagued by stupid mistakes, the "invaders" (as they came to be known), spent the better part of one day besieging Nate Champion, one of the men on their list. Although they finally killed him and a friend, the alarm had spread to townspeople and small ranchers around Buffalo, Wyoming. Shortly the invaders found themselves holed up in a ranch house, surrounded by an outraged mob of several hundred. Rescued by a unit of the black Sixth Cavalry—ordered in by political allies of the association when it became apparent that *they* were about to become victims—the members of the invading force were jailed for a short time and then released through a combination of political connections and legal maneuvering. Although the affair proved to be a debacle, almost a comedy, the sobering fact remains that they fully intended to murder their way out of their quandary.

THE MOUNTAIN WEST had entered the modern era, and the experience had proved traumatic for everyone involved. Frontier methods and values had collided with industrialization, mechanization, and capitalization. The mountain bonanzas had become overcrowded, at the same time the land and the national economy decided to take a capricious turn for the worse. The Rockies had lived high during the frontier years, savoring the delights to be found in only taking and never returning, moving freely with the time, space, and resources to shape almost any destiny. But when the golden era collapsed and the mountain West came face to face with the responsibility of maintaining a population and carving out a permanent role in America, the response was violent, selfish, and ultimately tragic.

CHAPTER 19

NEW RICHES IN THE ROCKIES

*An infant oil industry and new developments in irrigation and land
management that could end the uncertainties of boom-and-bust*

FOR MOST OF THE NINETEENTH CENTURY, the wealth of the mountain West was based largely on extractive industry, and therefore the fiscal health of the region was finite. Within the American experience in the Rockies, a man's success had been measured not by his ability to harvest the increase from the land, but by his efficiency in removing the wealth from it. Haste and competition had bred wastefulness in the fur trade, mining, ranching, and logging. Each pursuit of a natural resource had provided brief and spectacular success, but as each declined, the region inevitably sank back to the task of making a day-to-day living.

Industries that did not replenish themselves were not the region's only problem to be sure: greed, absentee ownership, a mercurial national economy, speculation by men who preyed on optimism, unpredictable weather, and impossible expectations of a dry land's ability to produce—all added a measure of instability to economic life. Railroads, which could never generate but only facilitate continuing prosperity, bred a false sense of optimism, generating booms that had to bust as soon as the construction bonanza had subsided.

But regardless of cause, the cycle of rise and decline—of prosperity that consumed itself—was simply a fact of Rocky Mountain life. If men were to continue to live in the Rockies, they had to do one of two things: either find new extractive industries or develop methods for living with, and profiting from, the land without depleting it. With the arrival of the twentieth century the mountain West found both.

Oil reserves, tapped as early as 1862, provided the material for the new extractive industry. The industrialization and mechanization that burgeoned at the turn of the century offered a market for the new resource. But at the same time the mountain West was repeating the old pattern of mining nonregenerating resources, the region also began taking steps that would provide a permanent, viable base for a high-country economy. The development of irrigation to insure reliable agriculture, and the organization of balanced grazing—along with measures to provide for the careful husbandry of other natural resources—were initiated and achieved under the direction of a strong federal government.

THE MINING INDUSTRY was largely responsible for the civilization that had developed in the Rockies. It was gold and silver that built the first cities, developed railroads, and drew the people that filtered through the mountains, sometimes settling to farm, ranch, or harvest timber. Mining was the genesis, and for four decades it dominated the region, earning and spending bigger than any other single pursuit. But by century's end the industry had begun to decline; torn by labor turmoil, suffering the vicissitudes of world economics, and efficiently ensuring its own demise by enthusiastically pursuing the last of the high-grade ores, the business was rapidly becoming a liability. But even as precious-metal mining began the long decline that continues to the present, the mountains that had proved so fruitful began to yield up a new mineral

*Hay ranch in Jackson Hole, Wyoming. The raising and storing of hay for winter feeding is only one
of many changes that have brought stability to pastoral industries in the mountains.*

233

Florence, Colorado, the state's lone source of petroleum for a quarter of a century, sprouted derricks right at the end of main street during the 1890s.

resource that would be more valuable and longer-lived—oil.

Petroleum was discovered in the mountains almost as soon as gold. Travelers along the Oregon Trail encountered seepage pools in Wyoming, finding the substance a workable, if not ideal, axle lubricant. They also found an occasional frontier entrepreneur who mixed the oil with flour and sold it as axle grease—a product that tended to lose its efficiency rather abruptly after the first cold rain. In Montana in 1864, an emigrant train on the Bozeman Trail near the Bighorn River, seeking a place to soak its shrunken wagon wheels, found a pool of water covered with oil, making it possible to swell the wooden wheel to fit the iron rim, and grease the axle all in one immersion. But what was basically a curiosity along the trail had already piqued mercantile interests in Colorado.

In 1862, less than three years after the nation's first wells were sunk in Titusville, Pennsylvania, a well began producing near Canon City. Although small amounts of kerosene and fuel oil were sold in the min-

ing camps, the find was almost valueless because it lacked a significant local market, sophisticated refining facilities, and a method of transportation. By 1876 the Florence field opened in Colorado, meeting with slightly more success because of a larger population and better intramountain transportation. Although never a big producer, the Florence field met the local need as the sole source in Colorado from 1876 to 1902.

Both of the enterprises had discovered the basic difficulty that would plague the mountain petroleum industry for many years—want of a market. Local consumption, because of the small population, continued to be low. The remoteness from outside markets, which makes any mountain industry a tenuous proposition, offered a further complication. Because of the bulk involved, shipping refined products to outside markets while remaining competitively priced has often been difficult—to ship crude oil has been impossible. Nevertheless, petroleum was the best alternative in a declining mineral economy, and when everything went well, the returns could be munificent.

234

"Shannon's No. 1," the first standard rig in the Salt Creek field near Casper, marked the beginning of Wyoming's long and profitable relationship with petroleum.

Before 1910, for the most part, the oil industry in the Rockies was exploratory, experimental, and minor. The most significant activity was in central Wyoming, near Casper, where petroleum claim location and litigation (both without either the intention of, or capital for, development) were being refined to a purer state than any oil in the region. In the late 1880s Philip Shannon, the first oilman in Wyoming with the capital to do more than locate claims, took up 105,000 acres around Casper, and began to sink wells in the Salt Creek country. By 1890 he had four wells producing ten to twenty barrels per day apiece; by 1894 he had built a refinery in Casper capable of handling one hundred barrels per day—making lubricants that ran from light oils to heavy greases. Even with no competition, Shannon had difficulties: not only did he have to haul fifty miles by wagon from field to refinery, but he had to pay almost prohibitive rail freight rates to the eastern markets.

By the turn of the century, activity at Salt Creek had grown, companies and wells had proliferated, and

by 1912 the field was pumping 1,000,000 barrels per year. Production could have gone much higher, but Salt Creek oils carried a disproportionately high amount of fuel oil, which wasn't worth the high shipping costs and which lacked a local industrial market for low-cost fuel. But in 1913 Standard Oil developed a sophisticated cracking technique that could extract gasoline from the fuel oil, and Casper embarked on a booming, if precarious, career.

In Montana, like Wyoming, interest in oil was mainly local and poorly financed until well into the twentieth century, and development lagged correspondingly. The Kintla field, found in the northern part of the state in 1902, was so difficult to market that interest died out in less than two years. Prospecting began again statewide after the Northern Pacific Railroad converted from coal to oil in 1910, offering at least a limited local market. By 1920 interest had grown enough to attract outside capital, and with this support Gordon Campbell brought in the Kevin-Sunburst field north of Shelby, Montana. Some of the new

Water for Ouray: Dam and flume on the Uncompahgre provide water for growth on the western slope.

investment capital also found its way to Colorado, opening the Wellington, Moffat, Tow Creek, and Greasewood domes—all in rapid succession—in the northern part of the state.

The mountains had the resources for a long-lived industry, but the region suffered from shipment and refining problems that made the business erratic. Because of their isolation and low-profit margins, the mountain states were always the last to feel the boom in the world price, and the first to suffer the squeeze of recession. In 1916, for example, the flow of gasoline from the Cushing field in Oklahoma was so great that it could be collected, refined, and shipped to Casper, and still sell for less than locally produced gasoline.

In the late 1930s, Montana lacked sufficient refineries and shipped crude to Canada for processing, but the industry collapsed almost completely after Canadian refineries found domestic sources. With the coming of war in Europe, Montana bounced back, only to suffer a temporary setback, again, when the war ended.

Production in the mountain states has risen steadily through the years, and in most cases has been an enormous boon to the economy, but it is still a precarious business. Rocky Mountain oil companies generally have to drill deeper, ship higher, and balance a narrower profit margin than any of their competitors. Like other natural resources, oil is finite, and the industry today depends on technology to keep the Rocky Mountain fields producing; even so, it must face the fact that some day hydrogenation of coal, or atomic reduction of oils, or nuclear blasts to clear natural gas will have been used—and will no longer be available as a talisman to shake against the future.

B UT THE FUTURE OF THE ROCKIES at the turn of the century lay not only in the direction of oil and other ultimately exhaustible extractive industries; there also was beginning to develop an awareness of the land and man's necessity to accommodate himself to its limitations. The legacy of the Rockies was the land—nothing more, nothing less—and man had either to find a way to use it without using it up, or to be willing, in the end, to abandon the region. The future of the mountain West depended in large part on finding ways of pulling a reliable living from the land without depleting it: of developing agriculture that didn't rise and fall at the whim of the weather; of husbanding the forests against the future, to grow and be harvested like any other crop; and of grazing that gets a maximum yield without risking a recurrence of the winter of 1886–87, or doing irreparable damage to the range by overstocking. These ends were ultimately achieved, but only after the federal government took a strong hand in directing and supporting the efforts—although some mountain folk will argue that the result is only the base-born offspring of Washington bureaucracy risen to plague their house.

The mountain West, in fact the entire arid and semiarid West, had been burdened with a land dis-

Headgate on Shoshone Irrigation Company canal, a cooperative enterprise near Cody, Wyoming. Most private projects failed for lack of resources, necessitating federal entry into irrigation.

posal system unsuited to their needs. This incompatible system, which Congress had alternately been too lazy, too ignorant, too frightened, and too venal to correct, had been based on the assumption that land in the arid, treeless, sprawling West could be used in just the same way as the humid, forested, close-coupled eastern woodland frontier. By the turn of the century, the need for corrective measures was obvious, and prompted by decades of prodding, some vigorous leadership, and an almost religious fervor for reform of any kind, the federal government set out to nationalize the West.

The implied rationale of the land laws since the time the federal government accepted the responsi-bility for disposal of the public domain has been to place every American on his own farm. Throughout the latter part of the nineteenth century, the govern-ment tried, with only limited success, to transplant the self-sufficient agrarian freeholder to the arid West, enacting legislation that was often counterproductive. Recognizing the need for irrigation, Congress passed the Deseret Land Act in 1877, which offered a full 640 acres at $1.25 per acre if the owner agreed to convey water to the site within a specified time. Largely un-successful, as individuals rarely commanded the re-sources for such an undertaking, the act did, however, open the door to fraud; ranchers and speculators alike took land, meeting the provisions usually with a fur-

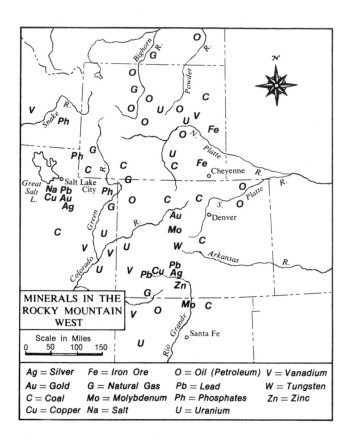

MINERALS IN THE
ROCKY MOUNTAIN
WEST

Scale in Miles
0   50   100   150

Ag = Silver	Fe = Iron Ore	O = Oil (Petroleum)	V = Vanadium
Au = Gold	G = Natural Gas	Pb = Lead	W = Tungsten
C = Coal	Mo = Molybdenum	Ph = Phosphates	Zn = Zinc
Cu = Copper	Na = Salt	U = Uranium	

ment was really equipped to supply. This fact was apparently realized and accepted in 1902 with the passage of the Reclamation, or Newlands, Act. The legislation, proposed by Francis G. Newlands of Nevada, a man who knew the West and irrigation firsthand, provided for the building of federal irrigation projects, with the settlers who benefited to eventually repay the costs. The biggest objections came from eastern and midwestern farmers who complained that it was unfair to subsidize one small group, and that the new agricultural lands would present unfair and unnatural competition for them. Ultimately it was Theodore Roosevelt's personal prestige that pushed the bill through Congress.

The first federal project under the new program was the Uncompahgre Project in southwestern Colorado. When the six-mile-long Gunnison Tunnel brought water to the Uncompahgre Basin, land values rose from $2 per acre to $800 per acre after the land was planted to fruit trees. Later the Pathfinder Dam on the Platte would serve both Colorado and Wyoming, while the Shoshone Dam and Jackson Lake projects would broaden agriculture in northwestern Wyoming. Montana would see the effects of the bill in the Huntley Project in the Yellowstone Valley, and in Sun River and Lower Yellowstone. Sadly, even this program fell slightly short of expectations as speculators began buying up the land at prospective sites as early as 1899, and netting tremendous profits after the projects were built. Nonetheless, the mountains were reaping the benefits of a stable, dependable agriculture—and the federal government had finally acknowledged its responsibility in the administration and disposal of the public domain in the West.

row plowed uphill from a dry wash, or a barrel of water "conveyed to the claim" by wagon and sloshed on the ground. Regardless of abuses, the act made no sense; even if a man could bring water to his land, 640 acres was too much land for him to handle with the intensive agriculture that irrigation generated. Land laws enacted by the East for the West seemed to invite fraud, for men saddled with inadequate laws sought ways around them, until an understandable bending of law blurred with a speculator's unscrupulous raid on the public domain.

In 1894 the federal government once again half-heartedly tried to encourage irrigation with the Carey Act, legislation that was supposed to shift responsibility to the states, ceding lands, sales receipts, and control if the states would solve the development problems. The states failed to pick up the task, and enthusiasm dwindled as everyone waited for someone else to move first.

Developing irrigation required money, organization, and planning, essentials that only the federal govern-

PROBABLY THE MOST OUTRAGEOUS ABUSES within the public land system concerned the forest lands of the West; the speculators who worked the forests didn't just hold the land to turn a profit, like most speculators, but instead stripped it of timber and then abandoned the land to avoid taxation. The fault, once again, lay with the law. There was no provision for the purchase of forest land, and men who wanted timber entered the land under such legislation as the Homestead and Preemption acts, never intending to settle but only to cut the timber. The laws encouraged, even necessitated, fraud, and many logging companies simply carried the abuse to its utmost degree.

As early as 1877, Secretary of the Interior Carl Schurz urged withdrawal of forest lands and close control of the harvest to facilitate both irrigation and flood control; but the bounty seemed so endless and so many people were getting rich that he couldn't get anyone to listen. But in 1891, in the course of some routine revision of the land laws, an amendment slipped in that allowed the reservation of forest land by presidential proclamation. Benjamin Harrison promptly created the Yellowstone Timberland Reserve in Wyoming. Grover Cleveland followed suit, setting aside thirteen new reserves. The West, led by timber men who convinced residents that this was the first step in an insidious plot to deprive them of the free and unbridled right to loot the public domain, howled for redress. Congress, striking a compromise that solved no problems, recognized no program, and even dodged the issue, suspended Cleveland's reservations for one year—in effect, throwing the land open for one final destructive splurge.

As a sop to western timber interests, Congress passed the Forest Lieu Land Act in 1897. The act—apparently acknowledging a belief that every American with investment capital, a sincere desire to better himself, and friends in Congress should be given statutory help in raiding the public domain--allowed owners of land within a reserve to exchange it for land outside the reserve, the clinker being that they would trade the land only if they wanted to. The net result was that over three million acres of untimbered land within reserves (mostly railroad grant lands above timberline) were exchanged for valuable forested lands outside the reserves. One interesting effect of the Lieu Law was the great number of people (including congressmen), who, although their land lacked timber, were so vitally concerned for the future of the forests that they offered their barren lands as reservations.

The situation began to change, however, during Theodore Roosevelt's administration. An ardent conservationist (although members of his organization had yet to coin the term) and opponent of corruption, Roosevelt unleashed his secretary of the interior, E. A. Hitchcock, on the fraud within the land bureau. Put-

Gifford Pinchot (right) and Theodore Roosevelt introduced conservation to the public domain.

ting Gifford Pinchot in charge of forestry, Hitchcock reorganized bureaus and created the Forest Service within the Department of Agriculture to give Pinchot the power and influence he needed. Pinchot began to clean up a corrupt and inefficient bureaucracy, and while encountering some setbacks, his era saw some remarkable changes. Coal lands, a traditional target of fraudulent entry, were closed from 1906 to 1909, classified, and then sold for $75 to $100 per acre, prices reflecting their real value; between 1905 and 1907 Pinchot withdrew 2,565 waterpower sites (on the pretext they were ranger-station sites) to prevent them from falling into private hands before the government could establish guidelines and preconditions for power generating facilities; under Pinchot's direction, Roosevelt withdrew 141,000,000 acres of land as forest reserve.

What Pinchot and Roosevelt had done, in effect, was to provide the foundation for a permanent public domain and to give the government a powerful lever in controlling land and resource use. Ultimately, federally controlled land, including parks, forests, and

Indian reservations, would amount to 30 percent of the land in Montana, 36 percent in Colorado, and 40 percent in Wyoming. Most of this land is not locked up tight but offers mineral rights, grazing, and timber-cutting—all for sale or lease—with the hope that the land will be used intelligently enough to permit use in perpetuity.

THE MOST PROFOUND EXAMPLE of incompatability between law and necessity in the mountain West is the grazing industry. After the decline of the open range, when it became necessary for ranchers to own rather than just control grasslands, there were no provisions for acquiring the large acreages necessary. Land laws geared to farming and a humid climate dispensed pitifully small parcels. Because a great deal of the land in Wyoming and Montana was suitable only for grazing—and, at that, upwards of twenty acres was required per cow—ranchers resorted to deceit and trickery to get and hold land. But worse than that, they competed for contested range by simply turning stock on to it early, or late, or too long, often resulting in severe overgrazing. The system was self-destructive—to the ranchers and the public domain.

Theodore Roosevelt, a former high plains rancher, recognized the problems and limitations of the land, and favored the fencing and leasing of the grasslands. Unable to find support, he directed Pinchot to pursue the policy in the national forests. In 1905 the Forest Service began charging fees for grazing in the reserves, instituted close controls on the numbers and types of animals, assigned suitable lands, and initiated studies of range management. For three decades, the closely regulated forest lands flourished, while open-range lands continued to deteriorate. Occasional attempts to get the land into private hands (on the assumption that private ownership might lead to *some* control of grazing), like the 640-acre Grazing Homestead Act of 1916, failed to transfer enough land to curtail abuses.

Finally, in Franklin Roosevelt's administration, Sec-

retary of the Interior Harold Ickes classified all of the remaining public domain and proposed a lease system like that used in the forests. Edward Taylor of Colorado, a former ardent opponent of government control, pushed the bill through and gave it his name. The Taylor Grazing Act of 1934 initially provided for federal control of 80,000,000 acres, to be superintended by local grazing districts that would dictate the specifics of type and number of grazing stock. In effect, the act applied to all of the remaining public domain; all of the nation's land was now either privately held or publicly controlled. The federal government, as long as it could regulate with reason and restraint, had begun to show some sense of its obligation to the land —and to the people.

THE MOUNTAIN WEST had lived with unstable economics through the entire nineteenth century, experiencing one boom after another, only to watch each subside as the resource being exploited was depleted. Impermanent, unsatisfying as it was, the practice of exploitation was what the land invited, and men made the most of it. When oil was found, and uses for it, the mountain folk resurrected the smoothly practiced habits and got ready to enjoy the boom. Cities grew, money flowed, land prices soared, and everyone planned big for the future. Although often hampered by isolation and frustrated by markets that seemed to defy control, oil has brought a greater prosperity than any previous industry.

The Rockies were rich in resources, but even as the oil industry grew, it became obvious that the parade of lodes was coming to an end, and with it the erosive impermanence of the boom-and-bust days. With the development of irrigation and federal control of forest harvest and grazing management, the civilization that had balanced so precariously for so long began to lay the foundations for a stable economy. It was in the cultivation of these renewable resources—agriculture, timber, and grass—that the future lay.

Sheep on spring pasture in the San Juan Mountains near Telluride. Federal supervision of grazing on public lands has reduced conflict and waste for the Rockies' livestock industries.

Although diminishingly profitable, cattle still stir pride and old visions of empire in mountain ranchers, who are often said to "raise cattle for respectability and sheep for money."

An abundance of dirt roads and logging trails leads four-wheel-drive enthusiasts into unspoiled regions of the Rockies. Recently controversy has erupted over vehicle damage of wilderness areas.

Steer-riding at an Evergreen, Colorado, rodeo.
Even small local events offer big excitement.

Overleaf: Trail riders in a sun-spotted aspen grove,
Upper Pecos Wilderness Area, New Mexico.

Swimming at Ouray: Undaunted by the crisp temperatures that prevail a mile and a half above sea level, tourists and local bathers enjoy warm waters in this pool fed by hot springs.

Harboring both power and sail craft, Dillon Lake, west of Denver, is Colorado's newest water sports recreation area. During the winter ice boats skim its frozen surface.

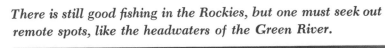

There is still good fishing in the Rockies, but one must seek out remote spots, like the headwaters of the Green River.

Salt Lake City—no longer a religious sanctuary in the wilderness but a bustling metropolis. The city that Brigham built now sprawls far across the valley and dominates the western slope.

Once a beacon for trappers and Indians, the Tetons and Jackson Hole now lure a tamer breed.

Denver, keystone of the urban concentration that represents half of Colorado's population.

Ski touring, winter's spiritual counterpart to summer backpacking, opens wilderness to year-round use.

Another dimension in winter backcountry travel, the snowmobile is useful to ranchers as well.

Although lacking the numbers of enthusiasts that skiing attracts, ice skating has experienced a popular renaissance—as on this portion of Evergreen Lake in Colorado.

While hardier types challenge the Tetons with rope and ice axe, many tourists prefer the quieter sports of power boating or simply basking in the sunshine at Colter Bay.

The canyons and rapids of mountain streams, once cursed for impeding river travel and retarding settlement, now excite white-water racers and river-rafting tourists.

The rugged cliffs and scarps above timberline in the Rockies draw an increasing number of mountain climbers to the region each year. This group rests above Aspen.

253

Sandstone monoliths shaped by wind and water, the "Kissing Couple" above Grand Valley are part of the arid and spectacular Colorado National Monument.

Lower Falls in the Grand Canyon of the Yellowstone. Once a wilderness known only to Indians and mountain men, Yellowstone Park now faces overcrowding.

CHAPTER 20

A MOUNTAIN PLAYGROUND

*The biggest bonanza of all—mountain recreation and tourism,
from nineteenth-century health spas to modern ski resorts*

BY THE END OF THE NINETEENTH CENTURY, the Rocky Mountains had experienced catastrophe and malady of every type and magnitude conceivable. The region was remote, by-passed, dubbed a desert; its beaver and buffalo had been slaughtered; its settlers had been killed by Indians, and then chastized when they overdid the revenge; it had lacked transportation, and then been victimized when transportation came; it offered gold and silver and abundance, only to suffer when too many wanted the wealth; it watched an empire of grass fall victim to greed, felt the weight of national financial collapse, and suffered the most violent of labor strife. The mountain West had been plagued with countless problems that were uniquely its own, and most of those that were common to the rest of the nation as well. Though its career had also been an invigorating, exciting experience, when it came to economics and the American dream, there was reason to suspect that the Rockies were the off-season pasture for the Four Horsemen of the Apocalypse.

But quietly developing in the late nineteenth century, and becoming louder as the twentieth began to age, was a curious complex of industries that could make money without depleting the land. People began to come to the Rockies just to be in the Rockies: to see, or to play, or to be cured, or to have the soul soothed. They needed services—mostly food, lodging, and instruction in high country diversions—and although catering to these needs looked like stealing to many of the mountain folk, they were glad to oblige.

Near the middle of the nineteenth century, a small eddy developed in the flow of the western migration, centering in the southern Rockies. For fifty years it grew, never ballyhooed by the contemporary press or latter-day historians—probably because it lacked mounted men in buckskin, clanking with the tools of conquest and empire—but nonetheless bringing more people to the mountain West than either the fur trade or the range cattle industry. The *dramatis personae* of this unusual influx shared a common denominator: they were close to dying, racked by coughs caused by a variety of ills, but usually diagnosed as tuberculosis. They came to see if it was true that air and climate might be an elixir for what ailed them.

Reports about the salubrious effects of the high country had begun to filter out of the mountains by the latter part of the 1880s. Mountain men plagued by coughs ascribed to a variety of causes from ague to consumption had been cured while in the Rockies. No less luminaries of the fur trade than the Sublette brothers and Bill Williams remarked on the miraculous cures effected, presumably by the mountain air.

In the nineteenth century it was estimated that tuberculosis killed one out of ten Americans. The disease was not understood very clearly, and in the search for a cure, a theory of climato-therapy developed which maintained that the pure air and altitude of the Rockies offered the greatest hope of arresting or curing tuberculosis. Most of the medical authorities of the day considered mineral waters to be of additional help in effecting a cure, a coincidence of considerable convenience, inasmuch as the region abounded with mineral

*Old Faithful geyser, magnet for over two million visitors a year, is the best known
and most reliable of Yellowstone's thermal sideshows.*

The Antlers Hotel, built by railroad magnate William J. Palmer, was Colorado Springs' first and most famous resort. Its formidable facade belied the gracious interiors.

Stately and sprawling, the Broadmoor—another monument to the wealth that found its way to Colorado Springs—evoked memories of a southern gentility.

The mineral waters and high-country air that attracted health-seekers also drew vacationers.
These idlers are gathered at the soda spring at Manitou Springs.

An artist's conception of the vapor baths at Glenwood Springs. Their efficacy in healing broken
limbs (witness the sling and crutch) might best be rated as marginal.

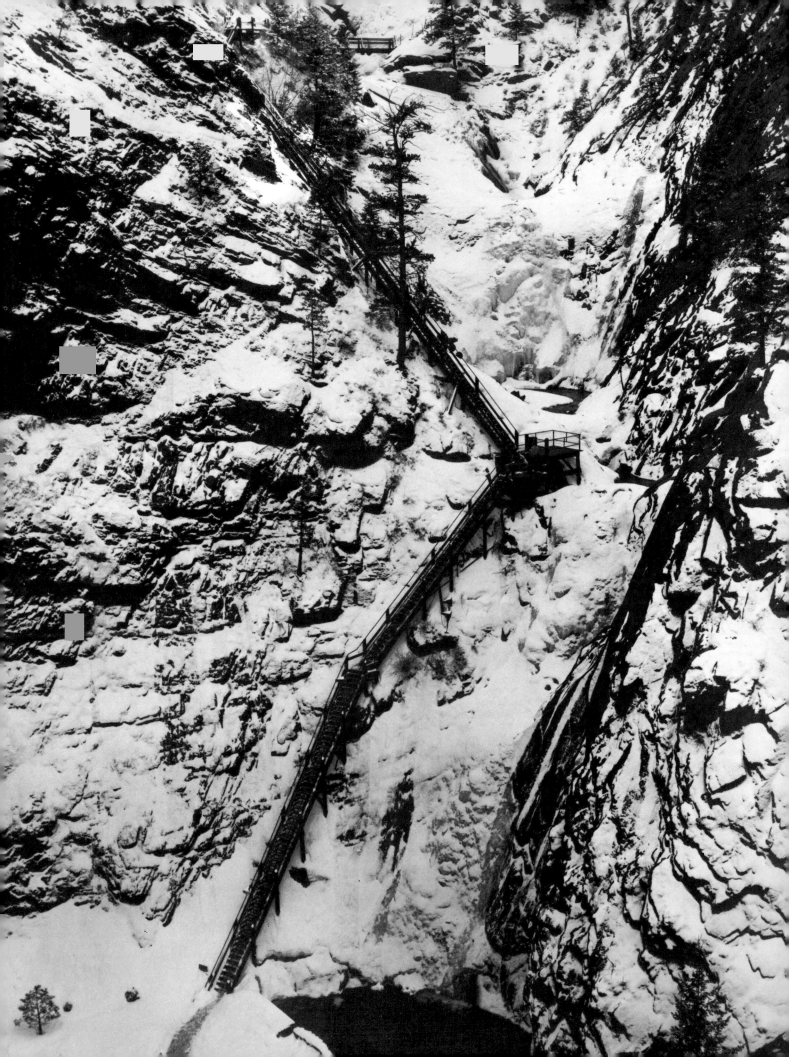

springs of every type.

The most successful of the Rocky Mountain health spas was Colorado Springs. Combining the energy, capital, and promotional instincts of William J. Palmer with the high, clear air and three medicinal springs—Iron, Soda, and Manitou—the town blossomed in one decade into a resort catering to the rich and famous as well as the ill. When Palmer ran the diminutive rails for his Denver and Rio Grande south through the site of Colorado Springs in 1871–72, en route to the encounter with the monolithic Atchison, Topeka, and Santa Fe, he built a small hotel around which a village developed. As enthusiasm for the cures mounted, Palmer enlarged his hotel, publishing promotional leaflets and advertising excursion tours to surrounding natural wonders. It was a bonanza for both his railroad and the hotel, and by 1883 he had built the first truly exclusive resort hotel in Colorado, the Antlers. Under General Palmer's fine and lavish hand, Colorado Springs acquired a reputation as the "Saratoga of the West," offering fine hotels with the best of accommodations. The advertising paid off, too, as the town registered 30,000 visitors in 1880, and by 1890 had increased the number to 200,000 annually.

Between 1880 and 1900, tuberculars flocked to the Rocky Mountain health resorts, and pursuing a fashion curious to the era, idle upper-class persons followed. For twenty years the resort towns enjoyed a healthy infusion of capital—lavishly spent by both the healthy and the ailing for accommodations that bordered on the opulent. It was a grand era, well stocked with money and sophisticated gentility, but it fell victim to the quiet persistence of a single man of science.

At the turn of the century, Robert Koch discovered the parasitic bacillus that caused tuberculosis, thereby proving that it was a contagious disease. When this information became common knowledge, boycott of the health resorts by the wealthy elite was almost instantaneous. In a self-destructive confusion, most resorts closed their doors to the ill, leaving themselves with no clientele at all. By the end of the Great War, few of the grand hotels remained, and those that did had lost the luster of the years that overflowed with the famous and wealthy.

The history of the rockies is riddled with transients: explorers who passed through en route to lands beyond;

mountain men pursuing a livelihood that precluded sedentary life; miners who came to tear at the ground like demented badgers, before moving quickly on to the next golconda; railroads that persisted in building right past the region until in frustration the mountain folk built their own. But then the tuberculars had come, and instead of taking the wealth of the land and moving on, they *left* money. It was the beginning of a new era, as visitors began coming to play, to look, and to relax. It was something called *tourism*, and it looked very profitable.

The lodestone of Rocky Mountain tourism was, and is, Yellowstone National Park. From the very beginning, the region had attracted attention, although for most people it remained unavailable. Yellowstone followed the pattern of most western discoveries; that is, the Indians followed the game trails to it, the trappers followed the Indians, the prospectors followed the trappers; and finally an army officer guided by a mountain man came along and "discovered" it. From the time John Colter emerged from the Yellowstone region in 1808 with tales of bubbling mud, boiling springs, erupting waterspouts, and subterranean fires, stories were told and retold of the amazing land where the earth burned. Mountain men, normally fond of stretching the truth, were scoffed at when they related what they had seen; some, most notably Jim Bridger, simply embroidered the truth a little more and were praised for their keen imaginations. It was not until 1870 that the region was closely examined and its wonders officially confirmed by a party of citizens from Montana led by Lt. Gustavus Doane and Henry Washburn. In the course of discussions about the best way to exploit their find, Cornelius Hedges, a member of the party, suggested that the area should be preserved for public use. Building on this suggestion and encouraged by William Henry Jackson's photographs and Ferdinand Hayden's report, made a year after the Doane-Washburn Expedition, Congress in 1872 created Yellowstone as the first national park.

At that time, the park was five hundred miles from the nearest railroad, contained no roads, and was still a favorite spring and fall hunting ground for Indians of varying degrees of hostility. For its first forty-three years, the park did not attract lines of tourists waiting to get in. The only people who visited in abundance

The cliff-clinging stairway down Seven Falls near Colorado Springs petrified early Rocky Mountain tourists as it does today's—with or without snow-glazed steps to add surprise to the descent.

Before chair lifts, stretch pants, and fiber-glass skis created a booming industry and crowded slopes, these turn-of-the-century ski tourers enjoyed relative solitude on a Colorado hillside.

were the poachers, who divided their time between slaughtering the game and eluding the park's management. By 1886 the problem had grown so bad that the secretary of war provided a detachment of soldiers to guard the park, with the commanding officer acting as park superintendent. The troops stayed for thirty years, finally securing the region against poachers and beginning the improvements that would open it to visitors.

The initial road system, built under the supervision of the Army Corps of Engineers, opened the interior of the park to visitors. Railroads built tracks closer to the park, and the Northern Pacific encouraged tourists by organizing wagon excursions from their line on the north. Horses were provided for transportation inside the park, and regular facilities for food and lodging were being developed. But despite these improvements, interest remained minimal: during the years before Henry Ford made mobility and the driving vacation a ceremonial—often sacrificial—rite in American life, there were no more than 20,000 visitors a year.

The boom in tourism in Yellowstone and the surrounding Rockies owes its existence to the automobile

and a war almost ten thousand miles away. The first cars were permitted into the park in 1915, and at the same time motorized bus service was established. World War I had already flared, vacation travel to Europe had ceased, and Woodrow Wilson added impetus to the obvious alternative by proclaiming his "See America First" campaign. In 1915 the number of annual visitors doubled to 52,000; by 1929 it had increased to over 260,000; 500,000 were recorded in the late 1930s; and over 3,000,000 tourists drove bumper-to-bumper in 1971. No longer a matter of encouraging tourism, the problem now seems to be one of dispersing the crush of visitors over various other Rocky Mountain vacation areas. All the ills of civilization are being visited upon Yellowstone: delicate plant life is being crowded; ecological balances are pushed past their centers of gravity; smog hovers over the roadways; and the people threaten to outnumber the other critters. Civilian rangers may once again give way to military troops, for they now find themselves forced to act as policemen instead of custodians.

Bordering Yellowstone on the south and intensifying

Winding a tortuous path through the San Juan Mountains between Silverton and Ouray, the "Million Dollar Highway" follows the route of Otto Mears's original toll road over the crest.

the area's magnetism is Grand Teton National Park. Although it lacks the natural curiosities of Yellowstone, Grand Teton offers the most spectacular mountain scenery in the West, and the broad valley of Jackson Hole, which has comfortably accommodated Americans since it was a center for the fur trade in the 1820s and 1830s, still attracts people who seek a peaceful retreat. Established in 1929, growing to include Jackson Hole in 1944, and stretching its boundaries still farther in 1949, Grand Teton Park is beginning to acquire the same problems as Yellowstone. Due to its ready accessibility during the winter, Grand Teton does not even enjoy the six-month respite that impassable snowdrifts give Yellowstone.

Relegated to second-class status by the overpowering combined grandeur of the Yellowstone–Grand Teton complex, Rocky Mountain National Park suffers undeservedly. Created almost single-handedly in 1915 through the persistent efforts of writer-naturalist Enos Mills against determined opposition, this park offers greater variety and is more readily accessible than any of the others. A textbook for glacial geology, it also offers rivers, canyons, forests, tundra and alpine plant and wildlife, and sixty-five peaks over 10,000 feet high.

Unlike Yellowstone and Grand Teton, where people generally go to *see,* Rocky Mountain is a park where people go to *do.* The park annually entertains over two million people—roughly equivalent to Yellowstone's patronage—but it accomplishes this by working year round. Essentially a wilderness park, it is best enjoyed from the trail, whether on foot or horseback in the summer months, snowshoes or skis in the winter. Since few roads penetrate the interior, many of the lakes, streams, and small valleys are protected from an overabundance of visitors that would destroy much of their pristine charm. But even for tourists restricted to highway travel, Rocky Mountain National Park offers one of the most extraordinary stretches of roadway in any park. Trail Ridge Road winds across the crest of the park, for eleven miles of it above 11,000 feet, and ultimately climbs to 12,183 feet, providing not only splendid panoramas but a measure of adventure besides.

The establishment of parks and promotion of tour-

263

A pack train from a dude ranch makes camp by Snowmass Lake, near Aspen.

ism benefited mountain residents enormously, as they seized the opportunity to provide vacationers with bed, board and entertainment. Almost as early as the concept of the parks was developed, parallel attractions in the private sector began to evolve—most notably, the dude ranch.

In 1880 Howard Eaton built a working cattle ranch in South Dakota. When his brothers joined him to operate the ranch, they brought several eastern friends to visit; charmed by the scenery and activity, a number of them returned year after year. Probably not wishing to outstay their welcome, several guests offered to pay for the accommodations. Eaton subsequently found the entertaining to be more profitable than ranching, moved the operation to Wolf Creek, Wyoming, and went into the business full-time with his brothers. The Eatons later built a little town—complete with houses, hotel, post office, and store—around their dude ranch. The Wolf Creek Ranch was popular and profitable, providing the archetype for a business that has grown steadily.

Building on a mythic heritage that had already spawned at least three Wild West shows and hundreds

of dime novels, and had vaulted the cowboy to the forefront in the American pantheon of heroes, the dude ranches in the Mountain West grew and prospered. What they attempted to offer was a facsimile of the old-fashioned cattle ranch, and it was not for want of dedication to the facade that the experience fell short of the essence. Initially, the dude ranchers played very hard at maintaining the appearance of a real ranch, but gradually the ranches added more diversions, dropping the pretentions to working-ranch status. Between 1920 and 1940 the business thrived; in 1938 over a hundred dude ranches in Wyoming that offered the usual horseback riding, pack trips, swimming, dancing, and guitar-strumming drugstore cowboy entertainments netted more than $2,000,000 in profits. Along the heavily traveled highways, some of the dude ranches are today little more than motels with a riding stable attached; others are tired ranches that have converted their outbuildings to cabins and replaced their cattle with tourists; a few eschew rustic pretensions entirely and specialize in $100-a-day suites, exotic cuisine, and tennis or golf—maintaining the "ranch" identification apparently as a concession to locale and humble beginnings. But most are in between, a combination guest and working ranch with the opportunity (but no compulsion) for the guests to participate in the activities of the ranch.

While the dude ranches generally offer simplicity and wilderness to their guests, there is nothing primitive in the ranch owners' approach to their business. In Colorado alone, the fifty-odd ranches have organized as the Colorado Dude and Guest Ranch Association, with combined resources for advertising, and market their product with a sophistication calculated to appeal to a broad range of clients.

Guiding and packing for hunters and fishermen in the Rockies has always been lucrative (in the latter decades of the nineteenth century minor luminaries like the Grand Duke Alexis of Russia and lesser potentates both political and financial paid lavishly to slaughter the wide variety of high country game). Today the bonanza has expanded, and the Rocky Mountain states envision only growing profits from the activities. Colorado considers hunting and fishing major industries, planning for the husbandry and harvest of wild game much as any rancher would. The state sells

500,000 fishing licenses a year to vacationers, who catch about 25,000,000 fish. To maintain this industry, the state hatches and stocks 600 tons of trout yearly. Hunting license sales bring in several million dollars every year, plus additional millions that accrue from bus and plane fares, supplies and equipment bought in the state, hotel and motel rentals, and guides and instructors necessary to service 700,000 to 1,000,000 hunters and fishermen. With nonresident licenses and permits reckoned in three figure denominations, it is easy to understand Colorado's expectations for continued bonanza.

The same industry that produced the dude ranches also provided the rationalization for yet another Rocky Mountain attraction: rodeo. Featuring events that directly or indirectly evolved from tasks and skills associated with the cattle ranch, rodeo has grown from an idle afternoon's excitement garnished with side bets to well-organized, week-long athletic events with purses sometimes in excess of $100,000.

As a spectator sport, rodeo received its biggest boost from turn-of-the-century traveling spectacles like Bill Cody's and the Miller Brothers' Wild West shows that threw in some bucking horses and calf-roping to vary the action. It was Bill Pickett, a black cowboy with the Miller Brothers, who created bull-dogging, an event that has since become a staple of the business. Dude ranches often offered small weekly rodeos for their guests, and during the summer months the Rockies are still dotted with the lineal descendants of these private events—small rodeos, with smaller purses, staffed by local boys, and contested more for the excitement and sport than the money involved. From such local contests grew the three- and four-day rodeos like the ones at Laramie and Cody, or the week-long brawls like those at Cheyenne, which draw top riders, thousands of tourists, and more of the entertainment dollars that have helped to resuscitate the mountain economy.

EARLY TOURISM, like most other mountain industries, flourished during the warm months of the year. For both residents and visitor, winter snows meant an almost complete halt to traffic and communication; man, like most of the other critters, either migrated out or holed up until spring. But the mountain-clog-

Fly fisherman near Hagerman Lake: Outdoor sports have become major industries in the Rockies.

ging snows, which formerly meant a four- to six-month respite from both work and income, are now beginning to look like white gold. Where once the high country settled in for a long quiet siege when the snow flew—enlivened only by an occasional individual on the rampage with cabin fever—now the mountains quicken with preparations for the annual invasion by a merry horde with money in its hands and skis on its feet.

Chief to benefit from the skiing boom is Colorado. Utilizing a 50,000-square-mile area that was once thought inaccessible in winter, skiing has grown to rival hunting and fishing in numbers of participants. Already handling more than one million skiing visitors annually, Colorado anticipates continuing for years the 15–20 percent annual growth in the ski business. The reason is simple: the Rockies offer the best powder-snow skiing in the world, and Colorado furnishes the best facilities in the Rockies. Colorado has built this reputation largely on the strength of two centers, Aspen and Vail, although there are a plethora of smaller, similarly attractive resorts.

Aspen had its first boom in the mining days of the 1880s when it was the cultural center of Colorado's

The Pecos Wilderness Area of New Mexico. Probably the Rockies' most valuable resources for the future are their unspoiled wild lands and the solitude they offer to an increasingly urbanized America.

western slope, with its own opera house, brick hotel, and impressive homes. After the Panic of 1893, it threatened to fade into a ghost town, until André Roch, a Swiss skier and engineer, made the first ski trail down Aspen Mountain in the winter of 1936–37. Developed in the forties and fifties, and popularized in the sixties, Aspen has grown into one of the finest ski resort areas in the country.

There are actually four mountains in the Aspen area: Aspen Highlands, Aspen Mountain (often called Ajax to avoid confusion with the Highlands), Buttermilk, and Snowmass. The four ski areas can accommodate an enormous number of people. Snowmass alone has thirty lifts and forty-seven runs, while the Aspen ski school at Buttermilk employs two hundred instructors at the height of the season. Other niceties such as heated pools and helicopter lifts to the top of otherwise inaccessible runs are additional garnishments on an already complete facility. When the snow melts, the resort becomes a summer lodge, mining the summer tourists for richer returns than the silver ores ever promised.

Vail, Colorado, was conceived in 1954 by Earl V. Eaton, former head of the Aspen Highlands Ski Patrol, who joined a friend, Peter W. Seibert, manager of the Loveland Basin Ski Area, to form the Vail Corpora-

tion. With the backing of additional investors, they began construction in 1962; by 1964 $15,000,000 had been invested in Vail to develop facilities and attract the chic—and the serious—of the skiing world. Vail's success has proved the investment worthwhile.

A more recent rival to Vail and Aspen is Steamboat Springs, infused in the early 1970s with Ling-Temco-Vought (LTV) capital that spawned a multi-million-dollar-resort building boom. Steamboat's Howelsen Hill run, predating World War II and boasting one of the first championship ski jumps in the West, has now been overshadowed by Mount Werner, focal point for LTV's $9,000,000 investment in gondola lifts, numerous new runs, the posh Thunderhead restaurant at the top of the mountain, and other relevant amenities. Since the opening of the Straight-Line Tunnel through Loveland, this latest haven for skiers is only three hours' drive from Denver.

Although skiing is not new in Jackson Hole, Wyoming, it is only recently that the area has been developed for intensive use. A ski town has developed at Teton Village, although habit and broader facilities still draw most of the off-slope activity to the traditional tourist center at Jackson Hole. While the area offers a sampling of modestly challenging runs, the mountains at Jackson are, for the most part, steep and dangerous;

only the most experienced skiers are in any degree safe on the upper slopes. Nevertheless, every year more thousands pour into the area, drawn by the challenge or misled by an overly optimistic self-evaluation of their capabilities.

It is probably impossible to reckon the amount being spent by skiers in the Rocky Mountain resorts, both large and small. Indicative of the demand, though, is the fact that at most popular resorts reservation must be made six months in advance for the holiday seasons. From all accounts, the Rockies are building a winter sports bonanza that will rival any other industry that the mountains have known—and one that may last considerably longer.

THE RECREATION EXPLOSION is not strictly a phenomenon of the private sector or a creation of developers and promoters. The single largest proprietor of recreational lands in the Rockies, catering to the needs of the greatest number of people, is the federal government. The public lands know no off season, providing facilities that range from almost urban campsites to pristine wilderness. The public domain, once principally the realm of the logger and the grazier, has in recent decades become an immense playground.

For a long time, the biggest users of public recreation lands have been hunters and fishermen. Through the summer fishermen swarm over lakes and streams, giving way in the fall to hunters stalking deer, elk, and pronghorn—and, to a lesser degree, moose, bighorn sheep, and bear. But these traditional visitors of the mountains are being joined in ever-growing numbers by wilderness campers, hikers, backpackers, and photographers—who range deep into primitive areas to experience the wilderness and escape the press of civilization. These pressures on the backcountry are being multiplied by the popularity of off-road vehicles. Four-wheel-drive trucks and jeeps, and all manner and size of motorcycles are pushing into areas previously accessible only on foot or horseback.

During the winter, the invasion is not perceptibly retarded by ice and snow. Building on the beachhead established by skiing, winter sports have proliferated in type and number of participants at a staggering rate. Ski touring and snowmobiles replace summer's hikers and jeeps in the backcountry, while closer to civilization ice-skating, sledding and tobogganing, and ice fishing have all enjoyed revival and growth.

Water sports have burgeoned, the beneficiaries of federal dam-building and the resultant reservoirs. Typical of the phenomenon is the town of Dillon Dam, a former wide spot in the road that, with the establishment of the lake, has grown to a small city of motels, cabins, and tourist facilities. Power- and sailboats, as well as fishermen, prowl the lake in summer, yielding to snowmobiles and ski-equipped sailboats when the surface freezes.

The mountains offer facilities for an almost endless diversity of outdoor activities, the only limitation apparently being the individual's imagination. The mountain West may have found a salvation in its geography—the same geography that plagued the region's development for over a hundred years. The Rockies were remote, cut off from the outside world by a lack of easy transportation; difficult to penetrate and often hostile to settlement. When men did come, they most often took what they could get and got out—often stripping the land, leaving it ravaged and useless.

But the very remoteness that discouraged cities and the twisted face of the land that curbed settlement may ultimately prove to be the region's salvation. The Rockies now offer wilderness, a place to escape the civilization that Americans so compulsively created everywhere they went. This opportunity to escape, to play, to relax even for a short time, promises to be more profitable to the mountains than any of the previous, extractive industries. And with careful management it may accomplish this without ever using up the basic resource. The challenge is not how to surmount the remote wildness that plagued the Rockies for so long, but how to preserve it.

CHAPTER 21

HIGH COUNTRY HERITAGE

*The growing industry and culture of a few islands of civilization
in a land whose greatest asset is still wilderness*

TRADITIONALLY, the mountain West has been a rather isolated and colonial land, supplying the rest of the country with raw materials at the cost of radically depleting its irreplaceable resources, and depending heavily on the goods, capital, and consumption of the outside world. Well into the twentieth century it has retained a wilderness character and resisted those who have tried to give it a sheen of high culture.

The last three decades, however, have changed the region dramatically: since World War II, the mountain states have done much to diversify their economies, ensure themselves stable water sources, and update their transportation. The area's culture, too, has taken on a new assurance and sophistication. What was once largely imported is now often indigenous; at the same time, the Rocky Mountains now draw many famous performers and artists from elsewhere.

Whether these moves toward more autonomy are basic and positive as well as dramatic remains debatable. Certainly traditional problems like aridity, remoteness, and dependence on outside capital still affect life here. And the quality of the Rocky Mountain future will no doubt hinge, like its past and present, on the quality of man's response to these basic realities of the region.

The most significant recent changes in the Rockies have come from attempts to diversify the mountain states' economies. Farming and mining, once mountain mainstays, have declined as sources of income and employment in all the states, and in states like Colo-

rado and New Mexico they are less important than manufacturing, trade, services, and government. In Montana and Idaho, where farming retains more of its old ascendancy, farmers are trying to broaden their economic base by supplementing the traditional crops with new ones.

States that still rely very heavily on turning out raw goods are trying to vary their production or to expand their manufacturing and processing facilities. Montana, for instance, has been attempting to add petroleum and lumber to its list of important raw products, while Wyoming and Idaho have been looking for funds to build processing plants for oil and agricultural products. One grasps the importance of these efforts when one realizes that in 1969 two-thirds of Wyoming's crude oil went outside the state for processing. One of Idaho's most important recent triumphs has been the creation of a major food industry out of its potato crop by beginning manufacture within the state. Governor Hathaway of Wyoming could have been speaking for the whole Rocky Mountain region, now and in the future, when he said in 1967, "Economic development of Wyoming is my number one goal. The fundamental problem in this state is that the economic base is not diverse enough."

Economic changes like these have gone hand in hand with the rapid urbanization of the Rockies. Perhaps surprisingly, people of the mountain West have traditionally been urban; mining and cattle-raising require urban centers, and typical western cities sprang full-blown out of the wilderness instead of evolving slowly

*The United States Air Force Academy at Colorado Springs, its chapel spires miming the
mountains in the background, is one of many military installations in the Rockies.*

Denver's high-rise skyline reflects the urban growth and increasingly cosmopolitan population gathered along the Front Range, both of which bid to dominate the once open spaces of the high country.

from rural villages. Rapid urban growth, however, has been the particular hallmark of contemporary Rocky Mountain history. Now, in every state except Idaho, more than half the people live in cities.

Cities have boomed and economies blossomed because the Rocky Mountains offer some things only a relatively undeveloped region can. Excellent recreation spots, space, and nearby nature lure individuals and families to the area; for companies, a recent article in *Fortune* reports, "it is the availability of good, cheap —and mostly unorganized—labor that provides the most compelling business reason for moving to the area. The mountain states have a hidden labor supply, bigger than work-force statistics show, of people who have dropped out of the job market or who never entered it because the kinds of work available until now were unattractive. In many places, the potential work force includes people thrown out of farm and mining jobs, farm wives looking for work outside the farm for the first time, and unemployed or underemployed Indians

and Spanish-Americans."

Almost all the Rocky Mountain states are leading producers of minerals and fuels essential to manufacturing; bringing businesses closer to the source of their raw materials is thrifty and efficient. Such decisions caused cities like Ogden, Brigham City, and Bingham to mushroom, as U.S. Steel, Kennecott Copper, and other metal industries moved into Utah after the war. In the fifties the town of Moab increased its size five times after Charles Steen found uranium nearby and the nuclear age offered a ready market for the ore.

The mountain region has seemed particularly alluring to the defense and aerospace industries because it provides inland security, a strategic location between east- and west-coast components suppliers, and uninhabited land for testing areas. And defense and aerospace, like other industries, have fully understood the advantages of the Rocky Mountain labor market.

These two industries have been extremely influential in most of the mountain states' economies. Colorado's

Aspen township, once a sleepy backwater in the Rockies, now entertains thousands of summer tourists and sprouts chair lifts from the edge of town to accommodate a growing winter sports industry.

1964 yearbook calls 1940 to 1960 the "Era of Defense," because during this time the outstanding economic developments in the state were the building of numerous military and other federal installations. The yearbook adds that more recently Colorado has grown economically by establishing manufacturing plants for defense and aerospace efforts. Of course, the federal presence in Colorado has been an impetus for population growth, which in turn has brought in the many other types of industry—retail trade, residential construction, and services—that now thrive in the state.

Denver's history illustrates something of this process. The most important modern economic changes in the city began in 1957, when the Martin Company opened a $27,000,000 plant nearby for the production of the Titan missile. Population in the area jumped, and Denver's reputation as an important center for defense and other industries was launched. Nowadays, it is said that Denver has "so many government bureaus that it is practically an annex of Washington." This largest

metropolis of the Rocky Mountains now houses a wide variety of impressive business interests, from American Potash and the Ideal Cement Company to the Gates Rubber Company, sixth largest in the nation, as well as a horde of consumer and service industries, like the Coors Brewing Company.

Some mountain cities, like Denver and Salt Lake City, have grown partly because of growth in other portions of the region; they are on the main east-west transportation routes, and thus important as supply and distribution centers for a developing mountain West.

THE WILDERNESS now sprouts steel and cement, and the kindlier reaches of the mountains attract people like magnets; the Rocky Mountains seem wealthier and more independent than ever before.

But diversification and urbanization have not wiped out two potentially hurtful realities: the region's reliance on extractive industry and its need for government

An oil refinery near Denver testifies to the region's continued dependence on mineral wealth.

money and regulation. For one thing, the mountains' basic output is still raw products like minerals, oil, foods, and lumber; many of these, obviously, do not renew themselves once they are extracted—they are simply gone.

Manufacturing in the mountains depends largely on what can be mined or farmed: Colorado, for instance, concentrates on food-processing and making sophisticated electronic equipment.

Government spending, too, is crucial for mountain economies: the important defense and aerospace industries rely so much on federal money that many fear the day when cutbacks will turn boom into bust. In fact, according to its 1964 yearbook, Colorado has already left the "Era of Defense" behind. This state was able to make defense spending the impetus for a more general flowering and diversification of its economy, but for other states federal cutbacks would be more hurtful. As Montana's Senator Metcalf noted in the sixties, "Federal expenditures have kept the Montana economy going. The Defense Department has spent hundreds

of millions of dollars in Montana at the Malmostrom Air Force Base, at the Glasgow Air Force Base, and the Minuteman complex in central Montana." At the same time, the senator added, the state's dependence on federal largesse spelled instability: "This year's bustling missile site may again be prairie within a decade."

The development of more diverse economies has not freed the mountain states of their traditional dilemmas completely because, finally, development depends and will continue to depend on improved water sources and transportation, neither of which will appear without government help.

THE AMERICAN ACADEMY OF SCIENCE reported in 1970 that cities and light industry use water in arid lands more profitably than agriculture uses it; recent economic developments in the Rockies, of course, mesh very closely with this finding.

Industry, nevertheless, needs enormous quantities of water, and the populations it entices to the arid lands require even more. Dam-building and water reclamation projects have never completely outstripped need and erased the western water problem, partly because the need grows so much and so fast.

Traditionally, moreover, lack of water has divided the mountain states against each other politically rather than uniting them into an efficient lobbying force in Washington. The mountain states have repeatedly had to rely on the federal government to supply what they were unwilling or unable to supply themselves: interstate regulation of water use and money.

There are signs, however, that the mountain West has begun to heed Secretary of the Interior Udall's warning that if the arid states did not cooperate with each other they would "shrivel separately." The region looks for future improvements in water management from the Water Resources Planning Act of 1965, which created federal-state commissions to coordinate planning of water use in the West. In 1966 the Western Energy Supply and Transmission Association (WEST) —a nonfederally financed organization—dedicated a thermoelectric plant in the Four Corners Area. WEST will serve most of the mountain states, and planners expect it to promote cooperation between public and private segments of the power industry. Ultimately,

Anaconda Copper still processes the metal that dominated Montana's economy for over three-quarters of a century. Only recently has agriculture outstripped copper's earning power for the state.

WEST is to mesh with Intertie, a federal project to connect federal, public, and private electrical systems.

Planners hope that a similar combination of cooperation among the states and federal guidance will create more water, as well as more power, for the thirsty Rocky Mountains. Federal and municipal engineers are collaborating on the $200,000,000 Fryingpan-Arkansas Project to bring water across the divide from the Fryingpan River to join water from the Arkansas River in supplying eastern Colorado towns like Pueblo and La Junta. The Western States Water Council, formed in 1965 by western state governors, plans to transfer water from the plentiful Snake and Missouri rivers to supplement overworked rivers in the southern mountain states like the Rio Grande, Arkansas, South Platte, and Colorado. Federal and local scientists even dream of tapping water from Alaska and western Canada; this giant project, called the North American Water and Power Alliance may be needed within the decade to supply growing mountain cities that have to compete with California, Arizona, and other booming states for water.

THE ECONOMICS of Rocky Mountain transportation is similarly two-sided. On the one hand, better highways and air travel encourage economic independence by promoting manufacturing, distribution, and that particularly important western industry, tourism. But on the other hand, the mountain states would be hard put to finance their roads and airports without federal aid.

Tourism is an important source of revenue for all the mountain states; it is particularly vital to states like Idaho and Montana, which contain some of the largest tracts of wilderness, and whose economies are not highly industrial. Many people in Wyoming, Idaho, and Montana cherish an ambivalence toward industrial expansion, fearing that the development their states need to meet rising federal taxes and inflation may threaten the clean air, nearby wilderness, and relative isolation that they sought in coming to the area. Tourism offers some solution to the problem, since it does not extract valuable resources from the region, create urban sprawl, or, in most cases, pollute and destroy nature.

273

The National Bureau of Standards laboratory in Boulder is part of a vast network of government installations in the Rockies to serve scientific, military, agricultural, and consumer needs.

The interstate highway projects of the last two decades have greatly improved communication with the rest of the country and among the mountain cities. Salt Lake City, Denver, Cheyenne, and Billings are on major east-west traffic routes, and all have one or more airports. Denver, of course, is the major distribution and transportation center of the region.

North-south transportation in the Rocky Mountains, however, remains less satisfactory than east-west. The map shows that major highways running east to west in the region outnumber those going north to south almost two to one; this may reflect the lack of regional unity that appears in struggles over water rights, or the region's continuing dependence on the outside world.

Clearly, further economic development of the Rockies will go hand in hand with transportation improvements funded by the federal government and the states.

CONTEMPORARY CULTURE in the Rocky Mountains, like economics, has gained a certain self-assurance and autonomy. In September 1970, *U.S. News and World Report* noted that "in the move of people westward, much of the nation's cultural leadership is moving with them. More than is generally realized, this part of the nation is catching up—and sometimes surpassing in creative thrust—the intellectual and artistic centers of the East."

Even in the earliest confused days of gold fever and cattle roundups, those who came to the Rockies to settle and be "respectable" enthusiastically courted "high culture" from the East and Europe, hoping that some of it might settle in their midst. As soon as the first materialistic rush had established the vague outlines of a settlement, frontier folk set about building churches and schools, and equipping their homes with the accoutrements of "civilization." On the frontier, speed was essential, and cultural symbols had to offer a concentrate of respectability, elegance, and obvious association with that most cultured place, Europe. Thus it was that the opera house emerged as the most potent sign of culture in a town.

Remote Montana had at least three important opera houses by the 1880s, in Helena, Butte, and Great Falls. Horace Tabor's opera houses in Leadville and Denver were the most lavish of all, with their frescoed ceilings, crystal chandeliers, and gilt-framed mirrors.

For all the effort and capital expended in giving the opera houses an elegant atmosphere, most of the culture merchants admitted tacitly if not openly that westerners preferred the boisterous conviviality of the saloon and popular entertainments like melodramas and light opera; bowing to public opinion, opera houses included much light entertainment on their bills of fare. Outside of San Francisco, no frontier town had more than a sporadic season of grand opera.

Serious painting and literature in the Rocky Mountains at first showed a similar lack of integration with the life of the region. Most of the artists and writers who took the West as their subject saw it romantically as a place where "nature" reigned and the ordinary rules of society vanished. Only late in the nineteenth century did men like Theodore Roosevelt, Frederic Remington, and Owen Wister begin to recognize a particular kind of civilization in the West, which could be recorded as "an entire era of this country's history." Such a concern, though inevitably colored by the patriotism, distrust of modernity, and interest in "true manliness" peculiar to these fugitives from eastern industrialism, nevertheless signaled a growing recognition of what really existed in the West—an indigenous popular culture that could affect the rest of the country.

Nowadays, the popular culture of the frontier has become an established—if still somewhat romanticized—part of American tradition. And in the urban centers of the Rockies one finds as much culture and intellectual ferment as one could want.

The high points of the Colorado cultural year are the opera, drama, and music festivals each summer in Central City and Aspen; famous performers from other parts of the nation and a cosmopolitan crowd of vacationers and music buffs come to these. The Aspen Institute for Humanistic Studies puts on a nine-month series of study programs in the humanities for business executives who wish to broaden their social perspectives.

Salt Lake City's Mormon Tabernacle Choir has been broadcasting over national airwaves since 1921; its records and concert tours have won much critical acclaim and popularity far outside the Mormon world.

Santa Fe and Taos, New Mexico, have attracted artists and writers since the 1920s when Willa Cather, Edna St. Vincent Millay, and D. H. Lawrence lived in the area. Writers like Oliver la Farge and Ruth Alexander have settled and written here; Peter Hurd, Theodore Van Soelen, and Randall Davey are among the well-known painters who make the city their home.

Santa Fe also has one of the finest opera seasons in the country. In a recent article on the culture of the West, *U.S. News and World Report* said that the company has received acclaim from eastern and European critics, both for the quality of works they offer, and for their willingness to produce little-known contemporary works seldom risked at major houses. Because of its excellence, the Santa Fe Opera Company continually draws visiting performers from top-ranking companies like the New York Metropolitan.

THE FUTURE OF THE ROCKIES can be envisioned from their present. It seems likely that current problems —meager water, need for better transportation, dependence on the government and extractive industry, and the region's ambivalence about its remoteness—will remain for some time. How these problems are confronted will decide much.

The question rouses passions, for the mountain West's problems are intimately connected with its unique promise: these states are still undeveloped enough to offer a reprieve from the mistakes of the East. As Wallace Stegner has said, "If only the image of Western virtue can be presented as an effort to avoid mistaken progress-at-any-cost, then inmigration may result in a good community instead of a merely growing one. It's the last opportunity we have in America."

GLOSSARY

alkali flat: an area of interior drainage where mixtures of soluble salts are present on the topsoil, characteristically found in arid regions.

alluvium: sediment deposited on the land by rivers and streams

caldera: a rocky volcanic crater with steep sides and a diameter many times its depth, usually produced by explosion or collapse of a volcano.

chinook: a winter weather phenomenon in which warm, dry winds on the lee side of a mountain range cause rapid evaporation of snow and soil moisture.

cirque: a steep-walled semicircular niche high on a mountain side excavated by glacial action.

conglomerate: sedimentary rock composed of fragments of pre-existing rocks, held together by a fine-grained cement.

cordillera: a system of related, often parallel, mountain ranges.

counting coups: an Indian system of reckoning military prowess by which such actions as striking an enemy, wresting a weapon from him, touching him after he had fallen, or vowing to stand steadfast in one place during a battle, all contributed to a warrior's honor; also, recounting such feats.

Desert Culture: the nomadic hunting-and-gathering society of primitive man in North America from about 7,500 B.C. until as late as the nineteenth century A.D. in some areas.

dike: a rock body that cuts through older rock, where it seeped while molten.

entrada: an entry, invasion, or incursion.

fault-block mountains: mountains bounded by one or more faults, where shifts in the earth's crust have produced uplift.

faulting: the process by which crustal rock ruptures, then slips along the line of rupture.

folding: the process of bending, wrinkling, or flexing rock.

gandy dancers: railroad workers, usually track-layers or section hands, engaged in ordinary construction or maintenance.

golconda: a source of great wealth; a rich mine, after the fabulously rich Golconda Diamond Mine of India.

granite: a common igneous rock that is coarse-grained and characterized by the presence of light-colored minerals (quartz and feldspar) with some minor dark minerals (biotite, hornblende, and magnetite).

hogan: an earth-covered lodge built of sticks and mud in a low, broad, cylindrical form; a hole in the mounded roof allows smoke from a fire to escape.

hogback/flatiron: a sharp-crested rock ridge that develops from the selective removal of weak adjacent rock layers by erosion.

igneous rock: rock formed by the cooling of molten rock material.

kachina: one of more than a hundred Pueblo Indian spirits; may also refer to a priest impersonating one of these spirits or a doll representing it.

kiva: a secret ceremonial chamber found in Pueblo Indian towns, usually circular and underground.

Laramide Revolution: the general mountain-building event, occurring from late Mesozoic to early Cenozoic times, which gave rise to the Rocky Mountains.

life zone: a region defined by its altitude, latitude, available moisture, and exposure to the sun, and identified by the flora and fauna that live in it.

limestone: fine-grained sedimentary rock containing calcium carbonate.

magma: molten rock material which lies deep below the earth's surface.

metamorphic rock: rock whose original texture or mineral composition has been altered by heat, pressure, or chemical action.

Montane Zone: the life zone of the forested slopes, falling between the foothills and the subalpine zone.

moraine: a general term for the ridge of rock debris that is deposited at the farthest advance of a glacier.

pediment: a sloping surface cut in the rock near a mountain base.

pika: a small, short-eared rodent that inhabits the rocky uplands above timberline.

placer mining: the extraction of free gold from alluvial deposits by the use of water; includes the processes of panning, sluicing, hydraulicking, and dredging.

rain shadow: the region of dry climate on the leeward side of a mountain range.

remuda: the horse herd on a cattle ranch; more specifically, the remounts, herded together and tended by a "wrangler," on a roundup or trail drive.

riffles: in mining, the ridges across an inclined trough, intended to catch gold particles carried by a flow of water; usually the last step in placer operations.

rite de passage: a social ritual that marks the end of one life stage and the attainment of another.

sandstone: sedimentary rock made of small quartz grains cemented together.

scarp: a steep slope, sometimes almost vertical, often resulting from a fault.

sedge: a family of grasslike plants, usually perennial; unlike grass, the stems are solid.

sedimentary rock: rock formed from an accumulation of organic and inorganic sediments.

Seven Cities of Cíbola: the fabled Seven Cities of Gold of North America, rumored to lie somewhere north of Mexico, which drew Coronado northward to the fringes of the Rockies.

shale: fine-grained, easily split sedimentary rock containing clay minerals and small amounts of quartz, feldspar, and other minerals.

shaman: among some American Indians and other primitive peoples, an individual who had received a personal vision giving him special wisdom or healing powers; a "medicine man."

Subalpine Zone: the life zone of timberline, above the forested slopes and below the alpine meadows.

uplift: the elevation of a mountain range.

Zion: the "promised land" of the Mormons, representing more the concept of an unthreatened Mormon community than any particular place, though it came to be identified with Salt Lake City and certain other Mormon communities in the West.

HISTORICAL CHRONOLOGY

10,000–5,000 B.C. The Ice Age enters its final phase. Big-game hunters migrate from Siberia into North America, and some settle on either side of the Rocky Mountains.

5,000–2,500 B.C. The ice recedes. Desert Culture dominates the Rockies, and the Anasazi (later Pueblos) of Colorado and New Mexico begin to farm.

A.D. 300–1300 Pueblo culture flourishes, but in the fourteenth century the Indians disperse throughout the Southwest, some to new towns along the Rio Grande.

1776 Escalante probes the interior of the cordillera seeking a new route to California.

1803–1806 Lewis and Clark's overland trek to the Pacific provides the first reliable descriptions of the Rockies to the new nation and encourages the advance of fur trappers.

1806–1807 Lt. Zebulon Pike explores the eastern fringe of the mountains in Colorado and New Mexico, but offers scant praise for the mountain region.

1807 Manuel Lisa establishes a fort and trading post at the fork of the Yellowstone and Bighorn rivers.

1811 Wilson Price Hunt crosses the Rockies en route to Astoria. The following year Robert Stuart, returning from Astoria, crosses the Rockies via South Pass, apparently not realizing what he had found.

1820 Maj. Stephen H. Long's expedition explores the area between the Missouri River and the Rocky Mountains, originating the concept of the "Great American Desert."

1822 William Ashley and Andrew Henry organize the Rocky Mountain Fur Company and develop the rendezvous system that revolutionizes the trade.

1824 Jedediah Smith rediscovers South Pass, first used by Robert Stuart in 1812. In the same year Jim Bridger and Peter Skene Ogden discover the Great Salt Lake and explore the surrounding region.

1835 Dr. Marcus Whitman leads the first expedition to include women across the Rockies to Oregon.

1841 The Rocky Mountain fur trade, which has been languishing for years, dies completely. In this same year the Bartleson-Bidwell party inaugurates overland migration to California through South Pass.

1842 Reflecting the growing continental aspirations of the U.S., John C. Frémont leads an official exploring party over the Oregon Trail to the Wind River Range and through South Pass.

1846–48 The outline of the Far West is completed with the acquisition of California and the Southwest from Mexico and the settlement of the Oregon question.

1847 The first Mormons reach Salt Lake Valley to establish Salt Lake City and the State of Deseret.

1851 The Treaty of Fort Laramie attempts to reduce intertribal conflict and guarantee the safety of emigrants passing through the mountain region. It is largely unsuccessful.

1857–1858 Democracy and theocracy rub elbows in Utah until the friction of disputed authority touches off conflict. The "Mormon War" was more threat than battle.

1858 Gold is found in Colorado; Pikes Peak gold rush begins, and the mining frontier in the Rockies opens.

1862 In an effort to place the immense new western lands in the hands of small freeholders, the government passes the Homestead Act; on it will be built a framework of experimental land disposal legislation that led westerners astray for forty years.

1864 Col. John M. Chivington leads the massacre of Cheyennes and Arapahoes at Sand Creek.

1865–1867 The Civil War ends and national attention is focused once again on the West: the transcontinental railroad plunges ahead; the "long drive" brings Texas cattle to the northern ranges; Clarence King and Ferdinand Hayden launch surveys in the high country.

1869 Maj. John Wesley Powell makes his exploration of the Colorado River. In the same year the Union Pacific and Central Pacific railroads meet at Promontory, Utah.

1870 The Denver Pacific and Kansas Pacific railroads both arrive in Denver.

1872 Yellowstone National Park is established.

1874 Joseph Glidden markets the barbed wire that will change the western cattle industry.

1876 Colorado becomes a state. Sitting Bull, Crazy Horse, and assembled tribes defeat Custer in the Valley of the Little Big Horn.

1880 The miners of Leadville form the Miner's Cooperative and go on strike for higher wages. Their bid is unsuccessful.

1883 The Northern Pacific Railroad is completed.

1886–87 The cattle boom fails, as serious drought and a harsh winter follow overstocking. Fenced ranching begins to replace the open range methods.

1887 Philip Shannon begins sinking oil wells in the Salt Creek area of Wyoming.

1889 Montana becomes a state.

1890 Idaho and Wyoming become states, and the U.S. Census report declares that the frontier is gone. At the same time the Ghost Dance sweeps the Indian reservations, culminating in a massacre at Wounded Knee.

1891 The Forest Reserve Act is passed.

1892 The repeal of the Sherman Silver Purchase Act and the formation of the Populist Party signal the beginning of a decade of political and economic readjustment for the mountain states.

1896 Utah becomes a state.

1902 The Newlands Act sets aside proceeds from western land sales to finance irrigation in the arid regions.

1903 Miners in Cripple Creek strike; the failure of the strike destroys the Western Federation of Miners.

1912 New Mexico becomes a state.

1934 The Taylor Grazing Act gives the federal government control of 80,000,000 acres of western land. With control of forests, irrigation, and grazing, the federal government assumes a powerful influence in the shape and quality of life in the Rocky Mountain West.

1957–present The Martin Company opens a Titan missile plant near Denver, heralding the beginning of a dynamic new era for the Rockies. From defense-related contracts and installations like NORAD, to scientific projects like the National Center for Atmospheric Research, the growth of aerospace industries and technical and scientific services generates prosperity for most of the region. The mountains, the last frontier, remain on the frontiers of experience; the use of a nuclear blast in 1969 to free natural gas deposits near Rifle, Colorado may mark the dawn of a new era.

NATIONAL PARKS AND MONUMENTS

COLORADO

Black Canyon of the Gunnison National Monument

Many geologists believe this canyon in western Colorado is one of the most remarkable scenic attractions within the San Juan Mountains. The Ute Indians called it "the place of high rocks and much water."

History: The gorge has been cut by water of the Gunnison River, flowing continually throughout several million years, incising its channel in one of the oldest bodies of granite rock known.

Key features: In places, the river narrows to a forty-foot channel, rimmed by cliffs that tower 1,730 to 2,425 feet above. Occasionally, a Rocky Mountain bighorn is seen on the pine- and juniper-studded ledges. There is a campground on each rim, and rangers are stationed there during the travel season.

Colorado National Monument

Twenty-seven square miles of canyons, escarpments, and free-standing columns attract the tourist to west-central Colorado. Campgrounds, picnic areas, and a visitor center are open year-round.

History: The canyon walls are sandstone, shale, and dark-colored igneous and metamorphic formations; the sedimentary layers were deposited while a series of inland seas and deserts alternately occupied the region. Vertical cliffs endure the attack of water and wind only where they are protectively capped by hard rock layers.

Key features: A scenic drive along the rim brings the traveler to Cold Shivers Point, a toadstool cap above vertical cliffs; the rounded domes of the Coke Ovens; Balanced Rock; fossil sand dunes; and Independence Monument, a towering landmark of free-standing sandstone.

Florissant Fossil Beds National Monument

In 1872 a unique deposit of fragile insect, plant, and animal fossils and petrified wood was found thirty miles west of Colorado Springs. In 1969 the site became a national monument.

History: Conditions for fossil preservation were excellent in the ancient lake bed at Florissant. First, volcanic ash rained down upon the lake; then lava sealed the basin, and uplift pressed the sediment to shale—with flowers, leaves, insects, fruits, and fish preserved between the layers.

Key features: This is a scientific monument, devoted to the biological and geological interpretation of the fossils and petrified wood found here. Over eight thousand acres are now protected.

Great Sand Dunes National Monument

This fifty-seven-square-mile region—part of the San Luis Valley in south central Colorado—contains the largest sand dunes in the United States.

History: Dunes have originated within their valley confines because prevailing winds are unable to blow over the Sangre de Cristo the sand grains they carry from the valley floor. So, the dunal area grows larger.

Key features: The dunes are most striking in appearance when lighting is oblique, emphasizing their flowing crests and hollows. Shifting sand permits little plant growth except in some dunal hollows, but bordering the dunes are cottonwood trees in luxuriant growth along the Medano River.

Mesa Verde National Park

The pithouse sites, cave structures, and villages of Mesa Verde represent thirteen hundred years of habitation by prehistoric Indian cliff dwellers; deserted stone pueblos remain as they were discovered two thousand feet above Montezuma Valley, in south-western Colorado.

History: The archaeological story is one of increasing skill as the Indian culture developed—from simple weavers and basketmakers to affluent creators of durable architecture, ornamental pottery, and an irrigation system. Tools, supplies, and food attracted enemies, but it was probably drought which drove the cliff dwellers from the mesa.

Key features: Spruce Tree House, Cliff Palace, and Balcony House are the three original cliff dwellings opened by the Park Service for inspection; atop the mesa are ancient pithouses and their ruins. Newly excavated cave villages have been found on Wetherill Mesa.

Rocky Mountain National Park

Four hundred ten square miles of some of the most spectacular mountain wilderness in the Rockies are set aside for public use and preservation; much of the scenery is reachable June through September by way of Trail Ridge Road.

History: A billion years ago this land was sea bottom, where sediments were collecting and being compacted into rock. Then uplift came and a range was formed. Millions of years of weathering wore down this range and an inland sea returned. However, millennia later, the pressures were restored, mountains again rose, and the Front Range was created. Water and ice have removed thousands of feet of the original mountains.

Key features: Within the park are sixty-five named peaks over ten thousand feet in elevation. Some are granite; others show evidence of ancient volcanism and metamorphic effects. Alpine lakes, small glaciers, mountain streams, wildflowers, and a varied wildlife may be seen on many of the park's trails.

MONTANA

Custer Battlefield National Monument

The last stand of Lt. Col. George Custer and 225 men of the Seventh Cavalry was fought against several thousand Sioux and Cheyenne here in the valley of the Little Bighorn River.

History: This battle was the last great Indian victory. Even while Custer was being defeated, Major Reno, Captain Benteen, and the rest of the Seventh Cavalry were winning another battle only five miles to the south.

Key features: The monument includes the ridge of Custer's last stand, the Reno-Benteen defense perimeter, a national cemetery, a historical museum, and a visitor center. Photos, maps, and dioramas depict the battle

Glacier National Park

Though it lies outside the Central and Southern Rockies, this park is frequently visited by travelers going north from Yellowstone.

History: At least five hundred million years ago silt, sand, clay, and lime were deposited here on the bottom of an inland sea. As they hardened into rock, ancient magma was forced into cracks and between layers of the sediments; then the earth rose into mountains. A million years ago the mountains were re-sculpted by alpine glaciers. Today, sixty small glaciers remain high in the peaks.

Key features: Emerald finger lakes, deep glacial gorges, and sheer mountainsides flanked by dense forests may be seen along a thousand miles of trail. Spectacular Going-to-the-Sun Highway is usually open from mid-June to mid-October. Fishing, riding, boating, and bicycling are among the summer activities; in winter, cross-country skiing is permitted but hazardous.

NEW MEXICO

Aztec Ruins National Monument

The valley of the Las Animas River, in northwestern New Mexico, was the site of a productive Indian civilization; immense stone pueblos still survive to tell of the culture.

History: Both the Chaco and the Mesa Verde Indians occupied Aztec, each in a separate period. They were farmers in a semiarid region, and irrigation was important. Their lives depended upon this way of life; thus, when a great drought came in the last quarter of the thirteenth century, the people were forced to abandon the village. In 1775 a Spanish Franciscan missionary and explorer made the first historical record of the ruins.

Key features: The Indians left behind their pueblos, with storage rooms, living quarters, and ceremonial kivas. The ruins have a self-guiding trail. Knives, stone hammers, pottery, and other artifacts are on display in the visitor center.

Bandelier National Monument

The monument contains two sections—the Frijoles Canyon floor and the Tsankawi section. They are part of an ash and lava plateau built by ancient volcanoes in the Jemez mountain region.

History: Indians came to Frijoles Canyon about A.D. 1383 to escape severe drought in the south. They occupied the canyon until about 1600, leaving behind combination cave and masonry dwellings on the canyon sides.

Key features: A road makes Frijoles Canyon and the nearly circular Tyuonyi Ruin accessible to the tourist. Other features—Painted Cave, Haatse ruins, the Frijoles Falls, and the Shrine of the Stone Lions—are seen only by trail. The Tsankawi ruins and cliff dwellings are in the monument's northern section.

Chaco Canyon National Monument

Twelve major ruins, each with one hundred or more rooms, 375 archaeological sites, and a sophisticated irrigation system remain at this great Indian population center.

History: The Chaco Indians inhabited this canyon about A.D. 825, and their culture flourished at its peak between 1000 and 1100. They were expert masons, farmers, toolmakers, and craftsmen.

Key features: D-shaped Pueblo Bonito ("Beautiful Village") is the most impressive of the large ruins; its workmanship is the finest of all southwest pueblos. Other large ruins are Chettro Ketl, Hungo Pavi, Peñasco Blanco, Una Vida, and Wijiji.

UTAH

Arches National Monument

Rock layers deposited millions of years ago have been eroded to spectacular arches of sandstone spanning canyons of the monument.

History: Great cracks developed in the 300-foot-thick upper sandstone layer; these were enlarged by weathering and gravity until perforations became openings, and the rock slabs or "fins" became arches.

Key features: A road leads to the Windows section, where the spectacular Double Arch and balanced rocks are primary attractions; then it moves on to Delicate Arch, Fiery Furnace, and Devils Garden. At road's end a trail leads to other features, including Landscape Arch, the monument's longest span.

Bryce Canyon National Park

Domes, pinnacles, figures, spires, windows, and walls of every description transform this half-bowl-shaped canyon into a badland.

History: Silt, sand, and lime of the Bryce formations were deposited in lakes of the Eocene epoch, sixty million years ago. It accumulated to depths of two thousand feet, and then the land rose. Upheaval cracked the rock, creating plateaus and speeding water erosion of the soft rock layers. Wind, rain, and frost action slowly wore the edges of the mesa into its unique pinnacles and spires. Iron and manganese color the formations.

Key features: A road rims the canyon from the visitors' center to Rainbow Point. Excellent views can be had from Sunrise and Sunset points; below is the unparalleled Queen's Garden. Sixty-one miles of trail may be followed on foot or on horseback. The main road is open in winter.

Canyonlands National Park

Canyons are more numerous and extensively developed here than in any other section of the Colorado Plateau.

History: The entire region has been uplifted, then deformed again by local upwarps, and intricately dissected by its rivers. The area is noted for its entrenched river meanders.

Key features: Much travel within the park is still by jeep trail or by float upon the two rivers—the Colorado and Green. A concessioner provides float trips. Hiking on the White Rim is nearly impossible, due to intense temperatures and lack of water, but a good road provides access to Grand View Point on the Island in the Sky mesa, and from there White Rim, Standing Rock Basin, the Needles, and the rugged canyons can be seen.

Capitol Reef National Monument

Colorful sandstone, appearing in many shapes and strange formations, is the main attraction of the monument.

History: These formations are all that remain of a group of folded mountains that were uplifted sixty million years ago. The reeflike cliffs of multicolored material and the rounded, weathered domes of sandstone are remnants of this ancient highland.

Key features: Sulphur Creek Gorge, Cohab Canyon, Grand Wash, Hickman Natural Bridge, Capitol Gorge, Cassidy Arch, and the Golden Throne are among many interest points; some are reached by the monument road, others by trail. Indian petroglyphs can be seen near the visitors' center.

Dinosaur National Monument

Originally established to protect a quarry containing the bones of prehistoric reptiles, the monument was enlarged in 1938 to include dramatic canyons.

History: Ancient rivers wound through this land along the Utah-Colorado border and carved its canyons. Uplifts during the Laramide Revolution tilted strata in the monument, exposing some layers of rock to rapid erosion and leading to the subsequent discovery of the dinosaur fossils.

Key features: A modern museum has been built over the original dinosaur quarry, but further exploration still continues. On the canyon rims, many promontories and peaks provide excellent vistas of the monument.

Hovenweep National Monument

Hovenweep protects a group of six separate prehistoric Indian masonry ruins in southeastern Utah; in the Ute Indian language it means "deserted valley."

History: Pueblo Indians came to Hovenweep in the twelfth century and left sometime between 1276 and 1299, while this part of Utah was unusually dry. The ruins which remain are unexcavated, so the complete story of the towers and their architects is not yet known.

Key features: The ruins of Square Tower Canyon contain more than twenty individual structures—two towers, two kivas, and many living and storage rooms; these are the most accessible ruins. Towers in other canyons are spectacular, but extremely difficult to find. Until they have been studied and stabilized, the public will not be encouraged to visit them. Roads to the monument are unimproved and impassable in wet weather.

Natural Bridges National Monument

Three sandstone bridges are the monument's key attractions; they may be conveniently viewed from a mesa-top loop drive.
History: Ancient rivers carrying sand-laden flash floods began undercutting rock of the river bend. Continuous erosion eventually produced openings and finally bridges. The thinnest span—Owachomo—is probably the oldest.
Key features: Owachomo, Sipapu, and Kachina bridges may be seen by road, or by a trail to the canyon floor. A collapsed bridge has left remains in White Canyon, beyond Sipapu Bridge.

Rainbow Bridge National Monument

Though Rainbow Bridge is reachable only by boat on Lake Powell and a foot trail, or by horseback, the charm of this natural feature is unequalled.
History: Bridge Canyon was formed by a tight, meandering stream that cut its bed while the Colorado Plateau was being uplifted. Seeking a straight course, the river wore through the canyon side wall, then enlarged its opening and created the graceful arch.
Key features: The massive red cliffs of the bridge are streaked with brown, and they span a twisting, turning canyon. This is the largest known natural sandstone arch in the world, standing 309 feet above the canyon floor. Visitors should check with Lake Powell Ferry Service, Blanding, Utah, for boat ride information, and Navajo Mountain Trading Post, Tonalea, Arizona, for horse rentals.

Timpanogos Cave National Monument

On the north slope of rugged Mount Timpanogos, surrounded by the Uinta National Forest, the monument offers beautiful vistas of the Wasatch Range, but three caverns are its biggest attraction.
History: Limestone rock of the caves was once a limy ooze forming on an ocean bottom over three hundred million years ago. As water dissolved the carbonate, fault zones in the limestone were widened, and the caverns were formed. Hansen Cave was discovered in 1887, the others in 1921.
Key features: Hansen, Middle, and Timpanogos caves are reached by a paved trail which climbs 1,065 feet above the visitors' center and picnic area. The caverns are noted for their unique and abundant "helictites"—pencil-thin calcite formations growing in all directions from the cavern walls—also stalactites, stalagmites, and aragonite crystals.

WYOMING

Devils Tower National Monument

Rising 865 feet above the plains in Wyoming's northeastern corner, Devils Tower is an imposing monolith.
History: The tower is part of an ancient lava dome which pushed upward from the earth's interior, then cooled and cracked into the vertical columns of rock now exposed by erosion. Established in 1906, it was the first national monument.
Key features: The light gray and buff columns are about ten feet in diameter and pentagonal in shape. A trail winds around the tower among ponderosa pine and fallen rock, but the top is reached only by rock climbers.

Grand Teton National Park

The Teton area is renowned for its dramatic mountains, glacial lakes, mountain-fed streams, and the resort atmosphere of Jackson Hole.
History: One forty-mile fault line is responsible for this spectacular topography. As the Tetons slowly rose west of the crustal fracture, land on the east was sinking to become Jackson Hole. Then glaciers invaded the peaks, carving the landscape into what is seen today.
Key features: Hiking on two hundred miles of trails with all range of difficulty, mountaineering, pack trips, fishing, boating, rafting on the Snake River, swimming, and general sight-seeing are delights in the Tetons. A park highway penetrates to many vistas east of the range and is maintained throughout the winter.

Yellowstone National Park

Thermal activity is the hallmark of Yellowstone, where the volcanic plateau is alive with steaming geysers and bubbling pools.
History: As mountains rose, they expelled an inland sea, then received the lava flows and ash that would create this great highland park. Today's geyser basins and hot springs are remains of that ancient period of volcanism.
Key features: A loop road passes many of the attractions—Old Faithful, the geyser basins, Mammoth Hot Springs, the Grand Canyon of the Yellowstone, Yellowstone Falls, and countless others—but to see more of this first and largest of the national parks, there are one thousand miles of trails, as well as organized pack trips, boat rentals, and many other activities.

SOURCES AND SUGGESTED READING

General

Beyond the Mississippi by Albert D. Richardson; American Publishing Co., 1867.

Colorado: Big Mountain Country by Nancy Wood; Doubleday, 1969.

The Grand Colorado by T. H. Watkins; American West Publishing Co., 1969.

The Fourteeners by Perry Eberhart and Philip Schmuck; Swallow, 1970.

Guide to the Colorado Mountains by Robert Ormes; Swallow, 1970.

Roaming the American West by Donald E. Bower; Stackpole, 1970.

The Rocky Mountains by Wallace W. Atwood; Vanguard, 1945.

Cattle, Ranching, and Land Use

The Agrarian Crusade by Solon J. Buck; Yale University Press, 1920.

Aridity and Man; American Association for the Advancement of Science, Publication 74, 1963.

Bankers and Cattlemen by Gene M. Gressley; Knopf, 1966.

The Cattleman's Frontier by Louis Pelzer; Arthur H. Clark Co., 1936.

The Closing of the Public Domain by E. Louise Peffer; Stanford University Press, 1951.

The Colorado Range Cattle Industry by Ora Brooks Peake; Arthur H. Clark Co., 1937.

The Conquest of Arid America by William E. Smythe; Harper and Brothers, 1900.

The Day of the Cattleman by Earnest S. Osgood; University of Minnesota Press, 1929.

The Farmer's Last Frontier: Agriculture, 1860–1897 by Fred A. Shannon; Farrar and Rinehart, 1945.

The Granger Movement by Solon J. Buck; Harvard University Press, 1913.

A History of the Public Land Policies by Benjamin H. Hibbard; Macmillan, 1924.

Our Landed Heritage: The Public Domain, 1776–1936 by Roy M. Robbins; Princeton University Press, 1942.

The Populist Revolt by John D. Hicks; University of Minnesota Press, 1931.

The United States Forest Policy by John Ise; Yale University Press, 1920.

Ecology and Wildlife

The American West: A Natural History by Ann and Myron Sutton; Random House, 1969.

Beyond the Aspen Grove by Ann Zwinger; Random House, 1970.

Deserts of America by Peggy Larson; Prentice-Hall, 1970.

The Ecology of North America by Victor Shelford; University of Illinois Press, 1963.

The Face of North America by Peter Farb; Harper and Row, 1963.

Field Guide to Rocky Mountain Wildflowers by J. J. Craighead et al.; Houghton Mifflin, 1963.

The Life of the Mountains by Maurice Brooks; McGraw-Hill, 1968.

Our Vanishing Wilderness by M. L. Grossman and J. Hamlet; Grossett and Dunlap, 1969.

Fur Trade

Across the Wide Missouri by Bernard DeVoto; Houghton Mifflin, 1947.

The Adventures of Captain Bonneville in the Rocky Mountains and the Far West by Washington Irving, edited by Edgely W. Todd; University of Oklahoma Press, 1961.

The American Fur Trade of the Far West by Hiram M. Chittenden; F. P. Harper, 1902.

The Ashley-Smith Explorations and the Discovery of the Central Route to the Pacific by Harrison C. Dale; Arthur H. Clark Co., 1918.

Bill Sublette: Mountain Man by John E. Sunder; University of Oklahoma Press, 1959.

James Bridger by J. Cecil Alter; Shepard Book Co., 1925.

Jedediah Smith and the Opening of the West by Dale L. Morgan; Bobbs-Merrill, 1953.

John Colter: His Years in the Rockies by Burton Harris; Scribner's, 1952.

Life in the Far West by George Frederick Ruxton, edited by LeRoy R. Hafen; University of Oklahoma Press, 1951.

Mountain Men by Stanley Vestal; Houghton Mifflin, 1937.

The Mountain Men and the Fur Trade of the Far West edited by LeRoy R. Hafen; Arthur H. Clark Co., 1965.

This Reckless Breed of Men by Robert G. Cleland; Knopf, 1952.

Tools and Traps of the Fur Trade by Carl P. Russell; Knopf, 1967.

Geography and Geology

Creation of the Teton Landscape by J. D. Love and John C. Reed, Jr.; Grand Teton Natural History Association, 1968.

Exploring Rocks, Minerals, Fossils in Colorado by Richard M. Pearl; Sage Books, 1969.

A Field Guide to the Rocks and Minerals of Wyoming by William H. Wilson; University of Wyoming, 1965.

Fossils of Wyoming by Michael W. Hager; Wyoming Geological Survey, Bulletin 54, 1971.

Geologic Atlas of the Rocky Mountain Region, United States of America; Rocky Mountain Association of Geologists, Denver, 1972.

Geological Evolution of North America by Thomas H. Clark and Colin W. Stearn; Ronald Press, New York, 1968.

Geology Illustrated by John S. Shelton; W. H. Freeman, 1966.

Guide to the Geology of Colorado by Robert J. Weimer and John D. Haun; Rocky Mountain Association of Geologists, 1960.

History of the Earth by Bernhard Kummel; W. H. Freeman, 1970.

Physiography of the United States by Charles B. Hunt; W. H. Freeman, 1967.

Physiography of Western United States by Nevin M. Fenneman; McGraw-Hill, 1931.

Regional Geomorphology of the United States by William D. Thornbury; John Wiley & Sons, 1965.

Rock, Time, and Landforms by Jerome Wyckoff; Harper and Row, 1966.

Traveler's Guide to the Geology of Wyoming by D. L. Blackstone, Jr.; Bulletin 55, The Geological Survey of Wyoming, 1971.

History

America Moves West by Robert E. Riegel and Robert G. Athearn; Holt, Rinehart and Winston, 1971.

Before Lewis and Clark by Abraham Nasatir; St. Louis Historical Documents Foundation, 1952.

Beyond The Hundredth Meridian by Wallace Stegner; Houghton Mifflin, 1953.

Colorado: The Story of a Western Commonwealth by LeRoy R. Hafen; Peerless Publishing Co., 1933.

The Course of Empire by Bernard DeVoto; Houghton Mifflin, 1952.

Exploration and Empire by William H. Goetzmann; Knopf, 1966.

The Far Western Frontier by Ray Allen Billington; Harper and Row, 1956.

The Gathering of Zion: The Story of the Mormon Trail by Wallace Stegner; McGraw-Hill, 1964.

The Great Plains by Walter Prescott Webb; Ginn & Co., 1931.

Great Surveys of the American West by Richard A. Bartlett; University of Oklahoma Press, 1962.

Health-Seekers in the Southwest, 1817–1900 by Billy M. Jones; University of Oklahoma Press, 1967.

High Country Empire by Robert G. Athearn; McGraw-Hill, 1960.

History of Wyoming by T. A. Larson; University of Nebraska Press, 1965.

The Journals of Lewis and Clark edited by Bernard DeVoto; Houghton Mifflin, 1953.

The Lost Pathfinder: Zebulon Montgomery Pike by W. Eugene Hollon; University of Oklahoma Press, 1949.

Mapping the Trans-Mississippi West (5 vols.) by Carl I. Wheat; Institute of Historical Cartography, 1965.

Montana: An Uncommon Land by K. Ross Toole; University of Oklahoma Press, 1959.

Montana: High, Wide, and Handsome by John Kinsey Howard; Yale University Press, 1943.

Narratives of Exploration and Adventure by John C. Frémont, edited by Allan Nevins; Longmans and Green, 1956.

Pageant in the Wilderness edited by Herbert Bolton; Utah State Historical Society, 1950.

The Rockies by David Lavender; Harper and Row, 1968.

Rocky Mountain Politics by Thomas C. Donnelly; University of New Mexico Press, 1945.

"Second Bonanza" by Don Douma in *Montana, The Magazine of History;* Autumn 1953, Winter, Spring, Summer 1954.

Vanguards of the Frontier by Everett Dick; D. Appleton–Century Co., 1944.

Western America by LeRoy R. Hafen and Carl Coke Rister; Prentice-Hall, 1941.

Westward Expansion (Third Edition) by Ray Allen Billington; Macmillan, 1967.

Westward Tilt by Neil Morgan; Random House, 1963.

Indians

The American Indian Wars by John Tebbel and Keith Jennison; Harper and Row, 1960.

Bury My Heart At Wounded Knee by Dee Brown; Holt, Rinehart and Winston, 1970.

Cultural and Natural Areas of Native North America by Alfred L. Kroeber; University of California Press, 1940.

Fighting Indians of the West by Martin F. Schmitt and Dee Brown; Bonanza Books, 1948.

The Indian Heritage of America by Alvin M. Josephy, Jr.; Knopf, 1968.

Indians of the Americas by E. R. Embree; Houghton Mifflin, 1936.

The Long Death; The Last Days of the Plains Indian by Ralph K. Andrist; Macmillan, 1967.

Man's Rise to Civilization as Shown by the Indians of North America, from Primeval Times to the Coming of the Industrial State by Peter Farb; Dutton, 1968.

The Native Americans by Robert F. Spencer, Jesse D. Jennings, et al.; Harper and Row, 1965.

North American Indians: A Casebook by R. C. Owens et al.; Macmillan, 1967.

Mining and Industry

General William Palmer: A Decade of Railroad Building in Colorado by George L. Anderson; Colorado College Publication, 1936.

Gold and Silver in the West by T. H. Watkins; American West Publishing Co., 1971.

Mining Frontiers of the Far West, 1848–1880 by Rodman W. Paul; Holt, Rinehart and Winston, 1963.

Rebel of the Rockies by Robert G. Athearn; Yale University Press, 1962.

Salt Creek Wyoming: The Story of a Great Oil Field by Harold D. Roberts; W. H. Kistler Co., 1956.

The Story of Western Railroads by Robert Riegel; Macmillan, 1926.

Weather

Climatology and the World's Climates by George R. Rumney; Macmillan, 1968.

World Survey of Climatology, vol. 2, edited by H. Flohn; Elsevier, 1969.

ACKNOWLEDGMENTS

The authors and editors wish to express their appreciation to all the individuals and institutions whose cooperation made this volume possible, with special gratitude to Alys Freeze, James Davis, and the staff of the Western History Department, Denver Public Library; Greg Chancellor, Colorado Department of Commerce and Development; John Barr Tompkins and the staff of the Bancroft Library, University of California at Berkeley; and Gene Gressley and Chuck Roundy, Western History Research Center, University of Wyoming.

PICTURE CREDITS:

Gene Ahrens: Pages 20, 22, 29, 90, 104, 106, 107, 111, 263. Bancroft Library, University of California at Berkeley: Pages 154, 156, 158, 160. Butler Institute of American Art: Page 141 (bottom). Harvey Caplin: Pages 18, 122, 212, 242 (top), 244-245, 266. Herbert Clarke: Pages 84 (center, right), 85 (center, left), 87 (top, left). Colorado Department of Public Relations: Pages 70, 131, 192, 222-223, 242 (bottom), 243, 250 (top), 251, 252, 253 (bottom), 264, 265, 272. Ed Cooper: Pages 6-7, 14-15, 16, 26-27, 30, 52, 56-57, 68, 78, 79 (top), 82 (bottom, left), 96, 98, 100, 101, 232, 253 (top), 260, 268. Denver Public Library, Western History Department: Pages 4-5, 114-115, 116, 120, 121, 123, 126, 129, 130, 132-135, 138-139, 140, 141 (top), 142-144, 147, 148, 150-152, 159, 162-163, 164, 167-172, 174, 176-183, 195-200, 202, 204, 205, 208-210, 214-218, 220, 224, 226, 228, 234, 236, 239, 258, 259, 262. Carlos Elmer: Pages 186-187, 246-247 (top), 274. Peter Fronk: Page 250 (bottom). Charles Grover: Pages 36, 190 (bottom). Frank Klune, Jr.: Pages 33, 38-39, 76-77, 246 (bottom). David Muench: Pages 2-3, 8, 24, 34-35, 37, 40, 46, 48, 58-59, 62, 73-75, 79 (bottom), 83 (bottom), 92, 119, 124, 137, 191, 241, 247 (bottom), 248, 249, 254-256, 270, 271, 273. NCAR Photo (National Center for Atmospheric Research): Page 60. Nature Graphics: Pages 84 (center, left), 86 (center, left; bottom, right), 112. William Staley: Pages 82 (top, right; center, left and right; bottom, right), 83 (top, right), 84 (top, left and right; bottom, left and right), 85 (top, left and right; bottom, left and right), 86 (top, right; center, right; bottom, left), 87 (top, right; bottom), 88, 99, 102, 109, 110, 190 (top). David Sumner: Pages 28, 80-81, 82 (top, left), 86 (top, left), 108, 185. Judy Sumner: Pages 83 (top, left), 94. Lester Tinker: Pages 188-189. Western History Research Center, University of Wyoming: Pages 219, 230, 235, 237.

INDEX

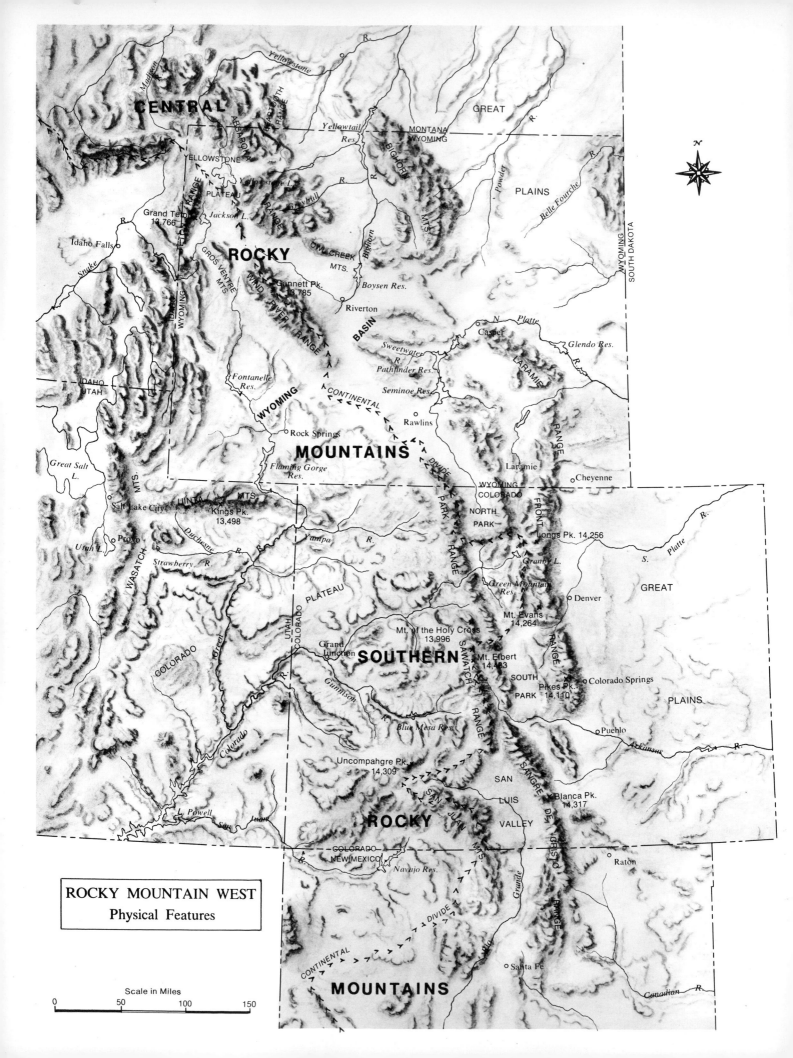

ROCKY MOUNTAIN WEST
Physical Features

Scale in Miles
0   50   100   150

CENTRAL

ROCKY

MOUNTAINS

SOUTHERN

ROCKY

MOUNTAINS

GREAT

PLAINS

GREAT

PLAINS

Madison R.
Yellowstone R.
ABSAROKA RANGE
BEARTOOTH RANGE
Yellowtail Res.
MONTANA
WYOMING
YELLOWSTONE
PLATEAU
Yellowstone L.
Greybull R.
BIGHORN MTS.
Powder R.
Belle Fourche R.
WYOMING
SOUTH DAKOTA
Grand Teton 13,766
Jackson L.
TETON RANGE
Idaho Falls
Snake R.
IDAHO
WYOMING
GROS VENTRE MTS.
OWL CREEK MTS.
Bighorn R.
Boysen Res.
WIND RIVER RANGE
Gannett Pk. 13,785
Riverton
BASIN
Sweetwater R.
Pathfinder Res.
Casper
N. Platte R.
Glendo Res.
IDAHO
UTAH
Fontanelle Res.
WYOMING
Seminoe Res.
CONTINENTAL
DIVIDE
Rawlins
LARAMIE RANGE
Great Salt L.
Rock Springs
Flaming Gorge Res.
Laramie
Cheyenne
WASATCH MTS.
Salt Lake City
UINTA MTS.
Kings Pk. 13,498
Duchesne R.
Yampa R.
WYOMING
COLORADO
NORTH PARK
PARK RANGE
FRONT RANGE
Longs Pk. 14,256
S. Platte R.
Utah L.
Provo
Strawberry R.
Green R.
Granby L.
Green Mountain Res.
Denver
COLORADO PLATEAU
UTAH
COLORADO
Grand Junction
Mt. of the Holy Cross 13,996
Mt. Evans 14,264
Colorado R.
Gunnison R.
SAWATCH RANGE
Mt. Elbert 14,433
SOUTH PARK
Pikes Pk. 14,110
Colorado Springs
Blue Mesa Res.
Pueblo
Arkansas R.
L. Powell
San Juan R.
Uncompahgre Pk. 14,309
SAN JUAN MTS.
SAN LUIS VALLEY
SANGRE DE CRISTO RANGE
Blanca Pk. 14,317
Raton
COLORADO
NEW MEXICO
Navajo Res.
Rio Grande
CONTINENTAL DIVIDE
Santa Fe
Canadian R.

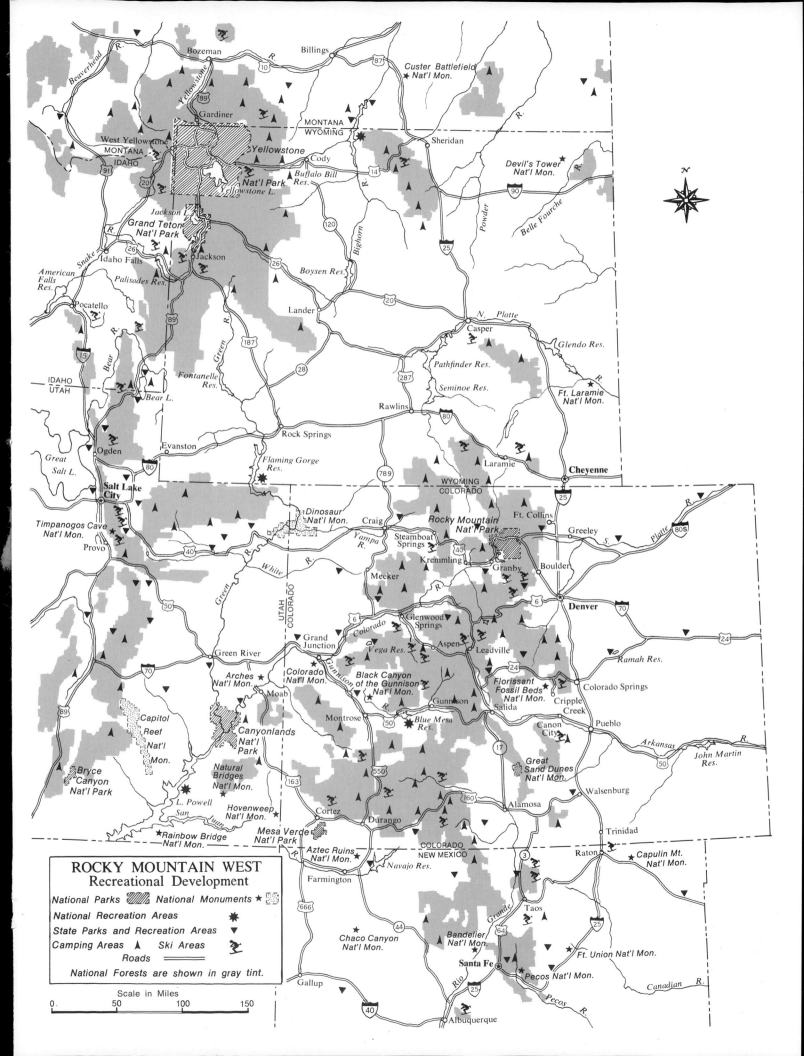

ROCKY MOUNTAIN WEST
Recreational Development

National Parks   National Monuments ★

National Recreation Areas   ✳

State Parks and Recreation Areas ▼

Camping Areas ▲   Ski Areas 🎿

Roads ═══

National Forests are shown in gray tint.

Scale in Miles

0   50   100   150

The type selected for this book is Baskerville, designed by English master craftsman John Baskerville in the mid-eighteenth century. Typography is by Hazeltine Typesetting, Oakland, California; color separations, printing, and binding by Kingsport Press, Kingsport, Tennessee.

Design by Arthur Andersen.